mastermind

by

Dmitry M. Arbuck, M.D.

To my patients; to my inspiration.

mastermind
by
Dmitry M. Arbuck, M.D.

ISBN 978-0-615-76131-2

1. Self-help. 2. Self-improvement. 3. Personal growth. 4. Mindfulness. 5. Memory improvement.

Printed in the United States of America.

First Edition.

First Printing: December 2012

Warning and Disclaimer

This book is not intended as a substitute for the medical advice of a physician. The reader should regularly consult a physician in matters relating to his or her health and particularly with respect to any symptoms that may require diagnosis or medical attention.

Bulk Sales

Please contact us at Info@MastermindMethod.com and we will be happy to discuss your bulk purchase needs.

MANAGING EDITOR
Paul Adams

EDITOR
Matt Jager

COVER ART
Nancy Noel

ILLUSTRATIONS
Jeremy Cranfill

MODELS
Jeremy & Kristy

PHOTO OF ČESKÝ KRUMLOV
Gennady Plotkin

Good to know you, Dr Burns!
Dmitry Arduch
3/6/15

"No one reached the Northern Star yet, but everyone who tried found the right way"

Mor Jokai, 1870

Part One: Basic Mastermind
Body to Mind

Part Two: Transitional Mastermind
Mind to World

Part Three: Advanced Mastermind
Mind to Mind

FOREWORD

As a child I was pale, fearful, sickly, and struck by rickets. I barely graduated first grade. My school only advanced me after my parents promised to transfer me elsewhere for the second grade. I never received a grade higher than a C until I was twelve years old.

That was when I stumbled upon a book about Autogenic Training, which is a system of putting automatic functions of the nervous system under conscious control. I discovered, then, that my feeble mind and sickly constitution was not a life sentence of weakness and inferiority. A brain can be reformed. Wounds can be healed. Memory can be sharpened, and intellect maximized. Thoughts can be induced, and then flipped off like a switch. Anyone can become anything.

That book was the first step on the long and happy journey of my life. Now it is possible for me to pass to you the tools I used to develop a dexterity in the art of being human. We are all tremendously complicated beings, knotting together memories and genetics and experiences and emotions. But every piece of us – physical, social, and mental – starts and ends in the mind. My challenge to you is to harness the native powers dormant within you, and use them to transform your life.

The skills you will learn are not binary. They exist on a continuum which spreads from insanity to brilliance. Wherever you stand on that continuum, however humble or genius you are, any learning creates endless joy and any understanding begets deeper understanding. In the journey of discovery to follow, you will turn the tables on what you think you know. You'll find that friends and enemies may both be equally good teachers, that hallucinations may not necessarily make you insane, and that it may be possible to look at a paperclip and see the whole universe within it.

You hold in your hands a system that increases in an organized and cohesive manner your physical, social, and mental wellbeing.

Use it.

Trust in yourself.

Be skilled in yourself.

Master your mind.

PART ONE

Basic Mastermind

Body to Mind

CHAPTER ONE

A Path in the Snow

It was getting dark. The squeaks and scratches of the city tram cut through the crisp winter air. An inch-thick layer of ice from the moisture of passengers' breath coated the windows, and everything inside the tram was washed in uneven blinking yellow light. We were nearing the edge of town. As the doors clunked and hissed open at each stop, I anxiously peeked outside to make sure that it was not my station. Finally, the tram screeched to a halt near my mother's office and I jumped off and ran inside as stream of frigid air blasted my face, leaving snowflakes on my eyelashes.

After school, I used to spend my afternoons at my mother's business on the brink of the forest. From one direction, the narrow windows of her building overlooked a city vista – towerblocks, lampposts, rooftops – and in the other direction lay snowblown fields and woods for endless of miles beyond. In those days, Siberian cities had no suburbs to buffer themselves from the wild. There was only city and taiga. Next short summer in the building season our city would expand and the frontier would shift outwards, but when I was six years old my mother worked at the border of civilization and wilderness.

I found her frowning over her desk chewing on the end of a pencil.

"Mama!" I said.

Her frown wiped away into a smile and she turned toward me. "Hello, little one." She pulled me close and kissed my forehead. "But you're early, aren't you?" She stood to check the wall clock, and then sighed. "Goodness, it's already so late. Tell me, how was school?"

I threw off my backpack and slid down her desk to hug my knees, saying nothing. School was always bad. I didn't like the tests, or the homework, or even the need for school. The happiest moment of my day was arriving here to be with my mother and all of her coworkers.

"Oh, it couldn't have been all that bad," sighed my mother. "Here, run about and then start on your homework. I am very busy today."

Suddenly happy and free, I jumped up to my feet and scurried around the office saying hello to people I knew.

My life outside of school was rather good. Only a few weeks earlier, I had found a diamond in a snowdrift near the door of mother's building. The doorman had nearly spat out his tea when I showed him the jewel. It turned out that a newlywed who worked in the same building had lost the rock from her ring. I didn't understand why everyone was so grateful, but the bride bought me an ice cream which seemed much more valuable than a sparkly little stone. Later that day, filled with hope for snowbound treasure, I dug out a handful of change from the sidewalk near the site of my diamond discovery. The coins were cold and wet from the melting snow at the palm of my hand, and worth enough for another ice cream. Success followed success.

After the office round I came back to my mother's desk, dreading the inevitable start of the homework, but my luck seemed to be endless that day. My mom wrinkled her nose:

"Dmitry," she said, "would you mind running across to the grocery to buy a bottle of milk? That way, as soon as I'm finished we can go straight home."

"Yes Mama," I said with a straight face – but on the inside, I was beaming. Goodbye, homework!

I dashed down the stairs, through the hallway, past the doorman warming his hands around a cup of steaming tea. "Find us another diamond today, boy!" he called as I skipped outside. The doors snapped shut behind me. Outside the crisp wind blew well below zero. Gusting snow blasted my cheeks, and ghostly drifts loomed over me. The grocery was situated on the far side of a snowed over field, distant enough that I couldn't quite make out the red lettering on its sign. Snowfall had buried the sidewalks completely, and pedestrians trudged with their hands stuffed in their coat pockets along the icy road that traced a long detour around the field to the grocery. Any other day I would have followed them, but they were dodging traffic and gesturing angrily at the cars. It seemed possible to cut directly across the unblemished emptiness of untrodden snow.

The cold didn't frighten me. I knew I was well equipped. My one piece woolen boots didn't have leather soles because the snow only melted once a year so the boots never got wet. Mama had lashed my mittens to my sleeves with rubber bands because I had lost so many pairs in the course of winter. Although boots and mittens are absolutely necessary precautions in winter, like all Siberian children I knew that warmth was generated from within. And so with the blind optimism of youth, I set out across the field.

On my first plunging step into the unpacked snow I sank down to my knee. Snow crumbled into my boot and clung to my woolen socks. After a few more steps it filled both boots, and my toes were like cold stones. A thought crossed my mind: If I was going to struggle through this field, I might as well make it a useful struggle for people. Packing the snow with each step, I advanced into the field, stamping out a narrow footpath so that any other grocery shoppers from Mama's office could follow in my path.

I have tried to think back to that moment, to recall what exactly was going through my mind for the stubborn, shuffling hour I spent stamping a trail through the field. I do remember that although no one in Siberia is raised ignorant of the dangers of snow, I had learned from the adventure of the diamond that in the frigid challenge before me was hidden potential of a wonderful reward. This adventure was a luxury! But I remember being frustrated too, about halfway across. I looked back, as my breath puffed out around me, wondering if I shouldn't have just followed the other pedestrians or at least made a shortcut without pathmaking. I was only a little boy who couldn't do his math homework, shivering and alone in a snowy field. But I had gone too far to turn around and take the easy path. The only way was forward.

The last fifty yards of my lonely adventure across the field were the hardest. I imagined the smell of bread inside the grocery. I wanted to spring into the air and fly to the doors of the shop, or clear the distance in two or three great leaping steps like a moonman. I resented all those people walking in and out of the grocery along the icy roads. They had taken the easy way, the safe way, the boring way. But of course from here there were no shortcuts, and I finished as fast as I could. The last few steps toward the open space were especially difficult, as the snow was deeper, packed, and harder to stamp down. When I finally broke through, I spared a look back, and saw to my surprise that someone was moving along the path, all the way back by my mother's office building.

I was sweaty and freezing. Inside the grocery I leaned against a wall heater and grabbed the heater bars with my naked hands while my mittens dangled from their rubber bands. My fingers, itchy and stiff and swollen from the cold, warmed against the surface. I stood still for a while until my body stopped shaking, and then it was already time to go back.

I paid for the milk, pulled the hat down tight on my head, donned my damp mittens, and stepped back onto the street.

The path I had blazed was strung with workers filing out from the dismal concrete office building and across the field to the grocery. On my way back I had to step aside for them to pass. After I returned to my mother's office, I spent the rest of the afternoon sipping sweet tea and drying my mittens and boots on the heater. Eventually I tackled my arithmetic homework.

When the workday ended, the engineers put on their heavy fur coats, fur hats, and fur gloves. My mother dressed me in dry clothes, kissed me gently, and holding my hand led me out of the office. It had not been even three hours since I had been outside, but already I saw my little path had widened to accommodate two people comfortably, and foot traffic travelled in either direction. I looked up to my mother. She did not know to be impressed. I don't think she even noticed. Still, I did not dream of pointing out what I had done. I felt strangely satisfied.

Day by day as I tramped into her office from the tram stop, I kept an eye on the path all the same. As winter stretched on, my path broadened until a few cars began driving down it, pushing pedestrians to the edges. And then it was summer, and then another one, and the road was paved and sidewalked, and then milk shopping was a quick and easy jaunt in any weather.

*　*　*

If I had been Superman, I wouldn't have needed to spend an hour stamping a trail through the Siberian snow. I could have stuck my fist in the air and flourished my cape and zoomed directly to the doors of the grocery. But I had no superpowers – just two legs, two arms, and a problem to solve. On that day, I learned that one doesn't need to be smart or big or mighty to make a road for others. If you know where you're going and you want to make things easy for others, the right things happen. Over the years since that day in the snow, I've encountered a lifetime of new problems and puzzles. In fact the whole experience of life can be understood as a continuing series of challenges. As a practicing psychiatrist, an exile from the USSR, a refugee, and an immigrant to the land of opportunity, I've seen that heartwarming lives are but a screw-turn away from bloodchilling horror, and also that tragedies can become comedies, and that the small can be huge and the mighty may be pitiful.

Throughout the experiences of my life and psychiatric practice, I've adapted a series of simple Mastermind exercises that have the potential to transform your life. Of course I'm not a fairy godmother. There's no wand anyone can swipe that will instantly transform you into a princess, or a billionaire, or a movie star. These Mastermind methods will not put treasure directly in your hands – but they *will* train you how to explore for treasure yourself. You will learn, throughout the course of stories and exercises, that snow doesn't just make you cold – that there are diamonds hidden in the drifts, and that challenges can be frustrating or invigorating depending on your outlook.

At its most basic level these methods are skills to be learned, like jumping rope or geometry or bike riding. Realized at its full potential, this ability allows you to master your own mind – hence the name Mastermind – through concentrated efforts in mental functions such as visualization, sensation, perception, and imaginative scenarios. Mastery will give you greater power and control over your career, your relationships, and your achievements. You may use Mastermind to adjust your physiology, moods, emotions, and positive thought patterns. Ultimately, with patience and focus, Mastermind allows you to be what you want to be, to build what is possible to build, and to believe in what you want to believe.

The Roman poet Juvenal wrote nearly two thousand years ago that a healthy mind lives in a healthy body. Modern civilization has taken this adage to heart. Consider our gyms and spas, our diets and our cosmetic surgical procedures. All are vigorous efforts to improve the sense of self-worth through external means – and they certainly can be effective. No one should deny the relationship between physical and mental health. Tai chi and yoga practitioners know that it is possible to improve the mind through the influence of movement or physical postures.

So the links between physical and mental – between material and unconscious – are real. Humans of every race and color have developed various methods of unlocking unconscious potential. You'll find such methods in ashrams and temples and bookshelves and infomercials, and more often than not they're pitching a magic bullet to solve all your problems in life. While it is true that many different methods can be effective with dedication and practice, in fact there is no single mantra you can chant to transform yourself. There are only tools that when applied in the appropriate conditions can effect that screwturn from problem to opportunity.

Consider Mastermind a jangling toolbelt, or a closet full of methods to wear depending on your needs. You must decide how to use them. For instance, a sturdy pair of boots won't pick up your feet and step for you, but they'll help you to maneuver comfortably the path you'll walk each day. In general it's a good idea to have boots – and shirts too, and slacks and jackets and hats and everything else. Once you have them, it's up to you to decide when you'll need a trench coat or when a t-shirt will do.

You will extract little enough mystery or exoticism in these pages. Rather, you'll read true human stories demonstrating a range of successes and failures. All of these stories have come from my life and practice, although I have changed names and details. Digest these stories critically. You may find that some of the people you'll meet have not balanced their desires with the possible, or have acted without careful understanding of themselves or the world. You may meet others who have made admirable decisions in difficult circumstances. Probably you will see as many flawless humans in these stories as you see driving on the freeway on your way home from work. That's because no one is born perfect. Our lot is to tend to those talents we have, and at best to maximize our potential. Through these stories you may gain an appreciation for missteps others have made, and also what remarkable things are possible when we begin to master the power of our minds.

The second component of this study is a series of matter of fact exercises descended from a mental training regimen developed in the 1930s by Johannes Schultz. This regimen is called autogenic training, and itself derives from the European tradition of self-suggestion. Suggestion is the oldest method of relieving human distress and treating diseases. The 3,500 year old Ebers Papyrus, recommends physicians to tell patients that "pain would disappear." Extreme suggestibility may be achieved through, among other methods, hypnosis, Haitian voodoo practices, Buddhist chanting, and the tribal dances of indigenous North Americans. Many physical combat systems such as Aikido, Kenpo, Hapkido, Gongfu, Wing Chun, and even some American schools of mixed martial arts are based on unity of the body and mind. The link between somatic and mental processes is the inheritance of nearly every human civilization in history.

Standing on the shoulders of many predecessors from diverse colors and cultures, and inspired by my own medical training, I have experimented for 20 years mixing novel mental and emotional concepts with Schultz' training methods. The results of this experimentation, applied over the many chapters of my own life, eventually became the chapters of this book – the Mastermind methods.

Use them pragmatically. Brittle and restrictive dogma has no place in Mastermind. In the same way that an eagle hunts with sharp eyes whereas the bat tracks his prey by ultrasound, humans have many different paths to self-satisfaction. Try to tell an eagle that he is weaker than a bat because he can't use ultrasound. He will probably peck you in the nose. Remember the lesson of diversity. Don't be a fanatic. Grow in yourself what you want to develop. Improve yourself according to your own standards and inclinations. The tools you will hang on your belt will be tailored to your own life experience, and if you apply them creatively in a way that does you good then you are on the Mastermind path.

So forget your limitations for now, and bridge the abyss before you as if it were a field of new snow.

CHAPTER TWO

The Alphabet Headache

W hen I met Jessica, she couldn't drive, cook, watch television, read books, or write. Six years earlier she had been a happy grand-mother with a large Irish-American family, a loving husband, a comfortable retirement, and a cabinet full of cookbooks. Now she was frazzled and bleary eyed, suffering splitting headaches on a daily basis.

The stimulus of her headaches was particularly strange. Just glancing at a written letter or word would cause her to double over in agony. She couldn't bear to look at name tags, or street signs, or even t-shirts with letters on them. Bizarrely, she only felt this pain in reaction to letters of the Latin alphabet – the ABCs you learned in school, and what I'm using to write this book. She could look at Cyrillic or symbol-based Asian writings pain free, but of course she couldn't understand them. She used to daydream wistfully of travelling to China, where she might stroll down a sidewalk without crippling pain from the signs.

When the problem first arose, she had met with an eye doctor who per-formed scans, lab tests, exams, and thorough evaluations. None of the results were abnormal. She visited another ophthalmologist for a second opinion, then a neurologist, a neurosurgeon, an internal medicine consul-tant and a pain specialist. She underwent MRIs, CAT scans and hormonal panels. Doctors hypothesized that Jessica had been poisoned by heavy met-als, or was allergic to dust mites, or infected by a rare fungus. She endured chelation therapy, and antifungal medications for months at a time. But no one could successfully identify the source of her disorder. When western medicine failed to have any effect, she turned to alternative therapies. She tried advanced homeopathy. She saw an herbalist and an acupuncturist and a chiropractor to work on her neck. None could pinpoint the origin of her sudden illiteracy. After six miserable years of isolation in a letterless world, Jessica turned to psychiatry. By the time she saw me, her reactions were so severe that even the thought of letters would spark a headache. If she as much as dreamed a letter she woke up and vomited in agonizing pain.

Jessica was not stupid. She knew her disorder was unprecedented. Neither she nor the medical community could offer any logical explanation for this ailment that had effectively ruined her life. By now she also knew that her headaches were purely psychogenic and that she was suffering from a mental, not an anatomical problem. There was no medical reason for her to be suffering.

We tried hypnotherapy to no avail. Medications were of no use. We tried cognitive therapy, analytical therapy, insight oriented therapy, and different medications. We analyzed and reanalyzed her. For a whole year, every incident of the headaches was evaluated closely. We reviewed possible stressors that could bring on the symptoms. We investigated her family relationships and childhood memories.

Could it be that she had her first headache just when she was reading something upsetting, which created a pathological association, which in turn caused her headaches? Was it an insulting letter she received? Was there possible news she was expecting and did not want to deal with? Was she abused in childhood? Was she physically assaulted? What could possibly have started this devastating chain of events? I had as much luck as the ophthalmologist did six years ago. Nothing. Jessica should have been a perfectly functioning grandmother.

Eventually we stopped hunting for the origin of this disorder. "We may never find out why you're suffering," I told her. "And it may be okay not to know why, and maybe there is no why at all. Let's just deal with what you have."

She agreed. We spent the next several months reprogramming her brain. We used more medications – antipsychotics, antidepressants, and anticonvulsants in various sophisticated combinations. We talked about electroconvulsive therapy and eye movement desensitization. Nothing worked. Some of the more radical approaches we ultimately dismissed as unreasonable.

So we became inventive. Rather than reading usual letters, we tested out writing with only half of a letter, pushing as far as we could without triggering the pain. Eventually we created a secret alphabet that was not based on the ABCs but rather different symbols that we used to represent each letter. In time she became fluent at reading our secret language without headaches, but functionally only she and I could read this language. We still weren't able to manage Jessica's daily suffering.

Finally we sat down and had a long talk evaluating all our futile treatments. Not only had we failed to identify the origin of the pain, we had failed to control it.

"Do you remember," I asked, "being a child and hiding under a blanket?" Of course she did. All kids do that.

"What happens when you hide under the blanket?" She thought a while, and then said that the longer she hid, the monsters seemed to grow bigger and uglier. "The longer you wait," she said, "the harder it is to look out from under the blanket."

"So how do you save yourself?"

"You needed to peek from under the blanket," she said, "and then switch on the lights, fast."

"And then?"

"And then no monsters."

"And after you turn on the lights, are you scared?"

"No."

"Does your heart pound?"

"For a while after."

"But not long?"

"Not long, no."

Jessica was stuck in a feedback loop. Out of fear, she hid from her monsters, and the more she closed her eyes under the blankets, the more fearsome and slavering the monsters became. The monsters governed her. She needed to turn the lights onto her fears, but was too anxious to even lift up a corner of the blanket. "Who is in charge of your life?" I asked her. "Is it you or your headaches? The letters or you?"

I taught Jessica a simple exercise called the Mask of Relaxation and asked her to practice fifteen minutes each day. In Jessica's case the Mask offered two benefits. It gave her a measure of control over herself, and also allowed her to quiet the frenzied anxiety in her mind. She told me after one week of practice that for the first time in years, she felt rational.

After she had mastered the Mask of Relaxation method, I suggested she try to read something pleasurable, but with two caveats – first, that she practice the Mask of Relaxation before the attempt, and second that she continue to read despite the pain. Jessica had told me earlier that the pain of reading letters made her feel like her head would explode, but I promised her that no matter how bad the pain got, her head would remain intact. She left, nervous with anticipation.

When I saw her next she was breathless. The very evening she left my office; she used the Mask of Relaxation and then opened up a cookbook. Right on schedule, the pain struck. Her head spun, she told me. Her eyes burned. Her brain throbbed. She felt nauseous and defeated, but nevertheless continued to read. She kept telling herself that the pain couldn't get any worse, that it was already as bad as it could be. She read the whole recipe, and then turned to the next page. Strangely enough, after fifteen minutes, her headache just stopped. Jessica couldn't think and could hardly breathe, but she had no headaches. She could read.

It wasn't an instant fix, of course. The pain returned periodically, but with effort and regular practice, its frequency declined and eventually petered to nothing. Armed with nothing but the power of her mind, the illiterate grandmother had retaught herself to read.

It's often possible to see the workings of the mind play out on a human face. Anxiety, joy, and fear are all visible. So there is a bridge linking the mind to the face – and it's not just open to one way traffic. The brain communicates with the muscles, and the muscles communicate with the brain. Curiously, a recent study showed that paralyzing with botox a wrinkle in between the eyebrows signifcantly improves depression. The less you frown, the less depressed you are. If you don't believe me, try this little test: Close your eyes, make a grimace of fear, clench your jaw, and observe what happens to your emotions. Within seconds you will feel anxiety. If you're not purposefully counteracting the natural physical response, your breathing may quicken and you may find that your fingers are curling into fists.

Your clenched jaw has just sent a message over the bridge to the brain. This muscle feedback, a link between instinct and consciousness that probably kept our distant ancestors safe from cave bears and saber toothed tigers, can have trouble adapting to the more delicate hazards of our twenty first century world. If your muscles tense up at your workdesk, for example, your body is communicating danger to the brain, which goes into crisis mode and prepares to defend itself from cave bears. Obviously this can lead to dysfunction.

But we can adapt the bridge between mind and muscle to our own benefit. In the same way that you used your jaw muscles to communicate anxiety to your mind, it is possible to reassure the brain that you are in a safe environment by relaxing your face. In fact your face has more distinct muscles than any other area of` your body – at least 52, depending on the system of classification. A larger proportion of your brain is dedicated to conversation with the face than any other part of your body – more so than your fingers, and much more than even your sexual organs. If you control your face, you are quite literally controlling about half of your brain's grey matter, as you can see in the illustration on the next page. This brains-eye view of a human being which shows where the brain devotes its attention is called a homunculus.

When Jessica practiced the Mask of Relaxation, she was laying the groundwork to master of her own life and mind. In her case exercising control of the face was enough to communicate peacefulness to a brain that was strung so tense and tight after six years of indescribable pain that it was of its own accord turning letters over and over in her dreams. Although Jessica and I went on to practice several other Mastermind methods such as dream programming (which you will learn about in Part Three) to control her pain, the beginning of life control for her and you is the Mask of Relaxation. Eventually you will consider it a stepping stone, but as Jessica discovered; it is a powerful exercise in its own right.

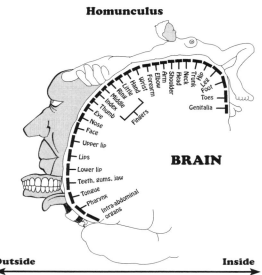

Homunculus

Try to plan about fifteen or twenty minutes each day to Mastermind practice. Eventually, once you have honed your skills, the whole series of body to mind exercises may take just a few seconds or less. At a high level, it is possible that you will be able to practice even while you run, or talk, or while you rub your belly and pat your head and hop on one foot. It may take months or even years of regular practice to achieve this extent of technical proficiency. You may not feel the need to push yourself that far. That's fine. What really matters is the fact and effect of the practice, not setting records.

Although Mastermind practice is at heart a solitary activity, you may find it easier in the initial stages to work through the exercises in a group setting where you can share your experiences and learn from other people's stories and observations. It is also beneficial to have a teacher who can guide you and the group through the process. Of course group study is not mandatory, but if you are working on your own, you must be disciplined. You must practice the methods diligently or your skills will not develop. Homework is important. Luckily, in this case the homework is fun and empowering.

For now, start in a quiet environment. Lie on your back or sit comfortably. If you decide to sit, choose a comfortable chair and make sure your hands do not hang in the air off the armrests. (You risk compromising blood circulation otherwise.) If you decide to lie down, do so with your body perfectly flat, with no pillow but a supportive roll – a rolled up blanket or towel will do – under your neck. Do not cross your arms, legs, fingers, or anything else. Position your arms alongside your body, bend them slightly, and rest with your palms down. Place another roll under the knees if possible.

Once you're settled comfortably in your environment, practice the mask as described below. Follow the simple steps, no matter how repetitious they seem. Do not progress until you have engaged your body in the sensations set forth in the lesson. Take a break after every chapter to experiment in the effects of the lesson.

After you are finished, spend two or three minutes to take some notes on the experience. Writing things down helps you formulate your thoughts, and makes certain subtle tendencies more visible. What are your thoughts? What are the sensations of your body? How do you feel about them?

Mask of Relaxation - Basic Benefits

- calms nerves
- gives you a sense of control over yourself

Mask of Relaxation - Extended Version

- Set a timer for fifteen minutes.
- Close your eyes.
- Behind your eyelids, roll your eyes toward the bridge of your nose. Don't strain.
- Smooth your brow.
- Loosen your cheeks.
- Unclench your jaws.
- Place your tongue on the inner side of your upper teeth.
- Focus your attention on the bridge of your nose.
- Slow and deepen your breath.
- Observe as your worries float away from you.
- Think to yourself, "I am here, and I am okay."
- Do not allow your facial muscles to tense.
- When the timer goes off, open your eyes and smile.

Mask of Relaxation - Short Version (when your skills are improved)

- Eyes closed
- Jaws unclenched
- Tongue is on the inner side of your upper teeth
- Open eyes and smile

Mask of Relaxation - Concentrated Version (fully developed skills)

- Eyes
- Jaws
- Tongue
- Exit

Mask of Relaxation

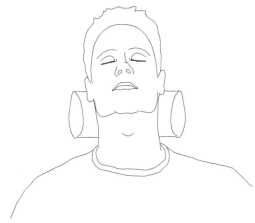

Mask of Relaxation - Body Positioning Examples

On the floor

- body perfectly flat
- supportive roll under the neck and knees
- do not cross arms, legs, fingers, or anything else
- arms beside the body, slightly bent, palms down

Seated

- hands in lap
- don't hang arms off armrests
- do not cross arms, legs, fingers, or anything else

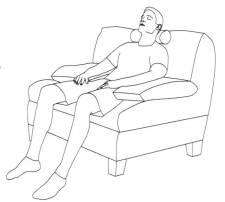

CHAPTER THREE

The Happy Death of a Virgin

When the attendants rolled Lois into my Indianapolis clinic, the musty smell of a nursing home followed. Her hair was grey and unkempt. I learned later that she hadn't worn makeup for almost a decade. She couldn't walk. She barely talked, and when she did it was in a slurring, breathy whisper. In our first appointments she said to me, staring blankly at the floor, "I'm a virgin and I always will be." Lois was clinically depressed. She was 42 years old and had been paralyzed from the waist down for nine years.

It took some time for the antidepressants I prescribed to take effect, but as they did, little stories from her past trickled out of her, and over the months the picture of her life came into focus. As a child, she had attended Catholic school where skirts were required to cover the knee, and nuns kept their eyes sharp and open for any hanky panky. Although Lois had kissed a boy once, it had been a tense and uncomfortable moment that filled her with regret. She was a good girl, and so to save herself for marriage she cultivated habits that others around her interpreted as standoffishness. By the time she graduated high school, no one competed for her attention.

At nursing school she studied hard and displayed some leadership ability. She befriended a classmate and as she said, "sort of dated him," but by the time she had loosened up enough to commit to him, he had lost interest. Heartbroken, Lois plunged back into her studies and finished nursing school a virgin.

After that, she applied all of her energies to her career. She volunteered for the long shifts at the hospital, took doubles, and worked weekends. She made decent money and was promoted ahead of her peers. As years passed she grew more and more confident in herself. Looking back, she said that in those early nursing years she had considered herself to be laying the groundwork for a fruitful life. Family and children, she knew, would all come once she applied herself to it.

But all of her relationships ended disappointingly. The men she met were either dumb, vulgar, sexist or alcoholics. She couldn't commit herself to losers, and so more and more she devoted herself to her work. Eventually she earned a promotion to the head nurse of the cardiac catheterization unit, where she trained nursing students and built her station into a well-oiled machine. But despite her success, her virginity tormented her.

Furthermore, strenuous physical work was triggering headaches. If she lifted an overweight patient or moved furniture, she'd pay for it hours later. Over the next few years the unexplained pain continued to worsen. Once she came close to going home with one of her friends, but fear of a head-ache caused her to decline his invitation. He dropped out of her life.

Eventually Lois decided to get a check-up for the headaches. On her day off she met with a neurologist at her hospital who promptly ordered an MRI and MRA scans, which revealed the source of her worsening ailment – a large aneurism deep in her brain. As a working nurse, Lois was well aware of the fatal consequences of a ruptured aneurism.

Suddenly her sexual torment didn't matter a whit. The aneurism in her brain wound Lois up so tight and tense that she told me later that it was like carrying a grenade in her head. The neurologist tried a few conserva-tive treatments that ultimately failed. Constant fear and obsession caused Lois to consider surgery, and she met with a neurosurgeon who carefully outlined the risks and potential complications of the procedure. She made the decision to undergo the operation in her own hospital under the hands of a surgeon she knew personally. She was 33 at the time.

Lois stroked on the operating room table. There is no way of knowing ex-actly why. Maybe with all the repositioning during the procedure a clot was thrown into her brain from the neck. Maybe a crucial vessel was accidently severed. Maybe one of the surgical instruments compressed something. She awoke in the recovery room paralyzed.

In the months and years after this horrific time, Lois didn't seem to care about anything anymore. She wouldn't even eat without being asked. She regressed into a childlike state where she would comply with requests, but otherwise laid still and motionless in her bed. Although she eventually learned to wiggle her toes, she never regained the use of her legs. The next nine years Lois lived in a nursing home, slowly picking up what fragments remained of herself.

I was a resident when she first rolled into my clinic. When she despaired at her virginity, I tried my best to help her process her feelings – to attend to her emotions, to reflect on her thoughts. As time strengthened our bond, she began to look me in the eye occasionally when we spoke, and even smiled once or twice. One day she came in wearing pink lipstick, and an-other day mascara, and another day she combed and braided her hair. She operated her wheelchair herself, cracked jokes, and became an easier and better conversationalist. Her celibacy, though, weighed heavily on her, and we didn't laugh about that.

Three years after I met her, Lois' condition had improved enough that she planned an adventure out from the nursing home to visit her sister in the hills of southern Indiana. All of Lois' caretakers were thrilled at the adventure, and her nurse later told me that Lois herself was bursting with energy. It was a perfect fall morning when Lois arrived at her sister's countryside home – sunshine, a gentle breeze, a table set with grilled corn and biscuits and gravy.

That afternoon, Lois startled the cat by dropping a glass of lemonade from the left armrest of her chair. Her arm had gone numb. She told her sister she was having a heart attack. Her sister called 911. The nearest hospital was an hour's drive away. Within minutes, a medical helicopter picked her up, and paramedics loaded her into the chopper where they administered shots and gave Lois an IV and oxygen for a short flight to a hospital.

Lois expired mid-flight.

She must have known that she was dying. She was a nurse, after all.

One of the paramedics sat down with Lois' sister that evening at the hospital and haltingly described Lois' last minutes of life – how Lois told him about a calming heaviness settling over her, how she thought he had a tight butt, and that she'd never had sex. She was laughing, the paramedic said. Moments before she perished she told him of her final wish – one of the very few wishes she had since the stroke. On her headstone, she asked the paramedics to tell her family to write three words: *Laid at last.*

* * *

When Lois' sister told me the end of this story, one detail struck me as particularly extraordinary – the heaviness that Lois felt in the helicopter. The sensation of heaviness is one of the pillars of autogenic training, derived from Johannes Schultz' ground-breaking discoveries at the turn of the twentieth century. He had determined that the sensations of heaviness in the limbs indicated an extreme form of muscular relaxation – or in other words, physical calm. As you know, the bridge from body to mind is a two-way street. It is no coincidence that just as Lois felt this calmness settling over her like a thick blanket, she finally felt secure enough with her virginity to joke about it. She had, in the last moments of her life, found humor in her deepest regrets.

That Lois, who had no feeling from her waist down, took enough comfort from this specific sensation of heaviness to be able to laugh at her affliction is especially remarkable. She had been paralyzed, after all, and during our sessions in Indianapolis she complained that her numb legs felt heavy and swollen. So she had felt two distinct forms of heaviness – one was imposed upon her and felt wrong, while the other one emerged spontaneously like a blessing.

As we've begun to see through the Mask of Relaxation exercise, it is possible to control the effect of those messages carried back and forth on the bridge between body and mind. In fact, truly masterminding your life *requires* that you take control of your body, your behavior and even your thoughts. I don't know if Lois ever managed to achieve this control consciously. The imposed heaviness – her paralysis – sent a message of regret and despair that often emerged during our sessions. But I strongly suspect that in Lois' final living moments, she had somehow arrived at a kind of peace that allowed her to end a tragic life with laughter. With practice, you can train yourself to feel that same release, and to allow what regrets and afflictions you have in your life to drift away.

Even if we are not so lucky as to meet our own passing with levity, at least it should be possible to greet the more minor inconveniences of day-to-day life with something more measured than the instinctive stress response.

Every time you encounter bad news or find yourself someplace strange or uncomfortable, your body tenses up. That muscular tension signals danger to the brain, and it, in turn, mobilizes the body for war. This is a survival strategy that serves us well in times of crisis. But stress that is not demobilized after the threat passes can over time alter your blood circulation and nerve activity. It induces long term muscle spasm which then causes grinding of the joints, and eventually turns into neck and back pain, headaches, and chronic knots in the muscles.

The method of stress demobilization, a paved road leading you to physical and mental health, is muscle relaxation. The practice of muscle relaxation has been proven to prevent, counteract, and even reverse the effects of stress on your body and mind. Of course that doesn't mean you should live your life as a soft lump, but instead that you should practice relaxing your muscles as much as you exercise them. That way, you are swift and springy when it is time to fight, and restful when you are out of danger.

So just relax. Sounds simple, right?

It is not.

Years ago in a Japanese study of muscle control, volunteers were verbally asked to relax, and electrodes monitored how the muscle interpreted commands. It turned out that although the volunteers were instructing their muscles to relax, true muscle tension actually *increased*. They discovered that even if you chant to yourself, "Relax, muscle, relax, relax," you may *feel* more relaxed, but physiologically your muscles are actually *more* tense than before. This is a natural reaction. Muscles spasm eagerly. That's their job. Relaxing is difficult for them. When in your mind you shout at the muscle, "Release!" your muscle suddenly blinks awake as if it's been caught sleeping on the job. "What?" it asks frantically. "Orders coming in? Contract, contract, contract!"

When you are communicating with your body, it is crucial not to fight against yourself. Communicating through sensations almost always works better than words. If you startle the muscle awake it will twitch into action. If you soothe it, it will relax. The most clinically reliable method of soothing muscle fiber is through the sensation of heaviness.

Feeling heaviness decreases muscular tonus – "the normal state of continuous slight tension in muscle tissue that facilitates an immediate response to stimulation" as it is defined in the encyclopedia. Heaviness is comfort and rest. It is the absence of tension. It is the opposite of stress, and it calms your mind as well as your body. Consciously activating this sensation of heaviness is the next Mastermind method.

How you conjure up that sensation will differ depending on your nature. Some rare left-minded people are able to simply chant to themselves to produce the desired heaviness. ("Hands are heavy. Hands are heavy. Arms are heavy," and so forth.) Others are only able to communicate to themselves through imagery. They will picture themselves laying beneath a heavy woolen blanket in winter, or laying on a beach covered by a mountain of warm sand. Others work through memory sensation, thinking back to how their body feels just before they fall asleep.

For most people, a combination approach works best. If you find yourself achieving results with a verbal approach, by all means continue using it. But also practice developing other methods. Work on your deficiencies. Add images to words or vice versa. It is important to rely on your natural strengths, but equally important to experiment with alternatives.

To familiarize yourself with the feeling of heaviness, make a fist and clench it as tightly as you can for several seconds, and then release. Pay close attention to how the muscle feels. You may feel something like what you would call "fatigue" or "muscle exhaustion" or "soreness." This is not heaviness. Parse apart those sensations, and try to zero in on the thread that is calm, relaxed and restful. It is pleasant and comfortable and safe. That is heaviness. Trust me, it's there. At first you may only feel it for a moment, but you will soon be able to relax your muscles at will.

Psychotherapeutic *progressive muscle relaxation* always includes tensing a muscle before relaxing it, and for your first few exercises you may need to tense a muscle before feeling heaviness. Ultimately, though, the Mastermind method requires that you learn to reproduce the sensation of heaviness without first creating physical tension in the muscles.

Try it out, focusing on one muscle group after the next, until the whole body is heavy. The order of these groups is constructed deliberately, so follow the order routinely each practice, and when you are finished write down in your notebook what images or words or memories are useful or not.

Don't worry if you fail to feel heaviness in the beginning. All practice ultimately strengthens your will and disciplines your emotions. So practice joyfully and explore the world within yourself.

Heaviness - Basic Benefits

- counteracts physical stress response
- eases muscle tension

Heaviness - Extended Version

- Set a timer for fifteen minutes.
- Lay or sit in the position described in the Mask of Relaxation.
- Sense the heaviness in your dominant hand.
- Sense the heaviness in both hands.
- Sense the heaviness in your arms.
- Sense the heaviness in your feet.
- Sense the heaviness in your legs.
- Sense the heaviness in your shoulders.
- Sense the heaviness in your back.
- Sense the heaviness in your buttocks.
- Sense the heaviness in your face.
- Sense the heaviness all over your body.
- Keep this sensation as long as you can, or until the timer goes off.
- Open your eyes and smile.

Heaviness - Short Version (when your skills are improved)

- Assume a Mask of Relaxation
- Right (or Left) hand is heavy (whichever is dominant)
- Both hands are heavy
- Right (or Left) foot is heavy (whichever is dominant)
- Both legs are heavy
- Shoulders are heavy
- Buttocks are heavy
- Face is heavy
- Heaviness is all over
- Excessive heaviness leaves the body
- Open eyes and smile

Heaviness - Concentrated Version (fully developed skills)

- Mask of Relaxation
- Hands and Arms
- Feet and Legs
- Shoulders
- Back and Buttocks
- Face
- Heavy all over
- Exit

Heaviness - Body Positioning Example (more starting on page 171)

Basic Heaviness Method - Arms

- flex both arms for one minute
- relax the muscles
- allow arms to fall to your lap
- feel heaviness in the muscles of the arms

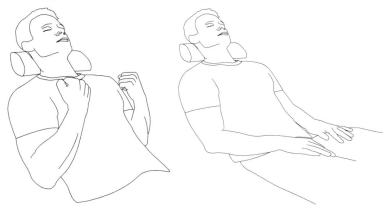

For other body part Heaviness exercises see pages 171 through 177.

CHAPTER FOUR

The Father Who Shared Warm Hands

Abram's beloved wife of forty years, with whom he had emigrated from Russia to the United States, had recently passed away, and he was suffering from grief and depression. During one of our meetings on a warm summer day, he told me a story from his childhood which was in some ways horrifically typical for men and women of his generation and descent. In other ways his experience was unique, because although he didn't know it, Abram had been practicing a Mastermind method for his whole life.

Abram grew up in a concentration camp. He told me stories of the cattle cars that transported him and his father and thousands of other Jews to the camps – the weeping and moaning, the hunger and thirst, the smell of urine and excrement, the awful shoving and pressing of body against body. Abram's father, who had been badly beaten by the Gestapo before being loaded into the train cars, must have been a magnificent man. Throughout the days and nights in the car, father connected to his son by holding his hand, or joining each other at the elbow or the hip, and every touch was a strength transmitted. Abram said that he hadn't cried at the time, nor did he now. He told me the story with matter-of-fact narration, looking at me calmly.

He remembered feeling happy to escape the stench of the car when they arrived at the camp. Hand in hand, he and his father stepped down from the train where they were deloused and washed with fire hoses right there at the rails. They were given prison uniforms, although Abram managed to sneak a light jacket underneath the striped pajamas.

Children did not earn their own bunks – father and son slept together on one narrow surface holding hands, and thusly they two lived for the next five months. Nazi orders were to exterminate the sick and elderly, and work the rest to death. But according to Abram, the commandant and guards instead kept population manageable by randomly selecting a hundred prisoners for death from roll call once or twice a week, depending on the inflow of new captives.

Abram and his father, along with all the other men in the camp, used to line up in rows and columns to stand waiting for the choice of either life or the oven. Those prisoners selected for death would plead or weep or stride stoically away to the crematorium. Father and son held hands tighter than usual in those hours. Abram remembered the feel of his father's heart beating in the palm of his hand.

On the day that Abram's father was chosen for death, the father and the boy were holding hands when SS commandant stopped next to them. The Nazi looked at the father and then to little Abram. He lifted his riding crop and poked into the father's chest. Abram squeezed his father's hand, and his father answered the squeeze. The Nazi pointed the tip of the riding crop toward the crowd of prisoners bound for the fires. When Abram's father didn't move, the commandant moved the crop to his left hand and reached for his holster.

Abram's father shifted his eyes down to his feet. The German returned the crop to his right hand and moved away. Father and son stood still holding hands. The guards, seeing hesitation, started toward them and one of soldiers took his submachine gun off his shoulder.

The father again gazed down at little Abram, shook his head and lost the grip. Abram let it go too. Sullenly the father quickly moved to the side and as soon as he reached the chosen crowd, turned around and looked at his son and smiled. There was a gap in Abram's memory here, but he knew that the prisoners were escorted toward the crematorium. Abram couldn't say how he felt inside, but through the numb blur he still felt the warmth of his father's hand.

It was the last time Abram saw his father. He forever remembered not the agony of his loss, but rather the feel of his father's hand holding his own. For years afterward, his hand would always warm up in times of trouble. Through this he knew that his father had never left him.

The day in my office that he told me this story, thousands of miles from the camp, decades later, Abram looked at his hands, palm up in his lap, and told me, "Even now, you see, my hands are warm."

*   *   *

We read about post-traumatic stress disorder or PTSD often enough in our headlines, especially in times of war. Combat veterans can be burdened by the disorder, and women who were sexually assaulted often suffer psychiatric symptoms for years to come. PTSD can seem to be an inevitable inheritance of trauma. But in fact only a minority of victims of trauma actually develop symptoms. Abram, for instance, lived through the Holocaust, yet managed to stay mentally healthy until the death of his beloved wife. We must learn as much from the healthy as from the sufferers. What allows them to stay sane through such horrors?

It begins with the mind's remarkable powers of suggestion. Your mind can send messages over the bridge to your body with the potential to cause real and measurable physical change. In extreme cases it can completely alter your hormonal balance. Consider hysterical pregnancy, a poorly understood phenomenon in which a woman shows signs of a pregnancy that medically does not exist. A sufferer of pseudocyesis, as the syndrome is known, will experience a break in menstrual cycle, her breasts will swell, and her belly protrude. About one percent even suffer labor pains. Most famously, Mary I of England, under social pressures to conceive an heir, suffered *two* hysterical pregnancies in her life. Studies have shown that placing such a sufferer under general anesthesia, which effectively shuts down the mind, causes the symptoms to disappear.

Abram's warm palms may seem less mysterious in comparison to hysterical pregnancy. It seems to me that his mind's power to warm his hands in a time of stress was a calming mechanism developed unconsciously to cope with extreme emotional and physical trauma. But imagine if he were the master of his mind – if he could consciously control the power to effect measurable changes on his body. This is not mumbo jumbo or comic book plots, but an actual, achievable aim.

I myself learned to warm my palms when I was twelve. I had stumbled across my mother's copy of a book about autogenic training. I experimented with manipulating my own hand temperature until I could hold thermometers in my fists and see the mercury rise. This is an exhilarating demonstration of the power of your mind.

As a teenager I used methods of sensing warmth to counteract my growing pains in my knees. I even learned how to fight cold sores. Warming up my lips through mental exercise would kill the viruses and dissolve the sores. In my early days, this experimentation landed me in the hospital. A few days after my first tests in raising my whole body temperature, my mother noticed that I was hot to the touch. She stuck a thermometer under my armpit and found my temperature was over 102 Fahrenheit.

I felt well, but she was sure that something wasn't right. The doctor couldn't find anything wrong with me, though. The labs were normal. I was just too hot. I spent the next month in the hospital being evaluated in every possible way and the cause was never found. It took about a month for my body to go back to normal. Of course I knew the cause of the temperature change, but had no intention in revealing it to any adults. It seemed to me that I had a good excuse for missing a whole month of school, and I wasn't going to ruin it.

Remember that the sensation of warmth is really just the way we send messages to our bodies. Just as we used heaviness to communicate relaxation to our muscles, the sensation of warmth translates physiologically into increased metabolism, more blood supply, and ultimately the engagement of various body defenses. Being able to consciously feel warm in different areas of your body means you are increasing blood flow to those areas. It is possible in this way to regulate healing, tissue recovery, bone growth, and even to fight infections.

An old legend of how Alexander the Great filled the ranks of his conquering armies speaks to the differing effects of blood flow in the body. As the story goes, Alexander chose the soldiers of his elite guard by lining up the recruits in ranks and insulting them. These soldiers knew better than to confront the emperor, so all they could do was listen to unfounded, unfair insults. But this was no aimless lashing out on the part of Alexander. He was watching carefully the reactions of different recruits. Those whose faces flushed red were chosen to stand guard around the emperor, while pale faced soldiers were selected to become officers.

It's all about circulation. When more blood rushes to the muscles and the face, it means that someone is ready to fight. When blood drains from the skin to the brain, one thinks clearer and quicker. (I like to think that those recruits who did not react at all to the insults became generals, because they displayed a balance in a time of stress.)

You will find that the sensation of warmth and heaviness are interrelated. Due to blood redistribution, feeling heavy automatically brings about a natural perception of warmth. Warmth means that blood is entering muscles which do not need to work hard any more, and are thus looser and supple. Muscles, then, are quietly resting while warmth is distributed to the skin. Heaviness and warmth in the arms and legs actually produces some measurable increase in their real weight, because of the increased blood volume contained in the extremities.

The additional flow of blood can produce more than just warmth – it nourishes the tissues and carries an anti-aging effect. The feeling of warmth becomes a powerful and quick tool that can normalize vital signs and mental state. I can't promise eternal youth, but if you can warm your face and supply more oxygen to it by bringing more warm blood to your skin, one side effect will be fewer wrinkles.

There are emotional benefits as well. You may know from your own experience of daily life that discomfort and stress results in cool and clammy hands. Using the principles we have learned about sending feedback over the two way bridge from your body to mind, you can extrapolate that *warming* your hands should then contribute to an *improvement* in mood.

As you proceed through the body to mind Mastermind methods, you will continue adding to the vocabulary of this new language of sensation that you use to communicate from body to mind. Applying this language may seem strange or uncomfortable at first. It may also seem like something ancestral, something you've always known and are only now viewing through a different lens. Either way, it is possible to hone this method of communication.

Just as we used the images of heavy blankets to feel heaviness, we can use the sensation of being buried in hot, dry sand at the beach to feel both heaviness and warmth. Creating vivid images and scenes in your mind helps your body to recreate the desired sensation. The sharper your image is, the stronger you will experience the sensation. Really try to experience the scene you are thinking. If you are using the image of buried in beach sand to feel warmth, imagine also the smell of the sea, and the shout of children playing and splashing in the ocean nearby. These details will help you materialize your self-suggestion.

At the same time, no image should be detached from emotion. It does not matter how clearly you think or what scene and sensation you invent, without a positive emotion attached to that experience, it is meaningless. If, for instance, your imagined scene of warmth is being boiled in a witch's cauldron, the sensation will not be pleasurable. Similarly, a steaming hot, wet towel on your face before a shave in a barber's chair can bring a pleasurable sensation of warmth to your cheeks. Imagined negatively, the wet towel over your face could easily become waterboarding. Therefore it is crucial to always know what emotion you want to nurture in yourself. For now warmth and heaviness should make you feel secure, as it did Abram.

Understanding the mechanics of an exercise is important, but it doesn't matter how well you understand the physics and mechanics of operating a bicycle – to actually ride one, you have to jump on and pedal. Similarly, you need to practice and learn the method of heaviness and warmth before advancing to the next chapter. It is crucial to actually experience these sensations, and then to practice them repeatedly. The more you send messages between mind and body, the more automatic and effortless it becomes. In the case of warmth, it is also important to practice reversing the sensation to normalize your body temperature (unless you want to miss a month of school.)

So try out the exercise now, and when you've achieved some success in it, move on to the next chapter.

Warmth - Basic Benefits

- increases metabolism and manages circulation
- countless applications for health

Warmth - Extended Version

- Set a timer for fifteen minutes.
- Lay or sit in the position described in the Mask of Relaxation.
- Apply muscular heaviness.
- Sense the warmth in your hands and feet.
- Sense the warmth in your arms and legs.
- Sense the warmth in your neck and shoulders.
- Sense the warmth in your back and buttocks.
- Sense the warmth in your face.
- Sense the warmth all over your body.
- You are relaxed, at ease, and it is pleasant and peaceful.
- Keep this sensation as long as you can, or until the timer goes off.
- Excess heaviness and warmth leaves the body.
- Hands and feet are light and rested.
- Excessive heaviness and warmth leaves the arms and legs.
- Neck and shoulders are light and back to normal temperature.
- Back and buttocks are light and rested.
- Face loses excessive heaviness and warmth.
- Excess heaviness and warmth leaves the body.
- You are in control.
- Open your eyes and smile.

Warmth - Short Version (when your skills are improved)

- Assume a Mask of Relaxation
- Right (or Left) hand is warm
- Both hands are warm
- Right (or Left) foot is warm
- Both legs are warm
- Shoulders are warm
- Buttocks are warm
- Face is warm
- Warmth is all over
- Excessive warmth leaves the body
- Open eyes and smile

Warmth - Concentrated Version (fully developed skills)

- Mask of Relaxation
- Hands and Arms
- Feet and Legs
- Shoulders
- Back and Buttocks
- Face
- Warm all over
- Exit

Warmth Method - Warm Hands Example

- imagine hot blood pouring into hands
- imagine hands warming from the inside, like hot water filling a balloon
- use a hand held thermometer to measure the warming of hands

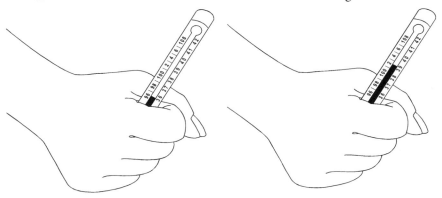

Warmth Method - Sunny Beach Example

- imagine yourself lying on a sunny beach covered to the chin in hot, dry sand
- feel warm inside and out
- feel relaxed, pleasant, and peaceful
- once you have mastered body warmth, integrate a sensation of heaviness alongside warmth with each muscle group

Removing warmth

- removing sensations is as important as creating them
- count to three, removing excess warmth and heaviness
- imagine warmth and heaviness spilling out, evaporating, leaving behind a strong, springy, healthy body

CHAPTER FIVE

A Strange Journey From Suicide to God

To be absolutely frank, when my mother's friend Natalya first told me of the winding path that carried her from a St. Petersburg bus to American immigration, I was bewildered. Natalya's obvious strength of will was stirred together with such human weakness and emotional frailty that I wondered what she might have left out or added in. But whether or not the events are verifiable, Natalya herself obviously believed the story had happened exactly as she told it. She began the tale in silence, breathing slowly and deeply, collecting her thoughts, and then she said, "I boarded that bus intending to kill myself."

Natalya had been born and raised in St. Petersburg, Russia, and she hadn't led an easy life. Her mother hated her, her husband raped and beat her, her daughter cried all day and all night, and her household was in debt and bankrupt. So one day she cooked dinner, cleaned their tiny galley kitchen, made the bed, arranged her daughter's toys, ironed her husband's pants, put on a dress with little blue flowers and short sleeves that had once made her feel beautiful, and she went to church to ask for forgiveness for her suicide.

At the cathedral she lit a candle in memory of her mother. She bowed her covered head and stood still. The sounds of the church – whispers, and the brushing of soft feet – reassured her. She saw forgiveness in the eyes of Christ, and the gentle face of St. Nicholas. For a moment she thought the icons themselves would speak. A feeling of kindness and contentment washed over her. This gave her confidence that once she killed herself, the afterlife would welcome her.

She boarded a bus toward a particular bridge over the Neva River where young lovers came in the evening to kiss and embrace. It would be a good place to die. Natalya settled into an empty seat. The bus seemed to be taken up by shadows. The whole world around her, she told me, seemed like so much meaningless decoration. She would meet God soon, and abandon all the misery of this life. "And then he touched me," she told me later, "and took my breath away."

Another passenger had laid a hand on her shoulder, a young man whose touch startled her and yanked her back into life. "I'm sorry miss," he asked. "Are you okay? I'm sorry. So sorry. I don't know you. But can I please talk with you?"

Even today, Natalya remembers thinking to herself angrily that he was lying, that he wasn't sorry for his intrusion. She was frowning when he said, "I'm sorry, but you are so beautiful. May I talk to you please?"

She glared at him, and he saw it as an invitation.

"I know it might sound crazy," he said, "but I saw you walking onto the bus and sitting here. And I saw such a mystery, such depth, such a sadness in you. Please listen to me. Please give me just two minutes. Please don't judge me. I don't even know your name – mine is Peter, I am so happy to meet you – but I saw you, I saw your eyes, and I instantly knew that I love you. I love you, miss."

Natalya was so astonished that she couldn't help but stare speechlessly. When the passenger next to her stood up and left the bus at the next stop, Peter slid beside her and took her cold hand. "I want you to marry me," he said.

Natalya laughed with me as she remembered the moment. "I almost fainted when he said that," she told me. "There I was, ready to leap from a bridge to meet God, and this man proposes! So irresponsible, I thought. So inappropriate. But he wouldn't stop talking, talking, talking. He told me his whole life story on that bus."

Peter had immigrated to the United States ten years earlier, and built a successful business in Los Angeles. His office life back home kept him so busy that he hardly had any time for friends. He wanted a soul mate, but couldn't find one among the Americans, so he decided to go back to his hometown to find a wife. For the past two weeks his family had set him up on daily blind dates, but he hadn't met a single woman he wanted to spend his life with. He carried on polite conversations, yes, and went to cafes and watched movies. He liked some of the girls, but nothing more than that. Now, tomorrow he was bound to return to Los Angeles, but he had seen Natalya on this trolley and it had changed his life. He'd never felt such deep and sudden love for another human. And he knew it didn't sound right, he knew it was impossible to believe him, he knew Natalya might find him obnoxious, but he was in love, and that was all. "Please," he begged, "please marry me, give me a chance."

"I'm married already." sputtered Natalya.

"You're not happy there. I know. I see it."

"I have a daughter," she said.

"I love children," he answered without hesitation.

And then she whispered, "Why are you doing this to me?"

"I want to spend the rest of my life with you," he told her.

Baffled, Natalya looked out the window – and discovered that the bus had passed the bridge she had resolved to leap from. Just a moment ago she had been calm and detached and separate from the world, ready to meet God – and now she could hardly collect her thoughts. "I missed my stop," she groaned.

"I'm sorry," he answered.

That made her angry again. "*You* are sorry?" she asked. She yanked her hand out of his and stood. Her daughter would be home soon. Natalya had to help her with her homework. Furthermore, if she arrived home late for dinner, her husband would be angry. She needed to hurry. "And that's why," Natalya told me later, "I didn't kill myself then. I resolved to do it the day after instead. Because on that day, my family needed me."

Natalya had stormed off to switch buses, and Peter followed behind her pleading that he loved her and didn't mean to complicate her life, that he would leave St. Petersburg tomorrow anyway, but that he loved her, he loved her, he loved her, and he wanted to spend his whole life with her, and wouldn't she please just give him her phone number so he could call her tomorrow to say goodbye?

"I should have slapped him in the face," Natalya told me, "but I gave him my phone number. My real number! And he called me the very next day, just like he promised. Then, bit by bit, I began to breathe again, low in my belly like an opera singer."

Peter called Natalya periodically, making little jokes and observations about his American life. She hardly said anything at all. But she didn't want to kill herself either. Something inside her had changed. She didn't despair any more at her husband's abuse, it only disgusted her. She felt sadness, not fear. A piece of the detachment she had felt in the bus remained with her. She knew the abuse had to stop, but she wanted to find a solution to the problem rather than flee from it. Every time she thought of her problems, she would lose her breath and feel dizzy and tingly. "It's not just my life," she thought, "I am sick."

Natalya filed for divorce, and in a few months it was granted. She moved back in with her father and maintained a casual correspondence with Peter. One day she told him about her divorce, and he was ecstatic. In her imagination, she began to see, as if through clouded glass, a life with Peter and her daughter together in sunny California. She realized that she missed him. She wanted to see him. After all, she'd been invited. "Come and visit me," Peter had asked. "I'll pay all your expenses, just come and visit me."

And then one night, God spoke to her. Natalya shuddered awake in a cold sweat with a sudden conviction that it was not Peter who had saved her life but God who had answered her prayers. Peter was only a tool. Natalya's desire to make a new life with Peter was a betrayal of God. She needed to devote herself to God, serve Him, and trust in Him.

But it was the mid-nineties then, and crime, poverty, and ongoing crisis made life nearly unbearable in Russia. Nobody around Natalya believed in the future any more. She had been recently robbed in the street by a couple of young hooligans. In the spirit of honesty, she told Peter of her concerns – that she didn't love him, that she loved God.

And he answered that even if she didn't want to be with him, he wanted to marry her anyway and bring her to Los Angeles. He said that he wanted her to be happy. He would help her daughter too.

Although she had never left Russia before and the mere idea filled her with anxiety, nevertheless she resolved to take Peter up on his offer. Upon her arrival in Los Angeles, she was surrounded by fondness, affection and care. With Peter, her life seemed so full of hope and security. More importantly, her daughter would have a safe life in California. At last Natalya agreed to marry Peter, and a few months later her daughter touched down at LAX.

For the whole length of their marriage, Peter never made a single move to be physically intimate to Natalya. They slept in separate rooms. Natalya kissed him once, and he answered with an embrace. He knew that she did not love him, that she wanted to serve God. There was never any argument about that. He only wanted her to be happy.

Shortly after she received her American citizenship, Natalya and Peter mutually agreed to divorce. She found a convent on the east coast, and he helped her move there. Peter legally adopted Natalya's daughter and agreed to raise her as a single father.

"And that," Natalya told me, "is how after two worldly marriages I became the devoted and happy wife of God."

*   *   *

I admit that hers is a strange story that even I do not completely understand. But most human behavior is strange and inexplicable. That does not make it unworthy of our attention.

On the bus in St. Petersburg, my mother's friend had made a reasoned decision to kill herself. While I do not endorse this choice and am thankful that she did not follow through, if we set aside our own judgments we can observe the results of her determination. By her own description, she was calm, content, and detached. After Peter's affectionate intervention, Natalya's same assertiveness was eventually redirected elsewhere – first into freeing herself from the abuse of her husband, and second in pursuing her relationship with God.

Traditionally *assertion* is understood as a reactive stance to some domineering figure or circumstance affecting you – a loudmouth coworker taking advantage of your timidity, for example. But as Natalya's story demonstrates, true assertion begins from within. No matter how we evaluate the *direction* of Natalya's assertiveness, at least we might admire the method of it.

There are so many people who have anxiety but don't see it. They don't realize that their arms are shaking until they spill their coffee. These people, if put in Natalya's circumstance, might have asserted themselves by shouting, stamping their feet, shaking their fists, and throwing glassware against walls, and adding to the ill will poisoning their relationship.

Instead of throwing a fit, Natalya acted in the way that she considered would best solve the problem of domestic abuse. She tried her best to think calmly and critically through a bad situation. Although she drew dangerously near to asserting herself through suicide, which is hardly a positive outcome, the love of another human drew her back from the brink. And after the fluster of interruption, she began to calm herself and once again sift through her circumstances both rationally and with assertion – breathing low in her belly like an opera singer, as she described it. (I never met Peter, but I suspect that his peaceful and loving determination also had a calming effect on his own body.)

Natalya's deep slow breaths communicated calm to her mind in the same way that your relaxed muscles sent a message of peace over the bridge to your mind during last chapter's exercise. In the same way, hyperventilation and other uncontrolled breathing patterns are steps on the way to panic. Your breath is the foundation of all metabolic activity in your body, and is worth a closer look.

People breathe in two ways – chest breathing or diaphragmal breathing. Chest breathing, which is produced by intense contraction of the chest muscles, evolved for one purpose only – to save your life. Chest breathing is engaged during extreme stress as part of your fight or flight response. In times of danger you have to bring more oxygen to your muscles, and you have to utilize deeper and faster breathing to intensify oxygen intake.

The process by which your chest wall forcefully sucks in air is quite involved. Large muscles are engaged to put the rib cage and joints in motion. Each rib is connected to the sternum in the front and the spinal column in the back, with joints at all connections. Moving this massive structure is hard work. If you have ever shot a bow, you know that it takes a lot of effort to pull the string. Surrounding your lungs are 24 ribs strung like bowstrings, and in chest breathing, all of them must move. Because of the rate of calories consumed and the demand in energy, chest breathing is exhausting. The faster you breathe the more energy you consume. On top of all that, if you aren't in the middle of intense exercise during the rapid breathe, you are likely to develop an electrolyte imbalance affecting carbon dioxide and oxygen levels in the body, with long-term potential to causing confusion, dizziness, blurry vision, ringing in the ears, and a dry mouth (among other unpleasant symptoms.) These are the physical signs of mental anxiety. These are the messengers galloping up to the brain shouting, "Danger!"

Your body actually employs deep chest breathing to mobilize for action. My theory is that the yawn is a last-ditch engagement of the chest wall that jiggles the yawner's body and mind more awake, in the same way that you might check if the door is locked before leaving the house. The yawn, then, is an unconscious use of the body to mind bridge – a built-in alarm system which warns against sleep and keeps you alert. That's why it is so infectious. Studies have shown that yawning is most contagious among friends and relatives. This is because your kith and kin are more reactive to your social signals to stay aware of a possible threat. We are social animals, and yawning reminds our bodies and our tribes to stay aware and awake even when the brain wants to sleep.

Diaphragmal breathing, or abdominal breathing, or what Natalya described as breath "low in her belly like an opera singer," is the natural, sleeping state of restful breath, and it sends its own soothing messengers across the bridge to the brain, whispering peace all the way. It allows the boney armor of your ribs to rest, utilizing the ergonomic power of your diaphragm to bring the oxygen in and to sigh out the CO_2. Whether you are sitting at your desk, or watching television, or standing on the subway, breathing diaphragmatically will communicate calm to your mind.

To bring your breathing under your conscious control, start off by placing your hand on your belly button. Try to bulge your abdomen out, pushing your hand away from you. Then suck it back in, pulling your hand back toward your spine. Play with the movement. Now coordinate inhaling with your abdominal bulge. Feel the air pulling into your abdomen as you push your hand away from your spine. Then as you exhale, feel the air pushing out of your lungs and pulling your hand toward your spine.

This breathing exercise can be practiced at any time, as frequently as possible, until you permanently switch to abdominal breathing. After a few such repetitions, an actual abdominal muscle effort will not be needed. Your diaphragm alone will do the job. Eventually, because your diaphragm is working instead of the abdominal wall, you won't have any visible belly bulge during abdominal breathing. Once abdominal breathing becomes second nature, you won't need to put forth any effort in maintaining it.

Chest breathing at rest will then feel awkward and ineffective. Deep chest breathing is ultimately harmful at rest and should never be used except when you need to mobilize for action.

By the time you master abdominal breathing, you will have four tools that you can employ to manage your anxiety. Physiologically, your face will be under your full control, your muscles will be regulated to produce a feeling of heaviness, your blood vessels will be regulated to produce a sensation of warmth, and finally your diaphragm and breathing will be regulated to soothe the mind.

It is very important not to view these first body to mind Mastermind methods separately from each other. They are one cohesive unit of self-regulation, and they function best when assembled into a single organism rather than dismantled in parts. The more you fuse these methods creatively, the more complex improvements you will be able to effect in your own body. Although each exercise has individual therapeutic benefits that you should be discovering for yourself, the successful performance of just one or another exercise does not necessarily guarantee a therapeutic effect. What matters is your application and kneading together of the whole set of exercises.

Try employing all four exercises you have mastered together – the Mask of Relaxation, heaviness, warmth, and abdominal breathing. Imagine yourself floating in a hot tub, breathing calmly and slowly through your abdomen. You feel pleasant, relaxed, comfortable, and in control. It is very, very difficult to feel anxious in such paradise. In fact you will be so restful that it may help to periodically remind yourself not to fall asleep before allowing the excessive warmth to leave your body and excessive heaviness to dissolve.

Abdominal Breathing - Basic Benefits

- allows you to change the course of events when feeling out of control, anxious, or fearful
- prevents hyperventilation
- actively prevents anxiety and communicates peace to the brain

Abdominal Breathing - Extended Version

- Set a timer for fifteen minutes.
- Assume the Mask of Relaxation.
- Sense warmth and heaviness in your hands and feet.
- Sense warmth and heaviness in your arms and legs.
- Sense warmth and heaviness in your neck and shoulders.
- Sense warmth and heaviness in your back and buttocks.
- Sense warmth and heaviness in your face.
- Sense warmth and heaviness all over your body.
- Breathe through your abdomen slowly and easily.

- Stay awake.
- Keep this sensation as long as you can, or until the timer goes off.
- Hands and feet are light and rested.
- Excessive heaviness and warmth leaves the arms and legs.
- Neck and shoulders are light and cool.
- Back and buttocks are light and cool.
- Face loses excessive heaviness and warmth.
- Excess heaviness and warmth leaves the body.
- You feel stronger, rested, and ready to move.
- You feel young, happy, and confident.
- Open your eyes and smile.

Abdominal Breathing - Short Version

- Assume a Mask of Relaxation
- Right (or Left) hand is warm
- Both hands are warm
- Right (or Left) foot is warm
- Both legs are warm
- Shoulders are warm
- Buttocks are warm
- Face is warm
- Warmth is all over
- Breathe through the abdomen
- Excessive warmth leaves the body
- Open eyes and smile

Abdominal Breathing - Concentrated Version

- Mask of Relaxation
- Hands and Arms
- Feet and Legs
- Shoulders
- Back and Buttocks
- Face
- Warm all over
- Abdominal Breathing
- Exit

Abdominal Breathing - Basic Method

- bulge the abdomen out and suck it back in toward the spine, just to feel the movement

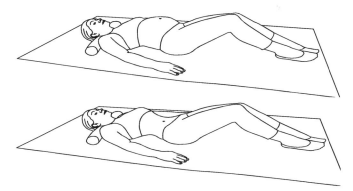

- repeat ten times
- inhale when abdomen bulges

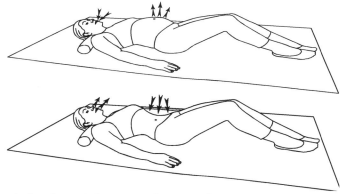

- exhale when abdomen sucks toward spine
- repeat as frequently as possible, any time and in any position
- eventually the body will switch to permanent abdominal breathing
- as that change takes place the diaphragm breathes and not the abdominal wall, so there is no unwanted belly bulge

See Quick Reference Guide pages 181 and 182 for additional information regarding Abdominal Breathing.

CHAPTER SIX

The Loser Who Kept Winning

Marlon, a recovered alcoholic, had been taking a schizophrenia medication Stelazine for forty five years, and he wanted to quit. He claimed that he hadn't had symptoms of any psychosis for the past forty years, and that if he could quit booze and amphetamines, then he could get by without Stelazine too.

I was immediately cautious. Of course there was a difference between alcohol and Stelazine. One was ingested recreationally and the other pragmatically. Marlon's medical records showed that fifteen years earlier one brave doctor had tried easing Marlon off the drugs with catastrophic effect. Marlon developed severe tremors, spasms, and paranoia. He was promptly restarted on Stelazine. It's possible but unadvisable to go cold turkey on alcohol to beat your dependency – the process can be life threatening – but beating mental illness means complying with treatment.

The more I dug into Marlon's medical history, though, the more doubts I had. It was possible that Marlon's tremors, spasms, and paranoia fifteen years ago had been the result of drug withdrawal symptoms. After all, he had been taking Stelazine for his entire adult life because of an earlier diagnosis.

Opinions in psychiatry differ all the time, because there are no real mental diseases, only syndromes. Psychiatrists can often agree on a syndrome – psychosis, for example – but disease diagnoses like schizophrenia or bipolar disorder can be misleading. The functional distinctions between diagnoses of bipolar, schizophrenia, substance-induced psychosis, or schizoaffective disorder are not very important from the perspective of treatment. In psychiatry we treat symptoms and syndromes, not diseases. And as Marlon opened up about his life, I became convinced that he had never had schizophrenia at all.

"Tough," and a shrug is how he described his childhood at first. His father was a local politician and an alcoholic. Family outings meant dinner at the tavern, a drunken argument between his parents, and then a beating for his mother upon their return home. At the age of seven, Marlon ended up in charge of his four younger siblings.

The family became progressively poorer, and they were always downgrading their houses until they lived without heat, and sometimes even without food for days. After several suicide attempts, Marlon's father, forty one years old, eventually drank himself to death on skid row. At twelve, Marlon became head of the household. He dressed his siblings, kept the fire in the stove, and worked hard to keep food on the table. He set pins at the bowling alley, caddied at the golf course, and gave the money to his mother, who would buy enough booze to keep herself in a stupor, and use what was left over for food. "I'll never be like my father," Marlon thought to himself. That same year, he got drunk for the first time and an addict was born.

When he was fourteen he earned his own way to a Catholic boarding school by impressing a priest with his remarkable spiritual curiosity. He lasted two years, studying hard but boozing as well. In his second year his mother told him that she couldn't take care of his younger siblings without him, and that she had no choice but to put them up for adoption. He dropped out and rushed home, but by the time he had returned home, his mother had placed out his two sisters. His sole remaining brother was a delinquent and a thief.

He started high school back at home, behind in every study due to his family responsibilities. He cut 54 days of his freshman year. His options at the time, he told me, were to cheat or flunk. Still drinking regularly, Marlon cheated and survived high school, although with grades and social standing that were not sufficient for further education. He showed me once a photo of himself at that age – a boy with his head at a stubborn tilt, disheveled blonde hair, and his big hands filling his coat pockets. He didn't look like college material, it's true, but there was some spark that guided him towards people who could help. A priest who respected the boy's scriptural knowledge and tough childhood convinced a college admission office to accept Marlon on a probationary basis for just one semester.

For that single semester Marlon didn't drink like he used to. Instead he binge studied, with a rare break to satisfy the addict's appetite that gnawed in his belly. He taught himself what he should have learned in high school and then excelled at his college courses. He was so outstanding in his effort and so much more mature than his classmates that the school decided to give him a full scholarship for the remainder of his studies. Setting himself impossible goals and then achieving them was becoming a habit. He studied at night and worked during the day, pushing his body as hard as he could. Sometimes he took amphetamines to stay awake to study. Upon graduation, Marlon applied for a teaching position with the very high school that he had cheated his way through. He got the job.

He maintained his maniac pace. He attended law school at night and taught high school in the day. He acquired a dependency on amphetamines to keep him awake, and on gin to put him to sleep. His younger brother, by now a cocaine addict, stroked at the age of twenty in a drug house. Both of his sisters were by now diagnosed with schizophrenia and locked up in mental institutions. Although when I knew him Marlon could only remember this period of his life in glimpses and snatches, he told me he remembered one hysterical evening he spent cowering behind a dumpster, panicking that gangsters were tracking him. He believed there were cobwebs stretching across his skin, and scratched at his face until it bled.

Marlon ended up spending a year in a mental hospital that was more jail than hospital. The facility was a product of its times. The doctors diagnosed Marlon with schizophrenia – as if no other mental diseases existed – and treated him with electroconvulsive therapy.

He emerged from the hospital frightened and guilty. He considered his mental illness and addictions moral sins. He had defied God with his dependence on the pharmaceutical cocktail of opioids and psychiatric medications. He would tell himself over and over, "Don't quit, Marlon. Don't give in. Don't give up. You'll win, Marlon. You'll overcome." And he did, in a sense. He found a job teaching algebra to middle school students and was named teacher of the year for three years running. Yet he couldn't sleep without Vicodin, and he couldn't smile without a mouthful of Percocet. He remembers a sweet taste of desire on his tongue, a warm anticipation of a drug in his belly.

Marlon being Marlon, he didn't know how to surrender. He found another job coaching football in the early years of racial integration. He was the first white coach in an all-black school. Despite his own failures, Marlon taught the kids that they could win even if they lose; that they could advance even at a disadvantage. He taught them that nothing was impossible with dedication and effort.

Although it was a successful first year, Marlon's hypocrisy gnawed coldly in his belly. He decided eventually that he couldn't be an addict and a role model at the same time. He quit drinking and quit all the drugs but his schizophrenia meds. He attended AA. He endured the pits of withdrawal, and then later the sweet temptation of relapse. Marlon indulged that desire twice, and then he quit disaster and chose life. "It's not the tenth drink that gets you," he explained to me. "It's the first one. You won't have the tenth drink if you don't have the first." And then he sighed and laughed a little and said, "What a life I had to live to figure that out."

He said that in the depth of withdrawal he had examined his own life and saw just three drops of hope in a glass. Those drops were all he had left. Over the next years he wrung himself dry, filling the cup to half full. He stayed sober. He married and had children. His addiction never left him

– even at seventy, when I met him, he still felt something within him pulling him towards painkillers. But something even deeper and more primal anchored him to his sobriety. Each day he didn't use drugs was a victory.

All that was left when I knew him was a daily dose of Stelazine, the schizophrenia medication, and at seventy years old he wanted rid of that too. Together we designed a plan of slowly lowering Marlon's dosage to reduce the effects of withdrawal that I hypothesized had caused his spasms, tremors, and paranoia fifteen years earlier during his last attempt at liberation. It took almost half a year, but eventually he was asymptomatic and free of the medicines.

Marlon is still damaged. He can't breathe well, he has pain in his joints, and his abuse makes him a high cancer risk. His body has absorbed a great deal of poison over the years. He continues to attend AA meetings religiously – 12,000 to date. It's taken him his whole life to correct damage that began when he was twelve years old. But he respects and values himself now. He has a happy marriage and a healthy mind and three well-adjusted children. He keeps learning every day. He knows he can fail any time, and the knowledge of it keeps him on his feet.

As he says, "I'm a winner, Dmitry, and I know it."

*　*　*

Although in his youth Marlon convinced himself that his addictions caused him to succeed – amphetamines to help him study, and alcohol to help him sleep – he eventually discovered that all of those successes had come in *spite* of his addictions. Marlon's ultimate realization that his most dangerous drink was the first was an acknowledgement of his own weaknesses. His solution – to not drink at all – was a protective mechanism that prevented the manifestation of those weaknesses.

Addiction, either to cigarettes or chocolate or crack cocaine, is unrestrained appetite. Once you have acquired that appetite, it lives with you, tempting and whispering from your shoulder for the rest of your life. What Marlon and all reformed addicts know, often through painful experience, is that to indulge that whispering appetite even once does not release any tension. To the contrary, the tension loads up again with each relapse, and every struggling day spent free from the object of that addiction will have to be relived. What Marlon knew was an irresistible sensation on his tongue, and in his gut – this pleasant and terrifying warmth of craving just before he gave up and submitted to it.

That realization is not limited to hard-core addicts. Consider the American pastime of dieting. If you diet strictly on raw vegetables for a month and then reward yourself with a splurge of corn dogs and fried Oreos, what have you achieved? If you've got the willpower to limit your splurges, then a system of austerity and reward may well be your ticket to good health. But most of us are creatures of habit, and if we're not careful, our occasional luxuries become future habits. Marlon learned to recognize the seductive warmth in his abdomen, which would trigger his conscious effort to "cool it down."

I've known – and maybe you have too – addicts of extraordinary inner strength and intelligence that with tragic regularity endure the struggle of withdrawal and desire, only to relapse later because they lacked a tool that would pull them out of their downward spirals. One cocaine addict I know had won five separate battles to get clean. In those addiction-free intervals he pursued careers in the Marine Corps, organic chemistry, a Colorado ski resort, construction and excavation, and real estate. But there always came a time when his appetite whispered to him, "Just once more," and every occasion he indulged that appetite, it took him on a long tailspin invariably ending on the streets or in jail.

Knowing your weakness is the better part of strength. The cocaine addict was blind to his own limitations. In fact, most of us are too. You may say to yourself, "I'll only visit this time-wasting website for five minutes." But do you really limit yourself to that time frame? Over time, does that small luxury become a habitual indulgence? Such pleasures seduce us into the trap of instant gratification. Marlon grasped at instant gratification through alcohol and pharmaceutical abuse. At great personal and physical cost, eventually he learned to harness his appetites. It may also decrease cravings, as Marlon found.

You won't find gratification by browsing Facebook at work, or lighting a cigarette on the porch after dinner, or chowing down fried Oreos at the fair. True gratification grows out from a planted seed. Care for that seed, nurture it, pluck the weeds out that threaten to choke it, and when its flower blooms you will know satisfaction. It took Marlon more than fifty years of dependency before he finally discovered how to control his appetites. Learn from his mistakes, and his hard-won triumphs.

Study yourself.

Of course, my recommendations can only go so far. Without your individual effort, advice is dormant. The fifth Mastermind method introduces you to your digestive system.

You might have guessed already the language you'll use to say hello to your gut. Most of us can chant, "More blood to duodenum!" all day long without effect. Our bellies don't speak English. The language of the body is sensation. If you want more blood flowing into your gut, you need to feel warmth in the upper abdomen. Warmth means blood.

The more nourishing blood that feeds your gastrointestinal tract, the better your overall health. Increased blood flow can neutralize symptoms of irritable bowel syndrome, Crohn's disease, stomach ulcers, acid secretion, and even intestinal cramps. If your gut is healthy, increased blood flow assists in digestion and regulates appetite. Warmth increases the activity of intestinal juices. Decreased blood flow which you feel as coolness in the upper abdomen, can decrease stomach acidity and knock down your appetite.

Your gut is deeply involved in stress, as you may know through your own experiences. We get nauseous when we are anxious, and can vomit when we are deeply frightened. Under stress some of us get "the willies" – gastrointestinal spasms, flatulence, diarrhea, and blood flow changes to the intestines that can over time contribute to the development of ulcers. All these symptoms are actually part and parcel of a healthy anxiety that helped early humans escape predators. When our distant ancestors were being stalked by a pack of wolves, a splattered trail of diarrhea could turn the predators off the trail. Who knows, you might be alive because one of your ancestors vomited in the face of a saber toothed tiger. But today in our modern world, nervous farts rarely solve problems. You need to be in control of your stress response.

The most valuable application of this exercise is increasing awareness of your body. With regular practice, you should be able to notice imbalances or minor aches. Maybe you will even learn how to regulate them. Test it out. Collect a bit of saliva on your tongue, and feel its warmth. Now swallow. Follow the warmth with your hand, as it moves down your esophagus and spreads in a pleasant wave of warmth in the upper abdomen. From here the exercise is conceptual, but try to feel the warmth travelling along the route of your GI tract. Tracing the shape of your digestive passages with your hand on your belly will help. The warmth eases through the bend of the duodenum, and the hoops of the small intestine in your gut. Imagine having a warm coiled garden hose inside of you filled with hot, floating gel. It reaches the large intestine on the lower right side of the abdomen, near the blind spot of the intestine where your appendix joins. Ascend with the colon up to the upper abdomen, kink to the left across your belly, and slide down on the left side. Feel the warmth travel all the way from the mouth to the rectum. The whole continuum, from throat to anal sphincter, should feel warm. Hold onto this warmth for some time, and then release it.

Remember that imaging helps – you may use the conceptualization described above, although eventually you won't need to swallow saliva or move your hand tracing along the path. Instead you might imagine a hand, or even a warm water bottle, or an electric heating pad, or the sun's rays – or anything else that works. Choose something you feel good about.

It's possible that in the process of feeling heaviness, warmth, and abdominal breathing, you have already begun to feel warmth in the upper abdomen. Your blood has been flowing, moved by the diaphragm, bringing in more warmth. All of these mind to body methods are interrelated.

Try combining them.

Warmth in Upper Abdomen - Basic Benefits

- increases blood flow to the gut
- improves nervous system function at the hub of the solar plexus
- improves digestion
- further manages physical stress response
- increases awareness of your body

Warmth in Upper Abdomen - Extended Version

- Set a timer for fifteen minutes.
- Assume the Mask of Relaxation.
- Focus your eyes on the bridge of the nose.
- Tongue resting on inner surface of your upper teeth, jaws unlocked.
- Sense the heaviness and warmth in your arms and legs.
- Sense the heaviness and warmth in your neck and shoulders.
- Sense the heaviness and warmth in your back and buttocks.
- Sense the heaviness and warmth in your face.
- You are floating in a hot tub full with steaming water feeling heaviness and warmth.
- It is pleasant and peaceful.
- Breathe comfortably using your diaphragm.
- The whole continuum from tongue to esophagus and other areas of the gut are warm.
- Upper abdomen is especially warm.
- Swallow some warm saliva to enhance the sensation.
- You are calm and under control.
- Enjoy it.
- Keep this sensation as long as you can, or until the timer goes off.
- Imagine the excess warmth and heaviness oozing out of you.It dissolves into the air.
- Muscles are strong and healthy.
- Body returns to normal temperature.
- Breathing remains abdominal, and stomach remains warm.
- Count to three.
- Take a deep breath in, and fast out.
- Open your eyes and smile.

Warmth in Upper Abdomen - Short Version

- Mask of Relaxation
- Body is heavy and warm
- Breathe with abdomen
- Tongue and esophagus are warm
- Abdomen is warm
- Excessive warmth goes away
- Deep breath in and fast out
- Open eyes and smile

Warmth in Upper Abdomen - Concentrated Version

- Mask—Heavy—Warm
- Breathe with the abdomen
- Abdomen is warm
- Exit

Warmth in Upper Abdomen - Basic Method

- collect saliva on tongue
- feel its warmth
- swallow
- follow the warmth with your hand as it moves through the upper abdomen, or "epigastric area"
- feel warmth travel down your esophagus and spread to the stomach
- linger here for a moment, at the solar plexus

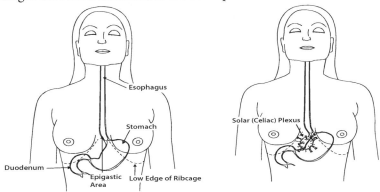

- trace the warmth with your hand through the duodenum and through the loops of the small intestine until it reaches the large intestine at the right bottom side of the abdomen
- feel the warmth building as the intestine ascends and turns to the left, crawls along, and spills into the descending colon
- feel the warmth floating down to the rectum and the anal sphincter
- the whole continuum should feel warm
- hold the warmth a moment
- release the warmth

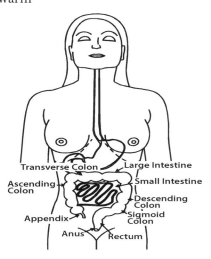

Warmth in Upper Abdomen - Integrated Method

- don't use your hand or your saliva to feel warmth
- instead use inner vision and visualization
- feel arms and legs heavy and warm
- feel neck and shoulders heavy and warm
- feel back and buttocks heavy and warm
- feel face heavy and warm
- feel warmth in the mouth, esophagus, and stomach
- imagine a heating pad on your solar plexus, or a warm water bottle

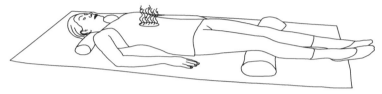

- feel warmth moving through the intestines to the rectum
- imagine a warm coiled garden hose in your gut, filled with hot floating gel

- imagine floating in a hot tub full of steaming water
- feel the heaviness and warmth all around you, inside and out

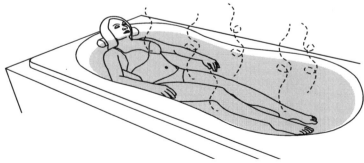

- when you decide to surface, imagine excess warmth and heaviness oozing out of you
- muscles are strong and healthy
- body temperature returns to normal
- breathing remains abdominal and stomach remains warm

CHAPTER SEVEN

The Family Without a Country

In 1988, Gorbachev's policy of Perestroika was gaining momentum. Private enterprise was permitted for the first time in the Soviet Union since the 1920s. I opened a business in the middle tier town in central Russia where my family and I lived, but it ended up being too forward thinking for that time and place. By 1989 my Soviet citizenship, as well as that of my wife and seven year old son, was revoked.

With little warning, my family and I were citizens of nowhere. The Soviet Union was sick. People were unhappy. The shortage of food and bare necessities made life cruel. Every day was dusk. The hope and enthusiasm that had once propelled the Party was gone. Red banners slouched and drooped. Empty stores housed canned sauerkraut and gallon tins of birch juice and nothing else. Even so, I didn't want to leave. This place had been my home for 30 years. But we had no choice.

We were left to manage our own way out of the country. Without citizenship we could not work, or live in an apartment, or stay in a hotel, or even fly on a plane to leave. Our passports were taken away and we were ordered to surrender our diplomas. There was no trodden path for us to follow, and no one to ask for advice. The only option we saw was to make our way a thousand miles overland to the Polish border, carrying anything we could along with us. My family of three was permitted to carry no more than four hundred US dollars with us out of the country. To carry any more foreign currency was to risk jail time. Although astronomical inflation made Soviet currency almost worthless, we cashed out our bank accounts for rubles. But we refused on principle to turn in our diplomas as we were ordered to do. We didn't even know what country would eventually take us in, but wherever we ended up, one thing we knew – money and credentials were absolutely necessary to begin our new lives.

We packed ten suitcases with canned food, kitchenware, books, clothes, toiletries, and a family-sized tent with two air mattresses. One luggage I filled with medications to be sold abroad for profit. We slipped our cash and diplomas into a secret pocket stitched into the lining in one of the suitcases.

Through a friend of a friend of a friend, I had gotten in contact with a group of Polish speculators who were roaming about selling western clothes in exchange for Russian gold. They were on their way back to Poland, travelling in a flotilla of ten Fiats. It seemed perfect – one suitcase per car – but the drivers were frightened to be travelling with émigrés. They couldn't risk any extra attention from the customs guards, or their gold might be discovered. My heart sank.

Through frantic negotiation, I struck a deal with two of the drivers. Poland was in as bad of shape as Russia at the time, and these two drivers were willing to bear the risk of transporting us in exchange for our color TV. But how could ten suitcases fit onto two tiny city cars? We had two days to find a solution, or the Polish convoy would leave without us.

Without papers we couldn't hire a bus or a minivan, and we knew no willing drivers who would pack everything into a car for a round trip to the border. With no other options, we stubbornly hoped for kindness or luck, and it happened. With less than twenty four hours to spare, a stranger offered us the use of his trailer with only one request – that the Poles return it to him the next time they were back to sell more clothes. This trailer, then, was our ticket to freedom. We loaded it up and said goodbye to our parents, our apartment, and everything that had once seemed so safe and familiar. With a moment of silence and a few tears, we left our home behind.

These tiny coffin Fiats were designed to be driven around the block and back, but I was only happy to finally be moving. My seven year old son was very quiet. My wife was anxiously talkative, but we couldn't discuss any of our true concerns – would my medicines be confiscated at the border, or our diplomas, or would they find our extra cash? – for fear that our Polish companions might not keep our secrets. So we discussed only small things. I could feel my heart punching inside my ribs. We weren't afraid of leaving Russia as much as we were afraid of our diplomas or cash or medicines being discovered.

We arrived in Moscow after dark. A vast and beautiful city of untold tragedies was draped in millions of windows which stared at us from all around. We arrived in the evening at a friend's flat. They served us hot tea and we chatted more about things of no significance. My family had no idea what lay ahead, and ignoring the vast unknown that lay in our future was a way of shielding ourselves from our fears. That first night we slept on the floor. At the time, the change we were undergoing seemed like it would continue forever.

We left Moscow in the morning crawling through rush hour traffic. I felt that some darkness was leaving me. The next stop carried us to my father's home, midway to the Ukraine. We drank tea and some shots of vodka, and slept on the floor, keeping quiet about our hidden treasures – the medicine, the money, and the diplomas. The morning after, we shed more smiles than tears. It was the business of departure, the meeting at base camp before the push to the summit. Sandwiches were packed, potatoes baked, eggs boiled, and cucumbers wrapped. We shared our last hugs and kisses and final looks. The political situation at the time was such that we had reason to believe we would never be allowed to return, so all these goodbyes were irreversible and permanent. We sighed and started up the cars. We moved forward with the hope of someone struck suddenly blind but grateful to be alive.

Goodbye, father.

That day we crossed into the Ukraine. The drive was long and exhausting. We drank vodka in the car and ate smoked sausage and sandwiches. It was one continuous last supper with sandwiches and alcohol – a long exit into the future and a farewell to what we knew of ourselves.

Kiev was as big and beautiful as Moscow, but my arranged lodging – friends of friends – fell through, and we were stuck wandering the streets. I stopped a local who turned out to be an elevator repairman, and I asked plainly, "I'm so sorry. Can you please help us?" He was a kind man, and took us around town to hotels whose elevators he had worked on. None would take in our motley band of foreigners and refugees.

This Ukrainian stranger was visibly upset. After the fifth hotel he got the point. "Okay," he said, "tonight you will sleep in my home." We hadn't expected that, but we gratefully accepted his offer. Although our food had run out, we certainly weren't hopeful for dinner. Food was expensive and scarce. Kindness and hospitality proved us wrong again. His wife cooked up a wonderful dinner, they shared vodka with us, and we slept another night comfortably on a floor. I felt a deep warmth in my heart for this selfless help these strangers offered.

The next day took us south and west. The closer to the border we drew, the more irrational fears were waking up in me. My heart thumped at the sight of tanks rolling out, barricading the roads and waving us to the side, police stopping us for a moment in a roadblock. I lost my appetite. We didn't speak much that day. Our last stop before the border was Lvov, a culturally Polish town within the boundaries of the Ukraine where our Polish companions knew of a safe place to rest.

It turned out to be a smuggler's den. The house was enclosed by a seven foot fence, topped with barbed wire. Western clothes and electronics were stashed in nooks and corners, and a whole arsenal of weapons scattered across one corner of the living room – bayonets, hand grenades, Nazi helmets, sitting in plain view. There was no sewer, but an outhouse holding a pit toilet in the backyard. This sullen hideaway did not fit into my understanding of Soviet rule. It screamed danger and illegal activity.

"A new life," I thought. "Great."

The vision of tanks and police raids visited me again, but the serious square face of the smuggler was reassuring. It plainly meant that he could protect us in case of emergency. Our destiny was at the whim of shifting winds, and all there was for us to do was turn up our collars and go on plugging. Let it be.

That was our last, restless night in the Soviet Union.

The checkpoint to the border with Poland was a long line of Polish and Ukrainian cars, patiently moving inch by inch with long waits stretching in between. My heart was in my throat as I imagined all sorts of possibilities. They might confiscate my medicines and the money, leaving me with four hundred dollars to provide for my wife and son. They might find our diplomas, and who knew how I could get certification of my credentials in whatever land I was heading to?

A mile away from the border, two of our Polish companions – women, both – asked if we had anything illegal that we needed to smuggle across the border. Having seen their safe house in Lvov, I guessed that they might know something about smuggling that I didn't. I told them about the money and diplomas hidden in the lining of our suitcases.

"That's the first place they'll look," said one. "Give us your money. Give us your papers." They arranged our papers and bills in tight rolls and with savvy smiles produced pink condoms. "We'll be right back," said one, and they disappeared into the roadside bushes. A moment passed, and then they were back.

My eyes were wide. "You?" I asked.

"Yes, yes," they said. "Don't worry. It's safe."

I sighed and did not think of thanking them. I was in awe of the many spontaneous kindnesses that had been shown to us on this journey.

When it came our turn to be scrutinized on the border, a customs officer immediately looked knowingly at the Polish girls. They did not blink.

"Hmm", he said.

Then he slowly opened the suitcase where our papers had been hidden to run his hand inside the lining. The Polish women didn't look at me, but silently I thanked them. Then he opened up my suitcase of pharmaceuticals and medical paraphernalia, neither of which were allowed to leave the country.

He looked up and asked, "Why?"

With my heart beating, I said, "I'm a physician."

"Ah," he answered, closing the luggage and reaching to zip it up. "It's fine then."

How did that happen? In those days, it was accepted in Russia to steal what you had access to. Still, I was shocked that this unwritten rule was respected even at the border. If i was a butcher, I would probably have been allowed to export a cow.

Let it be.

The officer gave us a hard time for trying to take a television out of the country – the color set that we had promised our drivers – but refugees were allowed to carry certain goods that foreigners could not, and since we claimed the set, we were all in compliance with the law.

He waved us through.

He didn't notice the license plate on the trailer hauled behind the Fiat until we had passed into no man's land. Our trailer, owned by a Russian, had Soviet plates. Without special licensing, a Soviet vehicle could not leave the USSR. We had gotten plain lucky that he didn't notice. But as they saw our cars rumbling toward the Polish border, an officer spotted it. He took off running toward our car, his overcoat billowing behind him. Two soldiers followed in his wake, chasing after the illegal load. The Polish guards got stiff – and then we were in Poland. The Soviet officer scratched at his bare head and watched for a moment before turning back to the Soviet side.

Goodbye, Russia.

A hundred yards into Poland, we stepped out of the Fiat and looked up. Never in my life had I experienced emotions as strong and clear. The sense of freedom and escape shook me to the point that I had to sit on the ground. It was freedom from the past I had lost, and freedom for the future I didn't have yet. It was a complete lack of obligations, plans, and worries. The usual chain of events had stopped. There was absolutely nothing we could do about our past, and nothing we could do at this time about the future. I talked to my heart as it was about to jump out of my chest. It listened and slowed down. Anxious trembling in me stopped. Palpitations calmed, replaced by comforting warmth. I stopped shaking.

We hugged our Polish friends. We kissed each other. We looked at the open faces of our car mates and knew that nothing could stop us from being happy. The two wonderful women disappeared again along the roadside, and emerged with our money and documents.

Hello, new life.

*   *   *

The long process of immigration as refugees from Poland to the United States was difficult in its own bureaucratic way, and at times along the road, my wife and I fell into pits of frustration and unhappiness. Being unhappy is part of human nature. Although you can limit it, most of us can't live without it. After all, unhappiness properly channeled can propel us to improve our world. At my Indiana clinic, for example, I ask all my employees to provide negative comments – but also to suggest solutions to improve. An employee who cannot find room for improvement in either himself or others is not honestly observing what is happening around him. But by identifying ways to change the environment for the better, we can transfer habitual frustration into a positive result.

I've found in my practice that the difference between the happy and the distraught is often not whether they feel unhappy, but how they manage their unhappiness. One of my patients who suffered from obsessive compulsive disorder was so demanding of himself that he considered "unclean thoughts" as a blasphemous betrayal of God. He wanted purity not only in action but in thoughts too. He was good, but not good enough. As Russian pessimists say, a teaspoon of tar spoils a bucket of honey.

It was difficult to help him, because pure thoughts just do not exist. Human beings are ultimately a mixture of good and bad, and it is impossible not to have some representation of those extremes. I compared his impure thoughts to waste. You have to produce waste to stay clean. You need to get rid of the rubbish. Unhappiness and frustration are waste too. Waste needs to be processed and discarded. This includes bad thoughts. The conscious presence of those thoughts is actually *good*. It means that they are not contaminating the unconscious, but rather are brought to light and "thought away." If we were blind to unhappiness within us, we would become toxic. Instead we should attend to our bad thoughts, dismiss them, and move on. Using this logic, *bad* thoughts become *good* deeds.

The fact is, we all live in varying degrees of uncertainty and unhappiness. At the time of my family's flight from the USSR, the disorder was severe. Maybe your uncertainty is provoked by a know-it-all teenager, or an incompetent boss. Life's changes probably provoke frustration in you. For that matter, so does the weather. While complaints and unhappiness won't move the clouds, if they spur you to bring an umbrella on your way to work, then you've turned your frustration into a mechanism that will help you stay dry on a rainy day. Focus on the solution, not the problem. In my case, my wife at the time and I are both grateful for the temporary frustrations of our canceled citizenship and the ensuing flight from the USSR. All the struggles since led us to our Indiana home. It has allowed us to build ourselves a fulfilling life.

* * *

The consequences of bottling up your frustrations over time can be dire. We've already studied how the human stress response tightens your muscles and disrupts natural breathing patterns. Your heart is equally vulnerable. The heart evolved to beat hard and fast under stress to give your ancestors the strength to fight or flee from the cave bear that woke you up from your nap. As you might imagine, all that extra pumping has less practical benefit when you're disagreeing with your spouse – or when you're standing before a Soviet customs post, praying the officer doesn't notice the license plate on the back of your trailer.

This chapter's Mastermind exercise will teach you how to put your heart rate and rhythm under your conscious control. This mental power is absolutely possible, and scientifically verified by Himalayan yogis hooked up by scientists to biofeedback monitors. In fact, some yogis have shown in published tests the ability to decrease their heart rate and body metabolism to such a low rate that they are in a condition of hibernation for a prolonged period, using practically no energy.

Slowing your heart rate to one beat per minute is possible, but not a plausible goal for all practitioners of this Mastermind method, for the same reasons that a beginning swimmer should not attempt to backstroke across the English Channel. A practical aim is to eventually be able to decrease your heart rate by a reasonable degree in a time of anxiety, or to increase your heart rate when you are tired, sleepy, and sluggish.

You know by now that commanding your heart to speed up or slowdown will be ineffective. Communication has to be achieved through sensation. If you can experience warmth in the heart area on the left side of the chest (or the right, if you are one of the rare individuals with right side positioning of the heart), the physiological effect will be to dilate cardiac blood vessels, making the heart muscle more efficient, thus slowing down the beats. The heart begins pumping stronger and more efficiently.

If you have mastered the earlier exercises, your body is prepared to receive targeted messages of warmth. The digestive warmth in your upper abdomen has already brought warmth to your esophagus. You can visualize your esophagus as a heating element. It is a short distance to direct that heat into your heart.

Concentrate especially on feeling warmth as you exhale. Draw out your exhalations while focusing on warming your heart. You can test the effects of this method with two fingers on your pulse. If you find your heart rate increasing, it means you are pushing against yourself. You may be trying to send a message of words rather than one of sensation. Remember – you are communicating not by overwhelming force of will but by soothing coercion. Take a friendly approach. Imagine your heart bathing cozily in the warmth inside your chest. See it slowing down in a soothing calmness.

Warmth is comfort.

Warmth is peace.

Warmth in the Heart - Basic Benefits

- regulates heart rate
- improves circulation efficiency
- improves health of the heart muscle
- further counteracts physical stress response
- communicates peace to the mind

Warmth in the Heart - Extended Version

- Set a timer for fifteen minutes.
- Assume the Mask of Relaxation.
- Focus your eyes on the bridge of the nose.
- Tongue resting on inner surface of your upper teeth, jaws unlocked.
- Sense the heaviness and warmth in your hands and feet.
- Sense the heaviness and warmth in your arms and legs.
- Sense the heaviness and warmth in your neck and shoulders.
- Sense the heaviness and warmth in your back and buttocks.
- Sense the heaviness and warmth in your face.
- Breathe effortlessly using your diaphragm.
- Slow breath in, slow breath out of the abdomen.
- Swallow some warm saliva.
- Feel the warmth travelling from esophagus to stomach.
- Move warmth all the way through the small and large intestines to the anal sphincter.
- Move the warmth from the stomach and esophagus into your heart.
- Feel the warmth in the left side of your chest.
- You are comfortable, in control, peaceful.
- Imagine yourself floating in a hot tub, or whatever imagery comforts and warms you.
- Enjoy it.
- Keep this sensation as long as you can, or until the timer goes off.
- Tell yourself what exactly you will achieve after getting back to life.
- Maintain this conviction. Embrace it. Assume it.
- Clear away excessive warmth and heaviness.
- Count to three.
- Take a deep chest breath in, and fast out.
- Open your eyes and smile.

Warmth in the Heart - Short Version

- Mask of Relaxation
- Body is heavy and warm
- Breathe with abdomen
- Abdomen is warm
- Warmth travels to the heart
- Chest is warm
- Remove excessive heaviness and warmth
- Deep breath in and fast out
- Open eyes and smile

Warmth in the Heart - Concentrated Version

- Mask—Heavy—Warm
- Breathe with the abdomen
- Abdomen is warm
- Heart is warm
- Exit

Tips

- sensation of warmth in the heart slows heart rate
- slow abdominal breathing slows heart rate
- heart quickens during an inhale, so by prolonging an exhale, heart rate slows further
- coordinate warmth in heart with the complete integrated method
- if your pulse quickens during the exercise, that means you are fighting with yourself; try soothing yourself instead

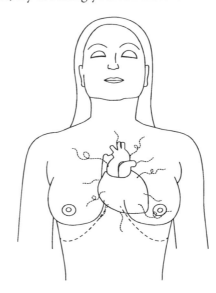

CHAPTER EIGHT

A Long Lost Friend

Although we grew up together, there was so much I would never understand about Ilya.

In our childhood in Siberia, he and I were like two ducklings, waddling about imprinting on each other, discovering the world together. We were inseparable for two years, which in childhood is an eternity. He was a little overweight boy with curly black hair. For some reason I remember him in green shorts and an untucked winter shirt. I wasn't sure why he wanted to be friends with me. He was much better at school than I was, but we played as equals. We used to have magnificent tactical battles on the floor of his parent's apartment, commanding toy soldiers and tanks and artillery against one another.

When my family moved away from Siberia into central Russia, the parting of Ilya and I was painful. We fought one last play-war, scattering our troops and equipment all across the floors of two rooms. I don't remember who won, but I do know that when my mother came to pick me up, Ilya and I both cried. Our parents smiled to each other. They had many friends. We just had each other.

Just before I left, I stole one of Ilya's toy cannons. I don't know why I did it. Maybe at the time I justified the theft as a trophy from our play-wars. Now, I think, I kept the toy to carry a memory of a dear friend away with me to a new home. At least this is the most convenient explanation. Whatever my motives, I felt terribly guilty about it. There in the bustle of central Russia, when I would see Ilya's cannon sitting beside my bed, I would call into question Ilya's judgment. Why would he want a thief for a friend? A year later I confessed my theft to him in a letter, so that I might assuage my guilt without having to make eye contact with him. He accepted my apology casually.

We kept in touch as pen pals for a while. But we were so young that we didn't have anything to write about besides new toys or broken toys. Our worlds drifted apart. Eventually as I settled into my new home and he found new playmates, our letters slowed to a trickle, and then we stopped writing altogether. The toy cannon I stole was eventually stolen from me, which seemed fitting enough.

That's how I lost my oldest friend. But even though we didn't talk, I felt him somewhere in the universe, the way you remember a long-gone childhood kitten which is forever alive in your heart. I made more friends, wonderful friends who were important and dear to me, but my first best friend could never be replaced. He was like my phantom limb. This sensation, I later learned, was a phenomenon scientists call *synchronicity*, which belongs to the field of *coincidence studies* and involves unspoken connections, vibrations, and hidden channels of energy. As was evident later in our lives, coincidence ruled us in unusual ways.

Thirty five years passed. I finished high school and medical school. I went through residencies and fellowships. I worked and I left Russia. Then I studied again and went through residency again and specialized again and started to practice in the United States. Ilya was utterly lost to me – an artifact of a past from the opposite side of the earth. But the world is smaller than it seems, and the past is never as far away from you as you think.

A friend from my Russian medical school who had ended up immigrating to New York in the 90s called me long distance to Indianapolis. "You know," he said, "I was talking to this pain physician guy who wanted me to come see orthopedic patients in his office in Manhattan. As we spoke, he asked me where I was from, so I told him about where we had gone to school. Do you know what this guy said? He said his best friend lived there. And he named you. I hope you don't mind, Dmitry, but I gave him your number."

It was Ilya! I could hardly believe it. We had both ended up in the United States, both doctors, and both still harboring a cherished memory of our shared childhood. Even more astonishingly, he somehow still thought of me as his best friend after our separation since the age of 10, and after my cowardly theft and after I quit sending him letters. He remembered me just as I remembered him.

Ilya called me soon after. The moment I heard his voice I knew him, although his deep and manly baritone didn't quite fit my childhood image of him. In my mind he remained the little overweight boy with curly black hair and green shorts and sloppy winter shirt. I asked him to send me a recent picture. Once I saw it, I knew him for who he was – my old friend, grown and matured.

Two weeks later I went to see him in Manhattan, in a refurbished apartment beside Central Park. He had a thriving pain management practice, like me. He had managed to find an impossibly cheap apartment which he restored to its full glory. We spent hours and hours catching up. He was married with three daughters. He had many friends, plans, and a wonderfully happy personality. We spent hours and hours catching up.

He was like a treasure lost and then found. There was no awkwardness in our relationship. We were together again, and I knew from now on that we had a future together. I came home excited beyond belief. I had found a walking, talking and smiling past that could now enrich my present. I could never have guessed how much could change in such a short period of time. I called my parents and told them that I had seen Ilya. My mother, who remembered the depth of our connection, was thrilled for us.

About two weeks after our reunion, Ilya called me again. His voice was strained. He asked for my help, saying that he had a problem that could not be discussed on the phone. I was on the next flight to New York, my mind racing. His wife wasn't at his apartment when I arrived.

"Well," Ilya said. "I have a secret, Dmitry."

I couldn't guess what he was about to tell me.

"I think I'm getting divorced. I'm having an affair."

I could tell by the pleading, wet look in his eyes that it was bad. Divorce always is. I wished he didn't have to go through with it. "I'm so sorry," I said. "How can I help?"

"I have to leave," he said. "I have to move away from this apartment."

"Does your wife know?"

"She does."

"And your children?"

"My wife will explain it to them in a few days. We don't want to tell them until it's finalized." His expression was agonizing.

How sad that his wife was losing him just when he returned to my life. The whole scenario sounded unfortunate, but it wasn't my place to argue or counsel him. I didn't know the details and I didn't have to. My role was to support my best friend, and to make sure that one of us kept a cool head. "Of course I'll help you," I told him.

The next day we moved some of the furniture, books, papers, clothes, and several sacks of daily necessities to an apartment a few blocks away. One of Ilya's friends, a tall fellow called Roberto, helped us. We three sat together sweating after carrying the last load into the apartment. It was obvious to me then that Ilya and I had much more catching up to do than I had originally believed. I invited him down to Indianapolis for a visit.

Ilya loved the idea, but was planning a trip to the Ukraine in a few weeks. He had an opportunity to get involved in a coal export deal. It sounded like big money, and he didn't want to miss the chance. Because I hadn't been back to Russia for more than twelve years, I asked him to take some photos to show me when he returned. He agreed. We arranged for him to bring his daughters to spend a few days with my family away from the press of the big city after he returned from the Ukraine.

All of it was still good. Complicated, but good.

Ilya and I hugged each other before I left, and he held on a little longer than I did. "I have to tell you something else," he whispered.

"Go ahead," I told him.

"Roberto," said Ilya, "he is my lover."

Roberto stood awkwardly behind us.

Talk about a shock! My best friend was gay. Of course I only wanted him to be happy, but in that moment I felt that there were mysteries I might never uncover about Ilya.

Back in Indiana, I got busy with my own practice and waited for his call after his scheduled return from the Ukraine. But when the New York area code popped up on caller ID, it wasn't his voice on the other end, but his wife's.

I started to greet her, but she interrupted me. "Can you fly in?"

What now? I thought, but I said, "What's going on?"

She was not delicate. She did not mince words. "So you met Roberto?" she asked.

"I did."

"And you knew he was Ilya's lover?"

"Tell me what's wrong," I said.

"Well," she said, "what I'm about to say must be kept in confidence, just like everything Ilya told you."

"Are you getting back together?"

"No," she said. "No, no, no. Ilya was killed in the Ukraine."

I fell out of my chair. "Killed! What do you mean?"

The story as she told it was bizarre. Ilya had been in a car crash – a head-on collision on an empty, countryside road. Ilya had been driving fast, passing a sputtering old jalopy in front of him. When they got to the top of the hill, the car they had been passing sped suddenly away, and Ilya's car smashed into a truck that was parked in the opposite lane, driverless, just beyond the crest of the hill. I couldn't believe it. Everything that had happened with Ilya and I over the last few weeks was so unfathomable. I didn't know whether his wife was so shocked that she couldn't think straight, or if there really was something sinister about the accident. I never did find out the truth.

Ilya's body was still in Kiev. It would be flown into New York within the week. I cannot express on paper the incredible sense of loss I experienced. I had only just reconnected with my best friend a month earlier. I could still feel the residual joy at my good fortune to have him back in my life. And now he was dead. I wept. "When is the funeral?" I asked.

Her reply was eerie. "I need you fly in as soon as possible," she said, "and not just for the funeral."

"What! What else can I do?"

She was so furious, she said, at her husband and her life and his sudden death that she refused even to *identify his body*. She would not allow Ilya's parents access to the corpse either. "They are not good people," she said. "I won't have them near my husband. You, Dmitry, must come to identify him. You are his best friend, and the only one with the right to do it."

I was stunned. I didn't want to ask more. There was so much mystery here that I lost hope of ever getting to the bottom of it. All that was mine to do was to stand beside my oldest friend. I knew that everyone who loved him was overwhelmed and depending on me. Despite my horror, I knew I had to remain cool and calm, for the family of my lost friend as much as myself. I agreed to her request.

A few days later my friend's body arrived. For the third time in several weeks, I returned to New York. His wife fixed me a bed in her apartment. All the furniture had been moved back. Roberto was gone. Ilya's secret was locked up. I went to the funeral home, feeling not myself. I looked down at him, my friend, my best friend who was dead, my friend who I saw twice after not seeing him for 35 years, dear Ilya, who spent a week shuffled between countries, whose funeral depended on me. It was him. It was him, but pale and cold and very, very much unlike him. I did not cry. My mind and forehead were cool, like his. I signed the paper. I went out and calmly notified his wife and his parents that it was her husband and their son back there in the coffin.

Because I was the only one not embroiled in any of the arguments or confrontations, they asked me to give the eulogy at the funeral. I talked about him, my friend, who I knew in a way that was somehow unlike how others knew him. It seemed that everybody at the funeral knew a different person and that whole crowd of personalities were jammed into one small coffin, together with my best friend.

I shouldn't have let him drift away all those years ago.

I should have written him more letters.

I shouldn't have stolen his toy cannon.

After the funeral there was a private gathering at his wife's apartment. People moved slowly trying not to touch each other, full of mistrust and anger. I was the only one outside of the simmering fury. I've never been touched as many times in my life as I was that evening. People held my shoulders, hands, and head. They hugged me, petted my shoulder, and shook my hand, thanking me for being his best friend.

I lived within a tragedy.

It was unbearable.

The next morning I discovered that one of Ilya's family members had stolen my aftershave from the toiletry bag I had left in the bathroom. It was expensive aftershave, but I didn't begrudge the culprit. In fact, I felt redeemed, and a little grateful.

*   *   *

Part of life is dealing with tragedy – the loss of a parent, or a child, or a spouse, or a best friend. Somehow we do survive these events, but very few of us are able to go through such losses completely unscarred. Our mind instinctively and unconsciously throws up defenses in the face of tragedy or extreme stress. In the midst of either physical or emotional trauma, self-preservation takes over altruistic behavior. We lose the ability to see things clearly. Long term planning is replaced by immediate and exaggerated action. Aggression rises. Social and ethical norms drift away. Language simplifies. Vocabulary decreases. Associations lose complexity.

A combat veteran will recognize these symptoms. So will Ilya's wife. Surely if she had been thinking clearly she would have granted grieving parents the right to say farewell to their son. But her mind, traumatized by the revelations of the past few months, just wouldn't cool down. The net effect was to turn what should have been a scene of mutual mourning into a tense, uncomfortable afternoon of blame which left few of the grieving with any kind of closure.

Of course we can sympathize with the reaction of Ilya's wife. Anger rarely arises from nothing, and emotions are infecting. Try thinking peaceful thoughts while standing in front of someone in a rage and lashing out at you. It's not easy. But on the other hand, you already know the negative physical effects of stress. Conscious emotional control is a skill worth practicing, it will limit your own mental strain, as well as prepare you for more difficult tests of mental strength. Smiling at your execution is an extreme example of this ability, and for most people may be more of an ideal than a reality. But experiencing events at a peaceful remove from the emotions surrounding you spares you undue suffering. Cats, for instance, are known to purr when they are sick or dying, not just when you are scratching their necks. They soothe themselves.

As a human being, you've got a larger, tougher brain than your cat. You are already communicating with your brain to consciously counteract the physical symptoms of extreme stress. The Mask of Relaxation counteracts anxiety, heaviness counters muscle tension, warm heart counters elevated heart rate, warm gut counters the tightening of digestion, and abdominal breathing counters frantic respiration. You've also learned that these methods will send a soothing message over the bridge to your mind. But by having a cool forehead – literally – you can exercise direct control over your mental stress response.

Regulating blood flow to the brain is the first step in managing your unconscious cognitive abilities. When you slow down or speed up blood flow inside your skull, you influence physiological activation or inhibition of the brain. Unlike other areas of the body, the brain doesn't like too much blood, and more often than not you will want to decrease blood flow rather than increase. Anatomically, you will be constricting blood vessels in the brain and thereby managing metabolism and brain function. But remember – your body speaks in sensations, not words. Your first task now should be to feel coolness in the forehead.

You should only begin this once you have mastered the other six exercises of Basic Mastermind. When it is simple for you to feel warm and heavy everywhere, then you are ready to cool your forehead. There are several different methods you can use to help feel this. You may ask someone to wave a fan over your forehead to sense that first draft of cool air and seize onto the feeling. Or you could try to put a wet cloth on your forehead, or sprinkling water droplets. Just like the previous exercises, these methods are your training wheels. After you begin to recognize and remember this coolness, the physical actions are no longer needed. You should be able to imagine and retrieve the sensation of coolness from memory.

Another method is to first experience coolness elsewhere on your body and move it to the forehead, as you did by moving warmth from your stomach and esophagus to the heart. Try inhaling through your mouth a few times, experiencing a cool feeling on the tongue. This is a natural sensation that you will always experience unless your mouth is completely dry. After clearly sensing the coolness of the air moving against the tongue, you can close your mouth and keep breathing through the nose. As you do it, it is not difficult to preserve a sensation of coolness on the tongue even with your mouth shut. Retain this sensation, feel it clearly.

Once you have learned how to keep the sensation of coolness in your mouth, which should not take long, move it through the bridge of the nose onto the forehead, spreading it as you go.

Again, after several repetitions you will be able to experience a cool forehead just by telling yourself that your forehead is cool and imagining such a sensation.

Because imagery is important in the Mastermind, once you do away with the training wheels it helps to imagine something cool actually lying on your forehead. My favorite image, which pretty much reflects everything that needs to be achieved during Basic Mastermind, is imagining myself floating in hot water with a cold towel on the forehead. It reflects everything you need to feel: heaviness and warmth, calmness and relaxation with a cool forehead. This, combined with all of the previous exercises, is the complete Basic Mastermind submersion method.

Submersion Method (Coolness to the Forehead) - Basic Benefits

- regulates blood flow to the brain
- manages brain metabolism and function
- influences physiological activation of the brain
- only use after mastering earlier methods

Submersion Method - Extended Version

- Set a timer for fifteen minutes.
- Assume the Mask of Relaxation.
- Focus your eyes on the bridge of the nose.
- Tongue resting on inner surface of upper teeth, jaws unlocked.
- A deep diaphragmatic inhale.
- Exhale long and slow.
- As you breathe, feel the worry and tension leaving your body.
- Sense the heaviness and warmth in your hands and feet.
- Sense the heaviness and warmth in your arms and legs.
- Sense the heaviness and warmth in your neck and shoulders.
- Sense the heaviness and warmth in your back and buttocks.
- Sense the warmth in your abdomen.
- Sense the warmth and heaviness in your face.
- Warmth floats in loops & hoops of small intestine and into the large.
- Warmth follows large intestine up, across abdomen, and down to the rectum and outside. Throat, esophagus, and stomach are warm.
- Forehead is cool, pleasantly chilled.
- The whole body is heavy and warm, other than the forehead.
- Imagine floating in a hot tub with an iced cloth on your forehead.
- See it. Feel it. Imagine it. Enjoy it.
- Thoughts are slow, pleasant, and comfortable.
- You are under control. You are full of hope and trust in yourself.
- Don't fall asleep.

- Keep this sensation as long as you can, or until the timer goes off.
- Take a deep and stimulating breath in with your chest.
- Forcefully exhale in a fast and decisive manner. Again 2 more times.
- You will succeed in whatever you set yourself to.
- Stretch and then open your eyes and smile.

Submersion Method - Short Version

- Mask of Relaxation
- Body is heavy and warm
- Breathe with abdomen
- Abdomen is warm
- Forehead is cool
- Excessive warmth goes away
- Deep breath in and fast out
- Open eyes and smile

Submersion Method - Concentrated Version

- Mask—Heavy—Warm
- Breathing
- Abdomen
- Heart
- Forehead is cool
- Exit

Tips

- in the beginning stages of this exercise, ask a friend to wave a fan over the forehead to feel the draft of cold air

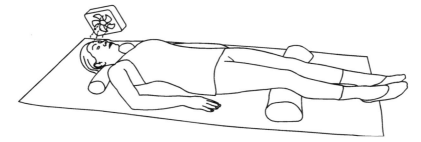

- or put a wet cloth or drops of water on the forehead
- as the sensation of coolness internalizes, physical crutches are no longer necessary

See Additional Tips/Examples starting on Page 188.

CHAPTER NINE

A World of Difference

Several years ago someone called me and said, "Birds sing goodbye my tie," and hung up immediately. Something about the little childish rhyme chimed inside me, and a memory of my first years in the United States flashed before me – it was an era in American psychiatry with few medication choices, and wards billowing with cigarette smoke, when eccentricities were treated by tossing medications and treatments at patients in hope of a miracle. There was one man, Jack, who suffered from schizophrenia who I had a soft spot for in those early days. I still remember the first words we exchanged.

"Nice to meet you," I had said. I expected him to react somehow to my accent. Some patients got quiet and confused; others would close their eyes and mouth my words back to themselves.

But not Jack. He looked at me with obvious contempt, frowned, wrinkled his nose, and after measuring me critically proclaimed, "I don't meat, I greet. I'm a vegetarian."

I was taken aback by the richness of the human mind. I immediately liked him in spite of his grouchiness.

For the next four months I stopped to visit him as often as I could. The hospital tried medication combinations, electroconvulsive therapy, and psychotherapy, but nothing helped. Jack only really felt well when he smoked, so he smoked relentlessly – two, three, four, sometimes even six packs a day. His mental associations were so jumbled that more often than not it was impossible to understand him. Sometimes we sat together just trading gibberish back and forth. It didn't matter exactly what we were communicating. The camaraderie was enough. We had fun together.

Jack had come from a large family of copper industrialists. When he was 23 his symptoms began – increasingly arcane and bizarre mental associations twisting any attempt at meaningful conversation into gobbledygook. What reasonable neural connections in his brain he retained were all from before the onset of his illness. But he did have the capacity to learn, and to observe. "You look smaller today," he said to me once. "Did you lose money?" After that, I found myself opening up my shoulders and lifting my chin whenever I received a paycheck.

Another morning I found him hunched over a book of lines and squiggles that he told me was a Thai-Sanskrit dictionary. I had no idea that such a book even existed. I don't know either if he was holding it right side up or not, but I like to think that he was. A thought that he could actually read and understand this dictionary was somehow disturbing. Sometimes he spoke about Chekov and Dostoevsky's characters. He could recite whole sentences and paragraphs from Gogol in the original Russian. It reminded me of high school. Genius and insanity truly are connected.

The hospital wasn't able to do much for him. Eventually his doctors discharged him to a large estate that his mother owned. She was a strange and off-putting woman who probably passed on a gene or two to him. After Jack was discharged, she put very little effort to his care. For her, Jack was already gone and there was no sense in trying to rescue him.

She did allow me to continue visiting him at his home. Jack had an incredible collection of musical instruments. They were all over his room: hanging on the walls, propped up in corners. He kept a mandolin on his desk and a cello in the bath tub. He would gather them up and set them in a line on the floor, playing them all in a row, one after the next. These performances were like his thinking – unpredictable, twisted and fascinating. Sometimes he just made sounds on the instruments, and other times the music was pleasant. That he retained such powers of mental and muscle memory considering the medication he was on – fifteen times the standard dosage of an archaic drug that probably no one else in the U.S. was on anymore – this spoke to his native intelligence (as well as a resistance to pharmaceuticals.)

He spent most of his time smoking in the sitting room with the shades drawn and listening to his records. The longer he spent in the care of his mother, the more his condition deteriorated. He stopped shaving. He wouldn't bathe. It was a battle to make him take his shoes off when he went to bed. He wouldn't brush his teeth, ever. Leaving the house came to be a major adventure for him. His lips would go dry and his tongue would stick to his throat. He wouldn't blink for the whole ride. After one such outing, he clenched his teeth and told me that he was ashamed of being me in his previous life. It took me a while to digest this insult.

I begged his mother to limit his cigarettes or trade him cigarettes in exchange for brushing his teeth, or not sleeping in his shoes, or taking a shower at least once a week, or changing his socks at least once a month. But for her it was too much trouble. Jack deteriorated into a snail-like existence. Eventually I gave up on him.

And then ten years later he called me and said, "Birds sing goodbye my tie," and hung up.

I guessed that his mother had died. Why else would he have called me?

I was right. Eventually his guardian called me back and arranged for me and a friend of mine, a behavioral therapist, to spend some time with him. The years had not been kind to Jack. He was filthy and wheezing asthmatically. His mind had cornered itself into a knot of unintelligible associations, and it took some casting about before he and I could communicate again. I did manage to teach him some Mastermind methods – relaxation, breathing, and heaviness. He would lie down in the silence with his eyes closed. We were glad to see him not smoking.

Gradually we limited his cigarettes, using them as carrots to encourage him to shave, bathe, and change his socks on a regular basis. His clothes went from literal stinking rags to passably clean, and then neat. We changed his medication from pills to a once a month injectable, removing the need for daily pills to be an object of contention. His mouth stopped drying out. His breathing improved. We began to play word games like we had in the old days – and on occasion we even had real engaging conversation.

He began to recognize his condition as something abnormal. In his usual witty manner, he deflected the behavioral therapist's casual comments about her own maladies, pointing calmly, "You should try my illness."

*   *   *

Jack's treatment wasn't easy and it wasn't quick. It's still not a perfect success. Even now I'm sure he smokes cigarettes whenever he can get his hands on them. But realistically, few successes *are* perfect. Improving your life does not just happen at the flip of a switch. It is a tangle of paths through a jagged landscape. Some will carry you to more contentment and balance than another. Some will do the reverse.

Jack wasn't able to evaluate for himself how to improve his life. His mental processes were so damaged both by his illness and his environment that he could not understand the relationship between tooth decay and poor dental hygiene, or the relationship between athletes' foot and never taking off his shoes. Jack cared about neither decay nor athlete's foot. Although Jack's is an extreme case, we all suffer our own handicaps. Maybe you can't resist that extra slice of pizza even though it's bad for your heart. Maybe, like some, you still smoke cigars even though you know that they lead to throat cancer.

Trust me, it's normal and even healthy to make mistakes. It's the ability to correct those mistakes in a timely manner – to prevent your own missteps from developing into crippling obsessions that brings about a humble mastery of life. You'll be paralyzed if you are too afraid to absorb a mistake. Inventiveness and experimentation is the way to success. Perfection is an ideal worth striving for, but if you cannot endure your own failures then your hunt for perfection will lead to stagnation. Only lawyers are truly repulsed by mistakes. They exploit them against you and they parasite on them, thriving in this pursuit. The lawyers are the only people who are diehard enemies of mistakes, because to them a mistake is exploitable. What happens in a society driven by attorneys is that the system punishes risks and mistakes that must accompany risk. This is the best way to kill the vibrancy of a civilization – by overregulation and punishment of initiative.

At the same time, there must be a system of checks and balances in a society. You should also always be testing your own notions and decisions. Mistakes in judgment are so common that you should always assume that you are doing something wrong. You need to constantly try to prove to yourself that the path you have selected is the right one. And to do that, you need to have both a clear head and an intimate awareness of how your own body interacts with your mind and your world.

That's the value of the exercises you've learned thus far. If you've mastered them – and you need to do so before moving on to the next set of methods – you've accomplished three things:

1. You're aware of your body in ways that you weren't before.
2. You've managed to put some unconscious physiological reactions under conscious control.
3. You've practiced fifteen minute long mental focus.

Congratulations.

You're getting to know yourself.

*   *   *

One of my girlfriends during medical school believed that her skin grew from a little scar on her abdomen. She had a theory that everything grows from one place, like a flower grows from a bud. As she understood it, her skin grew out of that one scar, spreading all over the body. Knowing what I do about embryology and anatomy, I can promise that her belief is ridiculous and false. But based on her body of knowledge, it was a perfectly logical and convenient idea.

But how often do we test our own assumptions? Could it be that we also have some ideas that are as untrue as the woman whose skin grew out of her scar? Before beginning the Mastermind exercises, you may have believed that it was impossible to consciously raise your body temperature. By now you know differently.

As you go on practicing the body to mind methods, you might encounter some strange effects that challenge the way you look at yourself and the world around you. For example, when you experience heaviness, warmth, and pleasant tiredness all over the body, you may get the feeling that your body is asleep but your consciousness is awake. During this state, the feeling of heaviness is strangely replaced by a sensation of lightness or weightlessness.

While the condition deepens, some people experience the perception of changes in their body structure. They may feel elongation of their arms or legs, or the head moving above the body, attached by a long neck. You may be surprised by having huge and disproportionate hands and feet, along with other bizarre body metamorphoses like those described in Alice in Wonderland. This frequently comes along with the feeling of hovering above the surface of the floor you are laying on, perhaps attached to it by a few points like the shoulder blades and tailbone.

The final progression is the sense of submersion – the total disappearance of the body while the mind seems to continue on its own without the need for the physical form. This is a dissociative experience which is unhealthy if it happens spontaneously, but is gratifying if done on purpose and reversed in a timely manner. It is possible to experience this after only a few weeks of regular Mastermind training.

This last sensation is a challenging one – but it is a real phenomenon, and worthy of your exploration.

See Submersion Examples on Pages 188 through 190.

*   *   *

The *inner flashlight* is the culmination of all the skills that you have practiced until now. It is the last tool that you will need to explore your body. Although it will help to first assume the complete Mastermind relaxation method before attempting this exercise, I'll give you no step by step instruction. Instead you can study and practice it according to your own needs, as it will eventually be highly personalized to suit you.

The inner flashlight method is what it sounds like. You will imagine a spot of light positioned somewhere on your body, say, on the palm of your hand. (It will help initially to first assume the complete Mastermind relaxation method from the last chapter.) When you have mastered it, you will be able to move the warm ray of light along your arm, leaving a warm trace behind – or just keeping the warmth at the spot that the light illuminates. Accomplish this first before moving on. Once you are ready, try to seep the warm spotlight through your skin and into the muscles. Move your spotlight into the bone at the elbow joint, and slip it higher, somewhere into your chest or abdomen, or anywhere else you like.

Imagining and experiencing this feeling trains you how to mobilize your attention and focus your brain on just one small area. The spotlight sensation of warmth uses the conscious control over your nervous system that you have already practiced to regulate the behavior of blood vessels in a very small area.

Strategic placement of warmth in a small spot gives you control over your internal organs. You may be able to dilate your kidneys for a stone to pass through, or to warm and heal a diseased gallbladder. If you know your anatomy well enough you can focus on any place that requires intervention. Bring local warmth to your inner ear when you have an irritating problem with dizziness or vertigo. Bring it to the lungs during a case of pneumonia. Warm an arthritic knee when it hurts. If you know anatomy and the function of the brain you can either stimulate or inhibit different areas of the brain. By doing that, you can directly influence vision, smell, pain, emotions, memory, and so on.

After you have mastered the use of the inner flashlight to experience concentrated warmth – physiologically speaking, local blood vessel dilation – you can reverse the exercise and learn how to constrict blood vessels, feeling icy cold in selected places. This would allow you to fight swelling and chronic inflammation, or help the same dizziness and ear ringing. It has the same effect as ice packs on strained muscles. All you need to do is to change your perception from a warm ray of light to a cold beam of light.

Now you're free to experiment. Remember that you are in control, not the method. Don't be afraid of mistakes, but be always testing and self-correcting. Use or modify this exercise according to your need. Venture across the bridge and back between your body and mind until you know it well.

And when you are ready to delve deeper into yourself, continue on to Part Two.

Inner Flashlight - Basic Benefits

- bridges the gap between body and mind
- the culmination of mental control over physical processes
- can be used for countless therapeutic self-treatments

Inner Flashlight - Concentrated Version

- Mask—Heavy—Warm
- Breathing
- Abdomen
- Heart
- Forehead
- Inner Flashlight
- Exit

Inner Flashlight Method

- assume a state of Mastermind submersion, using a boil down of the suggestion routine
  - face
  - calm
  - whole body is heavy and warm
  - warmth in upper abdomen
  - warmth in left chest
  - cool in forehead
- imagine a spot of light positioned on the palm of the hand

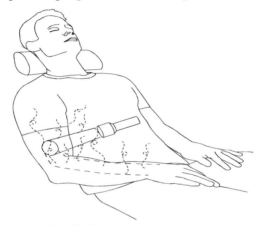

- feel the warm circle of light
- move the light along the arm leaving a warm trace behind or just keeping warmth at the illuminated spot
- brings *localized* warmth, or increased blood flow and healing power, to any place in the body

Tips

- with a working knowledge of anatomy, the inner flashlight gives control over internal organs
- with a working knowledge of brain function and physiology, can stimulate or inhibit different areas of the brain to influence vision, smell, pain, emotions, memory, and so on if to focus ray of light on particular parts of the brain
- try replacing the warmth with a spot of icy cool light to constrict blood vessels in targeted areas

PART TWO

Transitional Mastermind

Mind to World

CHAPTER TEN

The Girl Who Drew No Noses

A nna was a little four year old angel – pink cheeks, huge blue eyes, and bouncing golden curls. Her squiggled doodles ended up posted on nearly every desk and bulletin board of the rural hospital in central Russia. I even found one on the wall of the janitor's closet. Everyone loved her. That made her circumstances all the more awful, because Anna was dying.

I was in charge of the pediatrics unit of the hospital that first treated her. Her parents had exploded into the lobby bearing little Anna in their arms. Her lips were blue, and she struggled to suck in a gasp of air. Her mother was wailing and rocking back and forth as our aides bore Anna away, and her father wept quietly.

I had to pump Anna with intravenous steroids and keep her on the inpatient floor for days before she finally stopped wheezing. By then Anna had drawn a picture of me in my white lab coat, and the nurses, and the cleaning staff. She signed each one with a scribble and presented them solemnly to the subject.

Anna's asthmatic reactions had begun when she was two. Her mother tearfully told me how a fearsome German shepherd had barked and slathered at Anna while she lay in her stroller, triggering the first wheezing. The initial episodes were not very bad. Her parents did not seek help until Anna was in a desperate state. It sounded to me like a psychological trauma unmasking a natural, physical vulnerability.

Anna's attacks continued to worsen. Triage nurses came to expect the frantic, tearful parents bursting through the hospital doors, bearing their daughter in their arms like a load of firewood, the girl's mouth open and her eyes half closed. It was a scene of panicked terror. I managed to treat Anna each time, but as the disease grew stronger the medications became less effective. Consultants at the hospital concluded that sweet Anna's progressive and resistant condition was a death sentence. Children with Anna's medical history simply didn't last long.

Without any better options, I suggested to Anna's parents that we might focus on the underlying fear that had triggered the problem in the first place, rather than depending solely on the failing symptomatic treatments of IVs and steroids. I wanted to complement the hospital treatment with psychotherapy. Frankly, it was a theory born of desperation. But when you're dangling on the crumbling lip of a cliff, you'll grab on to any branch or twig within reach and pray it'll hold. Her parents agreed to try.

First I needed to coach them. I asked her parents to take their focus off Anna's breathing. "Do not panic when she begins to wheeze," I instructed them, "or fidget, or show your fear. Kiss her, yes, hug her, and take her to the hospital if you must. But do not cry. Keep your distress to yourself. Smile instead. You must be strong for your daughter." With trembling lips, Anna's mother agreed to comply.

For the next three months, I visited Anna twice a week. To her, our meetings were only games. We play-acted different scenarios. She would play a dog and I would play her, or vice versa. In every game she was either a victim or an attacker. She would be a rabbit and I would be the fox. She would play the bird, and I would be the snake. We had fun.

Our first order of business was always to review the pictures that Anna had drawn since we last spoke. She drew pictures of the characters we played, or of herself or her parents. Sometimes we brought her parents into the game, and that made Anna squeal for joy, especially when she was the attacker. Eventually she invented her own stories for us to play out. We would each act a part, and then swap roles until Anna had played them all.

One day during my rounds at the hospital, I noticed that one of Anna's pictures pinned to a bulletin board showed a nurse without a nose. As I strolled the corridors, I looked carefully and found that Anna *never* drew a nose. It was a hallmark of her work, and that struck me as curious. Even though four-year-olds are not the best artists, most do know the general shape of a face. But not Anna. Her subjects, whether rabbits or pirates or doctors, just showed a flat emptiness between the eyes and mouth.

At my prompting, Anna invented a character called Asthma. At first he was just a scribbled blob on paper, but over time he evolved into a clawed alien with a dozen legs and long dark hair and scaly armor. We made up a victim-attacker game with two characters called Anna and Asthma. In the first act, I played Anna and she was Asthma. She crept up and then sprang before me, clawing up at my throat and threatening me in a croaking wheeze. But the real fury was unleashed when we swapped roles so Anna played Anna, and I imitated the hoarse choking voice of Asthma. Anna lashed out at me like a cornered animal, thrashing and slapping and pinching until I yelled for mercy – first as Asthma, and then when she didn't stop, as Doctor Dmitry. "You won!" I cried, "Didn't you hear? The wicked Asthma surrendered to the brave hero Anna!"

The idea behind these games was to separate the disease from her, to make it foreign to her body and mind. I wanted her to feel like a healthy girl battling an enemy, and not an invalid losing a fight against a disease. Her parents didn't fuss over her any more. They hugged and comforted her whenever she suffered an attack, but Anna wasn't a baby. Over time she did in fact become less afraid, and increasingly confident that she could abolish the asthma all on her own. She knew that when Asthma attacked, Anna was a brave hero, a beloved daughter, and by golly she wouldn't be afraid of ugly old Asthma. As time passed, the episodes of suffocation became less frequent and less severe.

Strangely enough, the faces in her drawings started to show a little freckle of a nose – just a single pencil point in the middle of the face. Her noses grew into periods, and then two dots. They fattened and expanded into nostrils. After several weeks, the characters in her drawings developed little bumps, and then realistic noses. Some weeks later her asthma attacks stopped completely. She wasn't rushed to the hospital for steroids any more. At six weeks we weaned her off inhalers. After three months she stopped wheezing, and she didn't have any symptoms at all. The noses she drew then were great towering pyramids. The face and body of whatever she was drawing were vestigial lobes dangling from the noses.

I never mentioned the significance of these pictures to her. Anna thought she was just drawing for fun. But I knew that something deeper was at work.

*　*　*

Sigmund Freud led the practice of psychiatry into an abyss of endless rumination on the topic of the self. He reversed the focus of psychotherapy from what a person could *do* to what *had been done* to him. Leather sofa talk therapy is a direct descendant of Freud. Elsewhere in the world many Freudian theories have fallen out of favor, but in the United States conversation is still considered a keystone of psychiatric therapy.

The Freudian model extinguishes personal responsibility. You might say that Freudian psychiatrists in the United States have convinced Americans that they are the victims of their parents, of their schools, and of society itself. I do not consider that a productive outlook. Do you know anyone who was therapized into greatness? I doubt it. There are better ways to achieve health, stability, and mental tranquility than Freudian psychotherapy.

Consider the folly of psychological testing, such as IQ and personality tests. It is the tendency of our culture to quantify everything. We want classifications, measurements and certainty. But I don't know of any algorithm that can predict the full complexity of a human being. Psychological testing is not an x-ray machine. It depends on an enormous number of constantly changing subjective factors.

Many tests are even developed by pharmaceutical companies to identify candidates for the drugs they are selling. For example, you must be made of wood not to earn a confirmation of ADHD through testing. Every other child in America is diagnosed with ADHD, and the diagnosis is swelling even into adult life. More and more Americans are on pills. Psychologists, of course, know all of this, and will defer to a clinical evaluation over the results of psychological testing. But the lay public puts too much trust in the value of these psychological tests. The mind exists in constant motion. Asking someone else to measure it for you is the same as asking a friend to document your height while you jump on a trampoline.

This need to identify and medicate every fleeting symptom – from coughs to boredom to restless sleep – fills the coffers of pharmaceutical companies, and packs American veins with drugs. In fact, only symptoms that objectively impair life require pharmaceutical treatment. Not every cough needs cough syrup. Not every sadness means depression. Not every spat of inattention is ADHD. It is a normal function of the brain to feel sad sometimes, or bored, or to churn up an unpleasant emotion. If you use your brain at all, you cannot possibly hope to never feel emotional pain. Furthermore, emotional turmoil does not always respond to regular pain medications, and frequently worsens under the influence of drugs which interfere with cognition.

Psychiatry, like the fashion world, follows certain trends. In the 60s everyone was diagnosed with schizophrenia (remember Marlon?), in the 70s with PTSD, in the 80s with depression, and in the 90s with dissociative identity disorder. Today ADHD and bipolar disorder are the dysfunctions of choice. That doesn't mean these conditions are not real, or that they don't need treatment. Paradoxically, although over diagnosing and overtreatment are rampant, patients actually suffering from these conditions are *underdiagnosed* and *undertreated*. They are not many and they do not brag about their symptoms. They do not insist they are ill. They just are.

So not all medications are bad all the time. Anna would have certainly died without the steroids. The right drugs prescribed for the right reasons are wonderful, and it is always wise to seek information about a health condition from a specialist. A little knowledge from the internet is often more damaging than total ignorance. It's okay to have theories. Generate a bunch of them. But make sure that you test them against someone who understands the complexities of the human body and mind.

After all, Western medicine has developed an unprecedented capability to repair the hardware of the body. Our health care professionals are miracle workers on hardware. Our software, on the other hand, is a little more slippery. The present pain epidemic in the United States, for example, exists in part because even the mechanism of pain is not understood or appreciated. Mental disorders such as the physical symptoms of emotional distress (what scientists call "somatization") cannot be fixed with a needle or a knife. But almost any symptomatic unpleasantness in life can be reversed or prevented from the inside.

The way to defeat unpleasant emotions is not by talking in dizzy circles. The heroes around you have transformed their life using the Teddy Roosevelt model: looking forward and not backward, overcoming obstacles, and relying on a steadfast internal drive. They know that it is not what happens *to* you that matters. Even if every external force acting upon you were mapped out plainly for you to see, you still wouldn't be able to control them all. What matters is what you *do* with the platter you're served.

The question, then, is not how to track down the root cause of your symptoms, but how to change those symptoms. For the answer, look to your children.

* * *

A child's imagination is incredibly powerful. For more than a hundred years professionals in my field have been adapting play therapy for adults. We call it psychodrama, but that's just a fancy word for role playing. Children do this instinctively. They pretend to be what they want to be, which prepares them for real life experiences. The relationship between role-play and the real world can be direct, as in the case of the girl who walks with good posture because she pretends to be a ballerina. It can also have more subtle results as in Anna's management of her asthma.

We role-play less and less as we grow older. Modern adolescent culture, looking down on "posers" and emphasizing the virtue of being "real," discourages dreamers or role-players. Most of us leave make-believe behind as we accumulate real world experiences and obligations. Many American adults only exercise their imaginations through scripted fictions like television dramas or novels. But there is nothing childish about a mature imagination unleashed. The actor Michael Chekhov, nephew of the famous Russian writer, was known for enacting such comprehensive transformations on the stage that audiences swore he changed the color of his eyes depending on the role. It is testament to the power of role-play. Your native mental powers can be honed to produce astonishing results in your life.

In Part One of this book you explored the bridge between your mind and your body. Now I will take you across the bridge between your mind and the world. The foundation of this set of methods is visualization. The ability to consciously visualize within your mind rather than physically act is what will distinguish a child's make-believe from your mature Mastermind tools. The basic elements of this skill, which you'll learn in the next few chapters, are critically important and must be mastered before you move on to more advanced exercises. Your eventual goal will be to deliberately create and manipulate abstractions in your head.

The effects of using visualization and mental abstraction can be dramatic. Just look at Anna. She used the visualizations in the pictures to make real and measurable changes in her life. They turned out to be permanent. Thirty years after I finished my pediatrics work in that remote Soviet hospital, Anna's mother tracked me down on the internet and sent me an e-mail saying Anna hadn't suffered a single asthma attack since I saw her last, and also that the little girl with a death sentence had just given birth to a daughter of her own. Mind you, it was done without seeing Anna as a victim, without feeling sorry for her, and without ruminating about the traumatic experience she underwent.

*   *   *

Visualization will be easier for some than others. You have already practiced elements of visualization in your mind to body exercise – imagining yourself in the hot tub, for instance, or buried in sand. Mind to World methods require that you sharpen your control over these scenes. Think of it like conscious dreaming, where you are directing the action.

Because you need to be the director, there won't be set a list of step by step instructions as you used for the mind to body exercises. You, not I, are the creative force here. I will give you some ideas, but you're far enough along in your Mastermind training that you can scheme your own visualizations. These exercises must be stimulating and fun, so revise or program them according to your own specifications.

The first exercise is called **Capture Color**. Once you finish reading this paragraph, assume the Mask of Relaxation and pay strict attention to what happens next. Don't move your eyeballs, just consciously watch. What seems at first like darkness is actually a vivid scene of floating spots and planes of light and dark, all flaring and fading in to one another. To really shake things up, rub your eyes through your eyelids and observe the results. You may see colors, or shades, or hues drifting about. You may see geometric patterns too – spirals and circles arrayed in formation like abstract art. Try it now.

The first stage of the Mastermind capture color method is to preserve whatever color naturally appears to you while you are in a state of physical Mastermind submersion. Feel your heaviness and warmth in your body, a cool forehead, breathe with your diaphragm, and look for a color behind your eyelids. When you've found one, latch onto it and hold it there. Remember not to strain or command. You shouldn't be sweating or popping veins out of your forehead. Soothe instead. Think about that color you're trying to see as a pet cat you are enticing onto your lap. If you grab him and pin him down, he'll bite and writhe and won't crawl back easily next time. You must keep him by cooing and scratching him behind the ears. In the same way, make the colors you are seeing feel comfortable. When it floats away – and it will, at first – coerce it back. If you lose one color, then quietly observe for a while and try to keep the next color that appears. This will take brainpower, patience, and gentle focus. Eventually you will want to use your mind's eye more than your eyeballs. If you're sensitive, you may even feel your attention shift back away from your eye sockets and into your mind as you shift between one and the other. That's normal.

Once you're able to retain a color that you see naturally, practice spontaneously bringing a color to mind and holding it there. Your ultimate goal is to see yellow when you want to see yellow or green when you want to see green. It should be as brilliant and vivid in your mind as it would if your eyes were open.

You may notice that different colors have different effects on your body. Red, for instance, is widely known to excite and stimulate, while green is more calming and relaxing. Pink is associated with joy and comfort. Orange gives a sense of warmth. Blue is cooling and melancholy. Brown may increase the sense of heaviness. Explore these associations. They can be of some therapeutic value once you have mastered the capture color. If you are agitated, for instance, closing your eyes and simply seeing green or blue swathes in your mind can calm you.

Keep practicing. The very attempt of exercise invariably leads to its successful fruition. It strengthens the will and disciplines emotions.

With mindfulness and persistence, it is possible.

Capture Color - Basic Benefits

- trains attention
- trains memory
- helps with setting emotions

Capture Color - Concentrated Version

- Mask—Heavy—Warm
- Breathing and Warm Abdomen
- Heart
- Forehead
- Color
- Exit

CHAPTER ELEVEN

An Unforgivable Love

"I'm the forensic consultant," I told the guard.

"What's that for?"

"To determine if the patient is of sound mind."

"For the trial?"

"Yes, that's correct." I showed him my authorization.

He heaved a sigh and put his hand on the door handle. "Be careful," he muttered to me before nodding me into the hospital room where the prisoner was being held. "You know what he did, don't you?"

"I know," I said.

I stepped inside holding the chart, and waited to hear the door click shut behind me. The room reeked of medical ointment. Chips of paint flaked off the metal bed frame. An unwrinkled bed sheet softly covered the patient. Resting atop a pristine pillow was a pale face with a dimpled chin. His eyes were closed. Most of his hair was gone. A puffy red burn splashed down his head, across his face, and then onto his shoulder before creeping under the sheet.

I coughed.

He didn't move.

I cleared my throat as I flicked through his chart. "Hello, Ivan," I said.

He went on sleeping.

I looked out the window for a moment, not sure what exactly to do from here. When I turned back at him his steely blue eyes were open, unblinking. He was watching me. "Hello," I said again. "I'm Dr. Arbuck." He shut his eyes. The muscles of his jaws fluttered. When he finally began to speak, the voice came out monotonous and hesitant, as though he were reading from a prepared statement. The story began to unfold.

Ivan was a submariner. Life under the seas takes a stern mettle. Most men grit their teeth and endure the confinement, the prison-like quarters, and the sunless cruises. But Ivan thrilled to it. He loved the secret adventures and the kinship among his fellows, and even the handsome uniform which had won him the love of his young bride. The full horizon of Ivan's hopes and dreams extended from his living quarters to the double titanium hull. He aimed to command his own sub one day, and was well on his way to achieving that goal when his son was born.

He used to lie on his bunk shelf and imagine cradling his boy's little feet, and tickling his soles, and bending his toes in all different directions. When he smelled the harsh stink of the cleaning agents used on the metal of the sub, he imagined his son's hair. In the grumbling engines he heard his wife's laughter. What strange associations, I thought to myself when I heard them. He didn't say so, but he must have loved the sub like he did his own family.

For the first two years of the boy's life, Ivan was at sea more than he was home. The strain on his wife was awful, and during what would become his last cruise, it became clear from the tone of her letters that something had to change. Her early notes had been full of affection and anticipation of their bright future together. But they became sadder, and lonelier, and less affectionate. She seemed to be complaining all the time. And Ivan began to doubt the life he had chosen for himself and his family.

When his sub returned to dock, Ivan and his wife sat down and talked for hours about their family, their future, and their dreams together. She wanted a normal life, whatever that was. Ivan saw himself as a dutiful husband, and he wanted to be a good father. He decided, at last, that his goals of a career under the sea interfered with his family duties. And so for his wife and son he made the decision to walk away from his dreams. The paperwork took some time, but at last Ivan achieved his discharge.

He found a consulting job in the middle of the country, a thousand miles from the nearest salt water. He ate dinner every night with his wife and child. They went to see films as a family, and held dinner parties for their friends. It was as normal a life as could be had. Ivan loved his wife, and his darling son. The boy used to climb Ivan like a tree, hugging onto his strong legs, and dangling from his neck. And Ivan would laugh and laugh, like his wife had never seen. His old Navy buddies used to ask him if he missed his old life. "Of course," he'd answer, "and yet, there is always something new ahead."

But behind his brave face and his can-do soldierly disposition, Ivan suffered silently. Insomnia, a lingering souvenir of his submarining days, kept him awake at night. When the sun rose he was tired, and when it set he was restless. His wife grew less beautiful in his eyes. He tried to read books, but found himself rereading the same page a dozen times without ever truly understanding what was said.

The military precision with which he had once maintained himself and his things began to crumble. At first he misplaced small things like car keys or a magazine he'd been reading. Then he began slacking on household chores, and leaving a burner on through the night. And he got headaches, bad headaches that caused him to snap gruffly at his boy. He wasn't able to follow through with even basic responsibilities. He skipped work without calling in to alert them. He would spend the whole day just lying in bed fitfully trying to put himself to sleep. He drank more and more, hoping to knock himself to sleep each night.

Life outside the Navy, for Ivan, was pale and empty. There were no camaraderie bonds in civilian life to compare to what he had abandoned. Ivan's only sunshine was to hold his son. He told me in gravelly words that crumbled out of that burnt and puffy face, that he was not a good husband. He was an angry father to his son. The world his wife had brought him to was a greedy, heartless place. Ivan had given up everything to deliver his boy a joyful upbringing, but things only got worse. They would never turn around.

Ivan refused to see friends of the family. His chest ached all the time and pain settled deep behind his eyes. He lay in bed each night wishing that the sun wouldn't rise. The sun never rose in a submarine.

One sleepless Sunday morning, he slipped out of bed before the first blush of dawn. He went to the kitchen table and sat for a while with his head in his arms. He went to a cabinet where he had hidden a length of nylon rope. He knotted a loop into the rope with a sailor's dexterity, swung it up over a light fixture. Then he climbed up on a chair, made fast the slack line, slipped his head in the noose, and stepped away into the air.

The lamp crashed down over him in a hail of plaster.

A bedroom door somewhere creaked, and then he knew he had to finish the job quickly before his wife stopped him. He took up a carving knife and with a wide swing sunk it into his chest. Once, twice, three stabs. Twice he penetrated his heart. Ivan was a hard man and a young one too. Although his mind had shuttered long ago, his body wasn't ready to knuckle under. So Ivan doused himself in gasoline from a can he kept under the sink for the generator and then he ignited himself.

His son, barefoot in pajamas, stood in the doorway with his thumb in his mouth.

Fear hit Ivan like thunder – fear for a fatherless boy who had to stay behind and grow up in this torturous world, for a child who didn't know how awful and dry life truly was. Ivan knew, then, that he was the only one who could save his baby from years of disappointment and suffering. He took up the knife, toppled atop the boy, and stabbed him to death.

*   *   *

Defeat starts with self-doubt and ends in despair. That gory Sunday morning was the culmination of Ivan's lost hope. He didn't ask for help, or communicate openly with his old shipmates, or do anything useful. He wouldn't accept his own limitations. He wouldn't forgive himself for his failures. Instead he blamed his wife for stealing him away from the Navy. And then he got angry.

Anger is almost always a sign of defeat. It is a calamitous emotion which is only good for two things: to inflate a problem, and to hurt those around you. In Ivan's case, it did both. He lost his temper with his wife and son because he was angry at himself for his own weakness – and then vice versa. This catastrophic spiral of anger and self-loathing turned Ivan away from solutions and toward the demolition of self and family.

There are many different constructive methods you can employ during the worst of times so that you exercise some control over the only thing in the universe that is subject to your will: yourself. The Mastermind submersion exercise alone would have been invaluable to Ivan. Psychiatrists would call it *sublimation*, or a positive behavioral act which helps in a time of trouble. Doing heavy housework when things are not going well at the office is one example. *Humor* is another way to divert energy from destructive tendencies to something uplifting. And doing anything *altruistic* – doing good for the sake of goodness – has the effect of guiding the mind to healthy thoughts.

Suppression works too. When you wake up in a foul mood, consciously decide to delay feeding negative emotions so that you can cope with the present reality before you. Don't lay in bed all day bathing in your anger like Ivan did. Go into work with a smile on your face. Of course you must not bury your head in sand to ignore your problems, but rather reschedule the turbulent emotions to be dealt with at a more convenient time. Or you could anticipate them. Plan realistically for future discomfort. Realize that no life is free from trouble or sadness. At some time or another, everyone feels depressed, or anxious, or hurt. This foreknowledge is called *anticipation*. So if you have stage fright, prepare yourself to deal with the anxiety before you give a presentation. Or if you have a long night ahead of you, prepare yourself to stay awake.

Any of the Mastermind methods can be used for *thought stopping* to calm a mind threatening to capsize on stormy seas. They are simply sophisticated methods of *distraction*. When applied, the central regulation kicks in, and healthy phenomena such as calmness, heaviness, and warmth steady the rocking ship.

Blatant distraction is a powerful tool of its own right. Once, an angry drunk approached me in an unlighted street waving a knife about and threatening to kill me. He was raging and senseless. I tried to reason with him, but his blank eyes and morbid face weren't buying what I was selling. And so, as courteous as possible, I changed my approach. I asked him if he had ever sky dived. This question, completely out of context, made him think about something other than killing me. The distraction washed away his sick intent and ill thoughts. We spoke for a moment about jumping out of a perfectly good plane. He told me he loved me, hugged me like a close friend, and we peacefully parted. I do not believe he hurt anyone that night. His mind was temporarily redirected to a benign object.

Of course this sort of manipulation requires awareness and intuition. Your brain is constantly analyzing the endless input from memory and the sensory world around you. Think of it like a stock pot full of a boiling broth. Veggies, jostled by the bubbles, will turn and show and then sink away out of sight. And the pot's always on the burner. So even when you sleep, it's digging up thoughts and memories as old as you are, sputtering them to the surface, spinning them over and over.

Intuition is the brain's ability to analyze the simmering input from memory and the sensory world around you, and to then provide you with a conclusion. In short, this means connecting lines between little details to create a bigger picture. Like everything else in your mind, intuition can be trained and nurtured. Your brain is like Sherlock Holmes, and your conscious self is like Watson. Holmes did not always explain *how* he came to his conclusion – he just presented the conclusion itself, and together he and Watson acted on that knowledge. This sort of unconscious analysis is a natural function of the brain. This is why sometimes you only arrive at a solution once you stop thinking about the problem.

The more observant you are in your daily life, the better your intuition becomes. Consider the details you observe as data you are feeding to an adding machine. In order for the adding machine to function properly, it must be organized. The brain must be able to retrieve memories and images in order to function at its highest potential.

You can train the faculty of intuition by imagining the future in every detail. See it in progression. Unlike *preparing for the future*, in which you let your mind show you exactly what you want to come true, the *training of intuition* consists of the imagining future events without actual intention for them to happen. Create a movie of tomorrow in your mind, a movie that is built as it goes, without the framework of a given scenario. Consider yourself the audience and not the director. If the movie you have seen happens to actually match tomorrow's reality, it's not because you have compelled it to occur, but rather that your brain unleashed was able to make unconscious predictions based on minute hints of where things seemed to be headed.

Faulty intuition, though, can be pathological. If you base your actions strictly on automatic thoughts without testing them, your acts can detach from your motives. Ivan, whose outlook on life was increasingly pessimistic, is an extreme example of how someone's motives can be twisted out of recognition. Ivan loved his son. He wanted to help the boy, to spare him from an unbearable life – there's the gap between automatic thought and reality – and that's why he murdered him.

In fact we are all handicapped by the false assumptions our simmering mind turns up. Take procrastination. Maybe some Saturday afternoon you're planning to clean the gutters, but you've suddenly remembered a show you recorded, and you end up on the sofa watching television. Meanwhile, a task that needs attention lingers undone. So your motive to save yourself trouble during winter ice storms twists against itself, and you're actually giving yourself more work down the road. If you soberly observe your own thought process, you'll realize that it won't be any less arduous to clean the gutters next week than it would be today.

I remember a patient who suffered from depression for his whole life. He learned to control his symptoms somewhat using mental exercises similar to the ones you already studied – but one day his mind turned over an old memory of his classmates teasing him for his crooked teeth. He had grown up poor, and his teeth were in fact jagged and discolored. As a boy he compensated for the humiliation by learning to smile with his lips pressed closed. This became instinct. I don't think he even noticed any more that he laughed with a tight lipped huffing, or smiled thinly. That simply became the expression of his happiness. Thus he lived an adult life – working, going to the grocery store, seeing movies with his coworkers.

As he achieved a superficial understanding of his depression, he wondered casually why he didn't just go to get his teeth fixed. The longer he thought about it, the more heinous a problem his teeth seemed to be. They were the kernel of his unhappiness, and the reason for his whole life struggle with depression.

"If my teeth are so ugly," he wondered, "but fixable, why don't I just go fix them already?" He came into the office one day with a big, broad smile of pearly, beautiful teeth. He felt like a hero. No one would tease him. Despite concerned questioning, he insisted that he had no depression. What was there to be depressed about now? Everything was peachy. Everyone who knew him was very happy for him.

Two weeks later he killed himself.

I think we know why. He blamed all of the problems in his life on his bad teeth. The false reality that he had intuited became independent of the reality around him. (Although these stories are morbid, death is a huge part of life, and is worth learning from.)

*   *   *

You need to have an unshakable belief in your own fallibility. Whatever dogma or truth you hold dearest does have an alternative. Ignoring that alternative means that you are never testing your truth against the facts of the world. When you are dealing with a problem, you must dig deeply to identify its source. The answer may not be obvious. Your task as a Mastermind is to observe your own intuitions and weigh the evidence for and against them. Use your intuition the way you use Wikipedia. Both are good resources once you confirm that their information is reliable.

So how can you watch over something inside you?

Well, thoughts can be modified once they acquire shape. Consider how Anna, the little girl from last chapter, was able to unconsciously control her asthma through drawings and playacting. And now *you* have the ability to close your eyes and choose to see different colors. You've already taken the first step down the road to consciously manipulating your own thoughts. The coming series of exercises will sharpen your ability to create form with your mind. In the process you will be feeding details into your brain, which primes your intuition and allows you to produce more realistic and useful mental connections. Ultimately you can use these skills to change bad habits and dispel fears and anxieties.

Your practice begins with **Continuous Observation**. You'll be bringing the world into your mind. More simply put, you will observe a real object – something handy like a pencil or a cell phone or a paperweight – for five to ten minutes. Notice what makes this pencil similar to other pencils, and what makes it unique. If this pencil were aligned alongside a hundred others, how would you pick this one out of the crowd?

Your mind is bound to wander, but try channeling attention away from the concerns of children or household chores or work related obligations. If you're observing a pencil, for instance, guide your meandering thoughts to the wood of the pencil. Where is the tree from which this pencil was made? Who cut it down? What was that lumberjack's life like? After you drift for a while, bring your attention back to the pencil. Just look at it. Study it. Fixate yourself on it.

Remember: Don't force yourself! Straining will only make your task harder. Be gentle. It will help put your body in the state of Mastermind submersion that you learned in the Body to Mind methods. You may find that it is no longer necessary for you to be lying on the floor or in your recliner to assume the complete Mastermind submersion state. As long as you are able to achieve the physical sensations of warmth and heaviness and cool forehead, you can practice in any posture you like, or even during movement.

There are several practical benefits of this exercise. If you can practice continuous observation when everyone around you is in a state of anxiety, trust me, it'll be impossible for you to become infected by their stress. You have to be relaxed to achieve the kind of focus necessary for this method. You'll be the one with the cool head – literally and figuratively. Use this to change your mind, to master your attitude, and to calm down.

The pinnacle of continuous observation would be to discover all the laws of the universe by looking at something as insignificant as a paper clip. If your mind is open – if your Sherlock Holmes intuition is working at full strength – a paper clip can shed light on civilization and natural elements, technology and rules of gravity, fire and water, geometry and physics, investment and production, engineering and planning, death and eternity, biology and medicine and anything else. It all depends on how you open your mind to see not just a paper clip but what it is made of, its shape, its use, who made it, for what purpose, what stands behind its invention, the system of education and human needs and values behind it, and all the rest.

Don't lose hope if those answers don't come to you on your first try. That sort of observation is as much an ideal as a goal. But you will find that continuous observation directs your attention to the world around you in what may be a fresh or exciting new way. After a few days of exercising this method, you will find yourself in daily life noticing details that you hadn't before. You may observe how a bag bends as you lay it beside your desk, or remember the specific array of scratches on the face of your wristwatch. You'll be aware of the world around you in a way that you haven't been before. This is because you have been training your mind to observe and evaluate external stimuli that in the past you may have simply ignored. But now you're opening the bridge between mind and world. You may even find that your coordinating senses are heightened. Sound and smell and touch may become more vivid. Just for fun, exercise continuous observation for fifteen minutes a day three days in a row and then, after your practice, close your eyes and run your fingers through your hair. You'll feel each hair bending and pulling, and you'll feel that it's oily, or silky, or somewhere in between.

The sheer awareness is an extraordinary sensation.

It makes you feel alive.

Wallow in it.

Continuous Observation - Basic Benefits

- improves awareness
- enhances memory
- extends attention span
- stretches the mind

Continuous Observation - Concentrated Version

- Mask—Heavy—Warm
- Breathing
- Forehead
- Observation exercises
- Exit

Continuous Observation Method

- choose an object
- observe it for 5-15 minutes
- focus on the details
- what makes this object different from others like it?
- what makes this object similar to others like it?

Tips

- if the mind wanders, gently nudge it back to the object of your attention
- do not let the mind think about work or chores; instead direct it toward tangential wonderings about the object itself

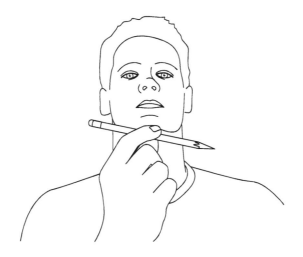

CHAPTER TWELVE

The Boy Who Looked a Spider in the Eyes

My grandmother always encouraged me in my flights of imagination. I would come galloping into the sitting room of her lake house waving a dustpan above my head like a saber, shouting at her that I would ride down all the enemies surrounding us. "Go on!" she would shout. "There they are, just outside!" I'd dash screaming out the door, my dustpan ready for battle.

Or I'd wriggle along the floor silently, holding my mimed musket in front of me. "Crawling across toward the enemy trenches?" Grandma would whisper, and I'd shake my head. She'd have a few more guesses – "Commando raid? Broken leg?" – Before I'd hiss at her that I was hunting bears. She'd hunch her shoulders then and raise a finger to her lips and say, "Stay quiet! I've heard one tramping through the woods just before you arrived," and we would sneak off together for a game of hunting. On one memorable afternoon, our bear turned out to be an escapee from the circus. We traced his sign through the house and down to the lake side, and then Grandma clutched her heart. "Did you see?" she gasped, "he's found a bicycle and ridden away! What a shock! Can you see it?" Because I was a child, I could, and I remembered the game for years afterward.

The lazy days at my grandmother's lake house seemed to go on forever. Time acted strangely, then. Grandmother had a large wooden picnic table in the backyard, which was the perfect place to play with my toy cars. I used to race them across the surface. I would wind up and release the car to shoot sideways along the table's edge too. That's how I learned elementary physics. If I shot my car fast enough, its wheels would hug the side of the table, defying gravity. Not enough momentum, and it would lose its grip and tumble into the grass.

One day I found a large spider web stretching taut between the side legs of the backyard table. The web was beautiful in its symmetry, strength, and alignment. It looked empty too. Nothing was stuck to it. Nothing marred it.

And it seemed strong. I had learned in school that a spider web could hold an angry wasp, and one of my friends had told me that clothes quilted with spider silk were bulletproof.

I wondered if the wheels of my mighty toy car, which were stronger even than gravity, could rip apart a spider web. I needed to set up a test. I would wind the wheels of the car against the tabletop, and then once they got spinning, touch them against the web. I would need a close point of observation. If the web broke I would need to halt the experiment immediately or the web would wrap around the wheels of my car and gum it up. I bent down to the web, primed my reflexes with a few practices and with my nose only inches away from the delicate structure, I scraped the noisy little wheels of my car against the wood and then began my test.

The web shook violently. In retrospect it should have been obvious that the web was newly spun. It was so pristine. Its weaver must have just finished making the trap, and she was hungry to catch its first meal. When she felt the shaking through the fibers, she came scuttling down from a corner beneath the edge of the table right up to the revving wheels of my toy car – and about three fingers-width away from the tip of my nose – just close enough that I had to cross my eyes to focus.

She was an ugly, fat bellied hulk of a creature. I was so close to her that if my car wheels hadn't been revving, I could have heard her long scaly joints creaking. She was alien, and huge, and the stuff of nightmares. My two crossed eyes met her eight, black, shiny, round eyes that piled out from her head absorbing my presence. If I close my eyes now I can still see them.

I think both the spider and I realized what had happened about the same time. She wasn't getting dinner, and I wasn't going to complete my test. After that odd shared moment, I screamed bloody murder and in my terror hurled the car away into the brambled woods and then took off in unbridled flight hollering for my grandmother. When I found her, it took a long bout of jagged, tear-swept panting before I was able to explain what had happened.

Grandma hugged me and patted my back. She reminded me of all the heroic bear hunters and soldiers I had played in my games, and asked me if they would be frightened of a little spider clinging for dear life to her web. "Not little," I said. The next day Grandma watched from the door of the cottage while I poked around the picnic table for my toy car. I found it, eventually. The web had broken, and sure enough the sticky strands had wrapped around the wheels and axle of the toy. I snuck a sidelong glance at the spider web at the picnic table. It was ripped and abandoned. I pointed it out to Grandma. "Mrs. Spider," Grandma explained, "doesn't have a grandmother to teach her not to be afraid of little boys with toy cars. She doesn't have a brain to imagine herself as anything other than an ugly eight-legged bug. Now she will probably always be afraid of little boys with toy cars. But you," she added, patting my head, "get to choose what you will be."

*   *   *

All self-improvement begins with make-believe. Say you want to get strong and muscled. You act like a fitness freak. You join a gym and lift weights. On the second day you will awake with a terrible soreness, but as long as you continue acting the way fitness freaks do – as long as you move how they move, behave how they behave, and talk how they talk – you will eventually find your knowledge increasing and your posture changing, along with your tone of voice and facial expressions, and eventually the way that you feel about yourself. What my grandmother taught me as a child, I have found through the experience of my life to be manifestly true: You choose what you will be.

By choosing to practice the Mastermind methods, for instance, you have chosen to become a leader. You have set goals for yourself, stayed on task, overcome challenges, thought for yourself, and controlled things that you once thought were as wild as a thunderstorm. You're learning what is possible and what is not. Leaders are not born in the Army or MBA programs. Those paths may help, but you can learn how to be a leader about as well as you can learn how to be an airplane. So unless you can grow propellers out of your wrists, you can only build yourself into a leader using that old trusty engine of achievement: hard work.

Hard work matures your childhood fantasies into adult aspirations. Being a hero or a leader does not mean putting on a costume and traveling back in time. It means knowing the importance of people, not keeping those who depend on you in the dark, delegating responsibility, solving problems, making decisions, managing life around you, and turning thoughts into reality. If you succeed, people around you will carve shavings off of your success and grow some of their own. The stronger you are, the more self-assured you are, the more you can influence others in a positive way. This influence may not be spoken, and it may not even be intended – but it is a fact of human nature that prosperity spreads. The same methods you use to listen to and understand yourself can be applied to understanding others. If you want to help others, help yourself. If you want to help yourself, know the world.

The observational powers that will help you do that must be developed painstakingly. For instance, look carefully at the passage of time. When you are a child, a good day can pass by in a couple hours, and a bad one can yawn on for months. Don't just shrug and accept the folksy wisdom that time flies when you're having fun. *Examine* it instead. What are these squiggling time lines, and how can you take advantage of them?

Once I fell off a running horse, and it took me a few minutes to land. Not seconds, but minutes. I flew next to the horse for a while, looking at its hair, muscles and muzzle. I remember the frozen eyes of the animal, the dust motionless in midair, the tall grasses bowed by the wind, and a complete lack of sound. When I finally landed on the ground, a horseshoed hoof landed on my hand. It sank down and lifted out, and when my time caught up with real time I was laying stunned but unhurt on the turf.

It's almost impossible to put into words the experience of these fits and starts by which humans perceive the passage of time. My descriptions of this event as I've experienced it may sound cinematic, but looking back on the actual experience, I can also describe the slowing passage of time as moments when I observed more in the period of one passing second than I do of some whole days. We remember certain sensations and images – the eyes of the spider, in my case, or the bending grass of the plains that cushioned my fall from the horse – with such intensity that the time seems to have slowed. You might say that in those moments we are so vividly aware of the world around us that other memories of, say, daydreaming at your workdesk or huddled in your cubicle, cannot help but dull in comparison.

As you sharpen your practice of Continuous Observation, you may find that time moves by strange intervals when you consciously direct your focus to the subtleties of the world around you. To take the example of my fall from the horse's back, the bending grasses and the flanks of the horse were always there. It was only in a moment of hyper awareness that I noticed them. The same may be true of the bite marks in your pencil.

Children perceive time slower than adults because for them the whole world is full of fresh wonders. As we grow older, our brain becomes more efficient by finding patterns in behavior and observation. For example, a seasoned driver might space out while behind the wheel, adjusting to the flow of traffic without thought. If you've been driving for more than a few years, you probably can't remember what you thought about on your way home from work today.

Ask a new driver on his way to school, and he'll know immediately. He was scanning his mirrors, struggling to maintain pressure on the gas pedal to keep a constant velocity, trying to stay in his lane, looking ahead for traffic and just in front of his front fender for potholes. His brain has not yet identified the traffic patterns or driving behaviors that an older driver incorporates unconsciously, and so he observes everything. Similarly, everything in the world is new for a child. Even simple things like table legs and pant pockets are magnificent discoveries to children. An adult hoping to achieve that slow passage of time may need to evaluate a pencil's bite marks, or scratches on your watch, or whatever else your brain seems to mindlessly skim over.

Of course in terms of physical realities, time may always be grinding forward at a regular pace. But to me, time is a *measure of our deeds*. In that sense, the same period of time that one person experiences as a straight line:

Someone else may live in dips and peaks.

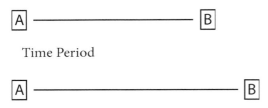

You may consider the first as a "time period," meaning the amount of time measured by the ticking of your watch. But the second squiggly line is the "mind period", or the way time can be *perceived*. Although both take place in the same number of seconds, minutes, or hours, by stretching out the perception it becomes clear that time is experienced slower in the "mind period."

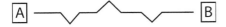

Time Period

Mind Period

Maybe you have discovered that a year in childhood seemed to last a lifetime, while a year as a parent flashes by. If you can observe and interact with the world using a child's curiosity and a mature focus, observant and hunting for discoveries, not only will the experience of your life become more colorful, time itself will seem to move slower. Mastering this conscious manipulation of your perception turns you into a time machine.

* * *

Intermittent Observation, this chapter's method, will broaden the bridge from the world to your mind by joining the principles of capture color with continuous observation. Your goal will be to observe an object and then to close your eyes and see the same object in your mind's eye. Leonardo Da Vinci, it is said, used a similar exercise to train his apprentices in visualization and concentration.

Hold whatever object you're starting with in your hand. Fascinate yourself with its smallest particulars, just like you did with Continuous Observation. Don't allow yourself to be distracted by anything else. Then close your eyes, and bring this object from the world into your mind. Recreate it. Remember how it appears in reality. Use your skills from Capture Color to make the coloring really pop. Open your eyes if you need to, study the object for a moment, and then close your eyes again to continue the task. Once you can see the object almost lifelike in your mind's eye, ask a friend to test you on how many scratches are on the side of the pencil, or where the bite marks are. Then choose a new object for study and recreation. After a few trials you will be amazed by how clearly you can see things when your eyes are closed. In addition to building skills that will lay the groundwork for advanced Mastermind methods, Intermittent Observation on its own has obvious memory retrieval and attention enhancing benefits.

It also enhances your ability to feed your brain information from the outside world. Many people try to treat themselves with little or no idea about what is wrong, or have a false impression of their problems.

At first you will find Intermittent Observation easier when your body is in a state of Mastermind submersion. As you know, the mind in a state of nature is constantly scanning for danger. Calming your body relaxes your mind and allows you to dedicate more brainpower to the task at hand. A body-calm will soothe the anxious twitching of your mind. I also recommend that you use a timer. It will be easy for you to lose track of time. And don't forget to smile at the end of your exercise. You're mastering your mind, after all.

Be happy.

Intermittent Observation - Basic Benefits

- improves memory
- strengthens architecture of the mind
- calms the mind
- extends attention span

Intermittent Observation - Concentrated Version

- Mask—Heavy—Warm
- Breathing
- Forehead
- Observe
- Exit

Intermittent Observation Method

- assume a state of Mastermind submersion
- inspect an object with eyes open
- commit details of that object to memory
- close eyes and recreate object in inner vision, looking for the smallest details in it
- repeat this process several times

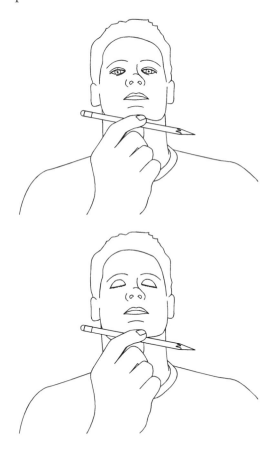

CHAPTER THIRTEEN

A Room with a View

In my childhood I heard many once-upon-a-time stories about what Russians called the Great Patriotic War. One which stuck in my mind all through the years is the tale of Sergey and Yakov, two wounded soldiers pulled from the front lines to recover in a hospital.

Sergey was an infantryman. The morning after his platoon had, in a bitter struggle, taken a farmhouse from its Nazis defenders, Sergey awoke paralyzed. No one could say why. During the assault he had been shot in the leg, but the bullet passed through his thigh, skimmed his pelvis, and exited cleanly without touching his spine. Such a wound was no excuse to retreat, not in those desperate times. All of Sergey's mates were wounded and bandaged up, and they went on fighting.

The morning he didn't rise alongside them, they told him to quit dawdling. But try as he might, Sergey couldn't even wiggle his toes, let alone grip his gun and climb to his feet. His platoon mocked him, poking and prodding while he groaned. Then the sergeant burst in, all brusque and soldierly. "Get up," he barked, "the motherland calls. We're laying wire against the counterattack." When Sergey didn't stand at attention, the sergeant became angry, kicking at him. "You weakling, you coward!" shouted the officer. "Do you want your comrades to work double for your laziness?" Sergey squeezed his eyes shut and clenched his jaw and groaned, "I will do it. I will get up right now." But he couldn't. The sergeant, who was a pragmatic fellow, tried another tactic. He squatted down and commiserated with Sergey in a gentle tone. "I know it's difficult," he said, "I know it's frightening out there son. We're all exhausted. But if you stay shell-shocked on your back, it'll take two men to carry you back to the staging ground and I can't even spare one. So you can lay here and rot while we fight, or you can help us defend this place."

His sergeant's efforts were all for naught. Sergey couldn't move. Eventually the sergeant left, disgusted. During the Nazi counterattack which lasted for three rattling, sleepless days, Sergey remained helpless on the floor, despised and neglected by his fellow soldiers. By the time an ambulance came for him, the wound in his leg was starting to stink, and he was taken to a city hospital where the gangrenous flesh was cut away. When Sergey complained to the doctor about his paralysis, he was examined carefully and eventually diagnosed with "war fatigue."

After the surgery, Sergey lay motionless in the hospital room staring at the ceiling. He waited all morning for the nurse to turn him, so that he might have someone to talk with. But during wartime no one, not even nurses, liked a coward. They kept Sergey isolated behind hanging sheets. A creeping madness born from his heartless treatment tickled at the back of his mind. "Can't you move me to the bed beside the window?" begged Sergey to the nurse, "I'd like something to look at if no one will talk with me." She snapped in reply, "Get up and hobble out from the curtain if you care to. But you're not swapping beds. We save the window bed for brave soldiers."

One such man arrived that very afternoon while Sergey napped. Sergey awoke to soft groans on the other side of the drapery. "Who's there?" Sergey asked. "Please speak to me kindly, comrade. I'm so lonely I'll go mad if you're as cruel to me as all the rest of them. Tell me, are you wounded badly?" The groaning stopped for a moment and then came an answer. "My name is Yakov," said the man, "and I don't care to speak of my injuries. Even if my toes were snipped off one by one by the SS themselves, how could I possibly feel any pain while such a beauty stands before me just out of sight? Hark! Even now I can see her. Such lovely blonde hair, and fair skin and bright teeth, oh, what breasts she has! Ah, I have in mind to leave this place and find her."

"A beautiful girl, loitering just outside the window?" cried Sergey. "Oh, how I've longed to take just a glimpse outside! Even ten seconds would do."

"A glimpse outside?" said Yakov curiously.

"Don't laugh at me, Yakov. You know they won't let me see out from behind these sheets."

Yakov paused to consider that, and then said, "I'm not laughing, comrade. It's just that in a quick glimpse you'd see only the girl with shining teeth and nothing more. But I'll tell you everything there is to see. I'll give you a good long stare, a whole afternoon. Look at the melon cart just outside the gates. See how perfectly round the fruits are, how they are stacked to a yellow pile. See the mustachioed old comrade tending to them. I'd like to buy one for myself. We could share it. There's so much juice that it dribbles down your chin as you bite and your hands are sticky for a whole day after. Can't you just taste it, Sergey?"

"Yes, yes!" said Sergey. "I've never eaten a melon as juicy as that."

While the sun drooped toward the far horizon, Yakov went on describing the scene outside. The old melon seller had a cat which prowled around the cart and brushed against his legs as he carved his wares for children skipping past on their way home. "They're singing," said Yakov, "a patriotic ditty." "I can't hear them," complained Sergey, "what is the song? Do you know the tune?" Yakov hummed a famous melody. In a quavering voice Sergey joined into the chorus and together they sang until they were out of breath.

"The window, the window," Sergey insisted. "It'll be dark soon."

"Yes," Yakov said with a sigh. "Yes, I suppose it will. Let me see what else is out there." The blond girl with shining teeth was still hanging about, he said. But she had a sweetheart now – an artilleryman, young and handsome. They were holding hands and smiling at one another. Sergey groaned at that, and Yakov added quickly, "Don't be disappointed. You would like him. He seems a kind man, with a thoughtful countenance. By the look of his uniform I'd say he hasn't seen any fighting yet."

"Lucky scoundrel," muttered Sergey.

"I think these two lovers have known each other for many years," said Yakov. "Maybe they even grew up together as neighbors, and ran touch-and-go about the hayricks when they were children. Their parents hoped they would marry. They had planned it that way. Had they stolen playful kisses as they lay together in the fields at dusk? Or touched the others' cheek with loving caress? I don't know. But when the war came, the young man had to march away to fight. Do you think she followed him all the way here to the fighting? Why would she? Perhaps she never received his letters, and he never received hers. You know how the censors demand letters of glorious victories and not heartsick pinings. Could it be that she followed her lover all the way from the fields to this place just outside our window? How lucky they are to meet again, Sergey. And how fortunate we are to see them together, wouldn't you agree? Although the Nazis can steal us young men away from our homes, you see, for all their aircraft and armored tanks they can't steal love away."

That night Sergey drifted off to a contended sleep, his first in days. The next morning he woke before the sun shone on his drapes. He waited eagerly to hear Yakov's stirring. The sun rose slowly, creeping across the curtains, and there was nothing. "Yakov," called Sergey, "are you there? What can you see?" Silence, that perfect silence, started the madness tickling in the back of Sergey's head again.

When the nurse came to turn him, he asked her where Yakov had gone. "He's passed on, the brave soul," she said, showing a hint of humanity which was quickly dashed away when she added, "better you had died than he."

"Please," Sergey pleaded, "do look and see if the girl with bright teeth is still standing about outside beside the window by Yakov's bed." The nurse stuck her hands under Sergey's bed sheet and with a grunt rolled him onto his side. "Girl?" she asked. "That window looks out onto the side of ward two. There's no view but a brick wall." Sergey made her repeat herself several times. When he finally understood, he was furious. The madness swarmed all around him and he could see nothing but his own rage. "That fraud," he slavered, "that cheat, he lied to me. Yakov lied about what he saw."

The nurse, distracted and annoyed, snapped back, "You keep that poor artilleryman's name out of your mouth. He's a martyr, you know. Leaves a fair young bride behind. He kept a picture in his billfold. Lovely lass, with a wide smile. And what are you moaning about, anyhow? Lied about what he saw, did he? You fool. The shrapnel had stolen both his eyes away. He was blind."

*   *   *

As a boy, I thought this tale was absolutely true. I later discovered that the premise was cribbed from an American short story written during the golden age of magazine fiction. "The Street" by Allan Seagers was slightly different from the story I remembered. In Seagers' original, the patient by the door envied the one by the window, and eventually watched him die without pressing the call button to summon a nurse. Only when he achieved his goal of a bed by the window did he realize that his perished roommate had been inventing the outdoor scenes of normal life to boost his spirits.

It is a fable of jealousy and altruism, and its ending is gut wrenching. I recommend it to you. Still, I think I prefer the story of Sergey and Yakov, maybe because it had such an effect on my imagination. I remember in my own little games playing a soldier or adventurer, laid up in some faraway convalescence, with only the power of invention to cheer myself and my mates. At the time, such a power seemed to be a survival skill as valuable as knot tying and rope climbing. Only later did I realize that imagination and visualization actually was a therapeutic tool in the psychiatrist's toolbox.

Think of your imagination as a vaccine. Viral immunization works by introducing your immune system to, say a weakened form of hepatitis. Once your body learns to fight the virus in small doses, it is then ready to take on the real monster itself. Similarly, you can use an imagination method that psychiatrists call **mental exposure** to vaccinate yourself against fear and trauma. This method can help with obsessive compulsive disorder (OCD), post-traumatic stress disorder (PTSD), phobias, and other disorders.

You've learned to bring colors and images from the world to see them in your mind's eye. Until now you have probably chosen to see objects that do not stimulate an emotional reaction – daily tools like a pencil or a paperclip. But what would happen if you saw something that filled you with horror? Imagine that you are terrified of snakes. Traditionally, to confront that fear head on, you would have to handle them, to feel them squirming against you, to see their wicked forked tongues tasting the air. Psychiatrists would call this *"in vivo"* exposure, and for sufferers of traumas or phobias it is absolutely petrifying.

Mental exposure, on the other hand, takes place in a safe and private environment. Think of it like an *"in vitro"* experiment, one that takes place in a sterile laboratory. You can bring the source of your fear into your mind, and confront it in a realm where you are king and it is nothing but a puppet or a jester. Once you can see it clearly and without fear, you are ready to tackle it "in vivo" or in the world.

Visualization, then, trains you for reality.

*   *   *

The past two exercises have broadened the bridge from the world to your mind, preparing you to interact with the world from within your own consciousness. The next observation method – **Mental Observation** – takes you the last step into pure imagination. You do not need to look at anything at all. You will put yourself in a state of Mastermind submersion, and then think of an object and recreate it in your mind's eye. The more realistic it looks in your head, the more successful you are in this exercise. To really excel at this method requires practice and focus, and your object must be interesting enough to maintain attention. Pick objects with absorbing shapes or colors or emotional subtexts. Examine a favorite doll from your childhood, or a family heirloom, or a pumpkin muffin your grandmother used to make.

Certain qualities of object you choose to create will have a therapeutic value. Remember the color associations from the capture color exercise: Red and yellow stimulate; green and brownish colors relax. Sharp edges and fast moving objects tend to stimulate, while smooth edges and peaceful objects relax. Animals like raptors, dragonflies, and toothy predators are more mobilizing. Plants such as trees, bushes, and grass are more calming, although there is a gentle movement associated with them which allows a sort of swaying stillness. Inanimate objects such as rocks, mountains, and buildings communicate heaviness and stillness. Landscape features like wide, steady rivers bring a sense of indestructibility, endlessness, and vastness. Of course these rules are generalizations – a volcano spurting lava is not calm or steady, and a butterfly fluttering from flower to flower is not very mobilizing.

Mental Observation, more than the two previous observational exercises, enhances control of your imagination and sharpens your ability to focus on details such as color, texture, reflections, angles, and so on. Because your senses are interrelated, you may find that the object of your attention becomes more vivid if you can hear it or touch it. Try shaking it in your mind.

What sound does it make? How does it feel against your imaginary finger-tips? Pay attention to how these senses interact with each other. Make sure to keep the visuals sharp while you listen.

You may also find that sound or tactile sensations emerge naturally from a vivid visualization. You may even feel the object drifting about in your mind's eye as you access different parts of your brain to add sensory details. Take pleasure in this realization. You are *aware* of yourself.

Once you've mastered this method, you can use a combination of the three inner vision exercises you've learned to date to immunize yourself against fear. Take the example of one of my patients who was so frightened of snakes that even the picture of one would cause her to shiver and weep un-controllably. We began her treatment with mental observation. She brought a picture of a snake – not the snake itself, but a picture of the snake – into her inner vision. She closed her eyes and imagined it. At first even this was frightening. But she was in a safe place, and gradually the picture became tolerable and even comfortable. She knew that she was in control. As she became habituated to the imagined picture of the snake, we progressed to intermittent observation. She would focus on a real picture of a snake for as long as she could bear, and then when she felt overwhelmed, she would close her eyes and retreat with the picture into the controlled laboratory of her inner vision. Eventually she graduated to continuous observation, in which she focused entirely on photographs of snakes out in the real world, and then even videos. By the time I took her to see a real, live snake at the Indianapolis Zoo, not only was her phobia cured, but she had acquired the skills to vaccinate herself against other fears and insecurities of her life.

As your ability to construct mental scenarios improves, you will be able to use exposure therapy methods to *detraumatize* events from your own past. The trauma can be either mental or physical. If, for instance, you were at-tacked and assaulted, the memory of the event may live on, haunting you for years after the event. Using Mastermind methods, you can change the way your memory of the events affects you. In this way you heal your pres-ent and build a more comfortable future. Psychiatrists call this "flipping psychological reality." The more vivid and realistic your power of visualiza-tion is when you attempt this, the more effective this method will be.

Begin by entering a state of Mastermind submersion, and when you are perfectly safe and relaxed, recreate the traumatic scenario in your mind. See everything as it was in the event. Feel your fright, your anger, your outrage. Remember it as it was. But then in the crucial moment, see you defending yourself and beating away the threat. You can pull your comrade out of the path of the bullet, or kick off your heels and flee to safety. What-ever ending you wish for that event, give it to yourself. When it is over, heave a sigh of relief that the worst never came to pass. And then repeat. After several repetitions, this new and imaginary reality can work toward neutralizing the wounds of the original offense.

* * *

Exposure therapy works. Don't be afraid to experiment with different combinations of observation methods besides what I have outlined for you. If, say, you're afraid of making decisions, recreate scenarios in your mind when you behave the opposite as you would in real life. In your mind you can give yourself a will of steel. Flipping psychological reality begins in the mind, but eventually spills over into your real life. You may never attain a will of steel, and you certainly can't change the past. But you can grow in strength beyond your normal abilities. It is your creativity and flexibility with these methods that will allow you to thrive in any situation, no matter how dire or hopeless.

For instance, try not just employing your inner vision, but inner smell, or inner hearing. I call this exercise the **Circles of Sound** (or circles of smell, touch, light, taste, time, memory, etc.) As you settle into Mastermind submersion, bring your attention to sounds. Very few places in the twenty first century are perfectly silent. Investigate the sounds in the small circle around you, and once you have identified those, extend your awareness to the whole room. You may find that things you hadn't consciously identified before – maybe the low hum of an appliance, or the rustle of curtains above a vent, or the ticking of a clock.

When you have thoroughly scanned the room with your hearing, listen to the whole building, or your neighbors. Draw a larger circle around yourself. Hear the squeaks and creaks and steps and knocks and scratches of life going on around you. Become acutely aware of every sound. Take pleasure in the guesswork of identifying each one. Continue extending the circles of sound, until you can hear in your inner hearing the birds and cars and wind. You can continue extending the circles to encompass the whole world until you can hear a landslide in a Brazilian jungle, and snow falling in the Himalayas, and a hoarse flute whispering on a Central Asian steppe, and a rare bird chirruping in the Hawaiian isles. The music of life does not consist of noise or silence. There is more to the music than just presence or absence of sound. These aural details will further enhance your intuition and awareness, as well as provide material to make your inner visualizations more vivid and lifelike. You never know when they will come in handy.

The story of Sergey and Yakov didn't go on to tell what happened after Sergey realized that Yakov was blind, although as a psychiatrist I can speculate. Sergey had propped his sanity against Yakov's imagination. Without counseling or therapy, once Yakov passed away, Sergey would have collapsed into depression. He had no developed mechanism to maintain a healthy outlook in his difficult circumstance.

But you, on the other hand, are accumulating tools that will enhance your life today and prepare you for the uncertainties of the future.

Mental Observation - Basic Benefits

- improves memory
- strengthens architecture of the mind
- calms the mind
- extends attention span

Mental Observation - Concentrated Version

- Mask—Heavy—Warm
- Breathing
- Forehead
- Observe
- Exit

Mental Observation Method

- assume a state of Mastermind submersion
- think of an object and recreate it in your inner vision
- conjure it with as many tactile details as possible
- add smells, or sounds if applicable

Tips

- different objects can be used to calm or excite the mind
- red and yellow colored objects are stimulating
- greenish, yellowish, and brownish colors are relaxing
- sharp edged objects stimulate, smoothed objects relax
- peaceful objects relax (like the flower below)
- fast moving objects stimulate (like the cheetah below)
- target imagery for therapeutic goals depending on the circumstance

See Quick Reference Guide starting on page 194 for more Mastermind exercises from this chapter.

CHAPTER FOURTEEN

The Obsession

At first Sandy didn't mind living with her mom. Coworkers at the doctor's office where Sandy worked wondered if forty five years old was too old to be living with a parent, but Sandy explained that her mother was living with *her*, not the other way around. It wasn't so bad. There was always someone to talk to, and her mom loved to reminisce about Sandy's upbringing.

Anyway, it was nice having someone to split the chores with. There was a lot to do every week to keep the place clean. Sandy hung around nurses at work, and she knew how important good hygiene was. Her mom balked sometimes at some of the tasks Sandy gave her – "But you don't have to steam clean the carpets twice a year," Mom would say – and Sandy calmly explained to her the virtues of sterile techniques and all the dangers of microorganisms and creepy crawlies. "You don't want to get sick, mom," Sandy used to say, "You don't want to live in an ant farm."

When Sandy told me her stories, she imitated her mother in a quavering whine, and herself as a matter-of-fact, long suffering, voice of reason. She ticked points off with her fingers and almost rolled her eyes at the tedium of explaining the escalating chain of events that led her to check her mother into a nursing home. In fact it had taken, in part, the constant nagging of Sandy's mother to convince her to even make an appointment with me. Sandy just didn't think there was a problem.

She came into my office with clothes that were crispy clean with colors dulled from over washing. Wrinkles drooped from her eyes. When she sat down her hands, callous and dry, locked in her lap. She shrugged and sighed frequently, and did not like to be touched. She was the kind of patient who believed that anyone with a different opinion than hers was a complete and utter loon.

The whole sordid tale began one August afternoon when Sandy saw a maggot in the garbage bin when she lifted the lid to dump in a new bag. (It was double bagged, like always, so smells didn't leak.) She had just caught a bare glimpse of the thing – like a pale, hairless fingernail clipping – and she slammed the bin lid shut and jumped back. Bile rose to her mouth.

"Disgusting," she told me, shivering a moment. "I never liked keeping trash in the garage. It's *so* unhygienic." She backed into her house and locked the door behind her. Immediately she went to the sink and washed her hands. After some good scrubbing, Sandy began to question her memory. Had there really been a maggot? "The light wasn't that good in the garage," she explained. With a lump in her throat, she snapped on elbow-length rubber gloves that she used for doing the dishes, snatched up a broom, and crept back into the garage to investigate. She approached the garbage can – "Like this," she said, scrunching up her nose and turning her face away – and lifted the bags one by one to see what was underneath.

Nothing but double bagged plastic.

He had gotten away.

With a pit in her stomach, Sandy took off the gloves and dropped them into the trash can. She tried to busy herself around the house, but all the while she felt the trash bin in the garage throbbing like a giant zit on the back of her neck, so she snapped on a second pair of gloves and trundled the trash bin outside into the drive. Then she dashed back into the house and locked the door behind her. But it wasn't enough. During a commercial break in her and her mother's daily ritual of the ten o'clock news, Sandy got her shoes and a third pair of gloves on, and she rolled the trash bin out to the end of the driveway as if it were trash collection day. Then she tossed out the gloves.

That night Sandy didn't get any rest. Her mind was cartwheeling. In every bend of the bed sheets she felt maggots wriggling and sliming against her, and she thrashed to swipe them away. The next morning, and the morning after that, she went to work feeling sticky and unclean. Only after two sleepless nights when the garbage men emptied her trash bin did she start feeling herself again.

At work she was alert, and at home too when she was busy doing the household chores alongside her mother. But in that quiet moment on the sofa during the ten o'clock news, niggling worries kept scratching at Sandy. She had seen a maggot, and then it was gone. And where there was one, there might be thousands. "I've got to clean the trash bin," she told her mother, and with that she quit their evening routine. Sandy washed the trash bin with soap and all-purpose cleaner, and then she bleached it just in case. Then she rolled it down to the end of the driveway again, and called for a new bin from the garbage collection agency as soon as the sun rose.

They stopped watching the news, after that. There was too much cleaning to do. Sandy convinced her mother to help her with a deep cleansing of the garage. They soaked every corner and niche and crack in disinfectant, and then sprayed it clean with a rented pressure washer. And then, Sandy turned her attention to the house. Anything might have been polluted.

At this point in the story, Sandy rolled her eyes and looked at me as if I might commiserate with her about wacky mothers. "But *Mom* didn't want to clean the house," said Sandy, drawing out the word 'mom.' "She would rather live with maggots. She's nuts, I know. But what could I do? She's my mom, after all. I gotta take care of her."

In the end, Sandy bullied her mother into throwing out all of her clothes, and replacing them. It soothed Sandy's compulsions for only a few days before she realized that the maggots might have nested in the carpet, and from there infested all of the new clothes. "So of course we had to throw them out too," said Sandy. "And Mom said, 'Oh my god, what's wrong with you, oh my god, you're going too far.' Can you believe it? There I was going to all this trouble just for her! For us! Trying to keep her healthy!"

Sandy stripped the house down to the bones. New carpet. Fresh wallpaper. A total fumigation. Replaced light fixtures, straight out of the box. Everything and anything from the past might have been touched by maggot larvae. All the memorabilia had to go. Photo albums. Wall hangings.

Sandy's obsession began to affect her job. She cleaned her desk more than she worked. She would sanitize her hands whenever she touched a pencil, or a keyboard, or a coworker. When the economy tanked, they let Sandy go. "Didn't bother me," she said. "It was filthy, that place."

The health of Sandy's mother deteriorated. They hardly spoke any more without fighting. Sandy blamed her mother's poor health on the maggots, and couldn't understand why Mom hadn't thrown out *all* of the old family photographs. So she put her mother in a home, and got rid of everything herself. She sold her house too, hoping for a fresh start. Just to make sure that no maggots had hitched a ride, she sold the car that she'd used to move into the new condo.

At last, after great effort and expense, Sandy was alone and clean and comfortable. She missed her mother, and visited the home often enough at first. But when she saw a fine golden cross hanging from her mother's neck, Sandy had to dash out of the room to keep from vomiting. The cross was an heirloom, an engagement gift from Sandy's deceased father – and it was a holdover from the days of maggot infestation in the old house. It was contaminated.

I know that Sandy loved her mother deeply. If she didn't, she just would have stopped visiting. But she didn't. Instead she developed a new routine to keep herself clean. First of all, she could never touch her mother. Then, just before leaving the nursing home, Sandy would change into new clothes in the nursing home restroom, stick the old outfit in a tightly sealed bag, and drop the clothes off at the dry cleaners on the way back. Once she arrived at her condo, she would vacuum the car, and wipe down the steering wheel and the seat and the door handles. *It would take an hour or two.* Then she would change clothes again and take an hour long shower. "The things we do for our mothers," she said, shaking her head.

I asked Sandy to read an article about obsessive compulsive disorder, and she couldn't relate to any of it. She refused medication. "Everyone tells me the same thing," she said, "But I swear, I'm not obsessing. I'm just thorough. What kind of person wants to live with maggots? Why should I take pills instead of a shower? I'm not crazy, Dr. Arbuck. I just need to clean."

*　*　*

Sandy's case is a classic example of the perils of self-diagnosis. The medicine that she chose for herself – cleaning – *hurt* her. By unintentionally indulging her OCD, Sandy lost her job, lost her house, and lost a healthy relationship with her mother.

Her reality had split apart from the reality around her. She walled herself off from the world. Her imagination rambled along self-made paths behind the battlements, so the choices she made and the opinions she formed were never measured against any standard beside her own inventions. Those of us who besieged her castle – her mother and I, among others – hammered at the walls, begging to be let inside. But she refused to lower the drawbridge. Without external inputs, Sandy couldn't identify the disconnect between the false reality she had constructed in her mind and the true reality of her own disorder. Instead she constructed a strange playground of her own behind her moat, where she was reasonable and thorough, and everything outside was filthy. She lost control of her life without even knowing how.

From a practical standpoint, Sandy needed to listen to professionals. But in our own daily lives, all of us need to keep the bridge between mind and world open. That is true on the small scale – we need to pay attention to the world around us so that we don't, for instance, stub our toes. But we also need to treat all of our beliefs as theories, and constantly test them against evidence in the world. Sandy had people offering her different perspectives – her mother, and the friend that recommended me to her. But she wasn't willing to give them a fair hearing, and so her circumstances continued to worsen.

You might find in your own life reason to reevaluate some of your own responses to the world. Consider how you respond to anger. Do you resort to the silent treatment, or do you rage and bluster? Do you release a burst of hot fury, or a soft and simmering contempt? Observe also how your reaction to anger affects the people around you. Are you solving problems or worsening them? Analyze how your anger makes you feel. Does it stay with you, or drift away? Afterwards, are you satisfied, or regretful, or neither?

In part three of this book, you will learn how to actually modify your emotional reaction to certain stimuli. For now, it is enough to observe yourself, the world, and your place in it. You may already have found that your heightened awareness is changing the way you experience the world. You may be recognizing tics and mannerisms in yourself and others that you hadn't noticed before, or having fun doing tasks that used to seem tedious – washing the dishes, maybe, or cutting the lawn.

Savor that awareness. Nurture it. Cultivate it. That is what makes you feel alive.

But now I'm going to contradict myself.

There may be a time when you *want* to close the bridge we have spent so much time opening and widening. Take a closer look at Sandy's example. She lived in a house that most of us would consider immaculate, and yet somehow managed to convince herself it was a pigsty. Sandy lacked a reasonable awareness of the world around her. But turn her story inside out, and consider the opposite potential. If you live in a truck camper or a cramped New York apartment or even a federal prison, by consciously implementing visualization and imagination exercises you could live as contently as though your home was Buckingham Palace. Or if you're blind and dying in a hospital, a bit of creative visualization can be a valuable skill that actually improves your life.

I don't recommend unconscious delusion, but it is worth experimenting with intentional manipulation of your environment. Psychiatrists call that *therapeutic escape*. Like Yakov the artilleryman, at times you may need to retreat into the sanctity of your mind. Detachment from harsh reality can be achieved *on purpose* when you are unhappy, tired, upset, angry, or annoyed. The better the furnishings within your own mind, the more satisfying a place your escape becomes.

*   *   *

In a psychiatrist's terms, Sandy was unable to "mark" her unrealistic beliefs on hygiene. There are two therapies a psychiatrist might use to treat her. The first is cognitive therapy, which involves the identification of such abnormal behaviors. For Sandy, that entails identifying her dysfunctions through journaling or activity listing, and then the development of approaches which might confront her obsessive cleaning habits. Delaying, for instance, just for a few minutes the urge to wash her hands, would have given her a measure of control over herself. But cognitive therapy requires a certain understanding or appreciation of a problem, and Sandy was unable to understand the nature of her delusion.

Behavior therapy was a better fit for Sandy. By merely modifying behavior and leaving cognition unchanged, we accomplished significant and positive changes. In the same way that an elephant can be trained to walk on its hind legs as a conditioned behavior, the insight of what exactly causes a problem is not essential to changing the symptomatic behavior of that problem. It doesn't matter if you, or the elephant, understand the mechanics of how to walk upright. It's the mechanical skill of keeping your balance as you put one foot in front of the other that's important.

Today's world of psychotherapy orbits around the past – why abuse happened, who did what, what was involved, why you reacted the way you did, and so on. But really, you rarely need to know *why*. What happened in reality is less important than how you function today *in spite of* what happened in the past.

Behavioral therapy brings you to the here and now. It allows you to move into the future without looking backwards. Clinically, methods based on these principles are more effective and take far less time than multiple psychotherapy sessions which analyze childhood. Of course, sometimes it is important to know the reasons why things happened, but more likely than not those reasons can't be retrieved from memory without distortions and unconscious falsifications. Therefore your actions are often far more important than their reasons. Problems and memories are used only as fuel for a solution.

*   *   *

The **Item Combination** exercise further sharpens the visualization skills that you use to, among other things, debug yourself in methods like therapeutic escape. The goal is to split your attention between two or more objects, and then to twine those objects together in your mind's eye. This ability exercises the mechanisms that act on multitasking, as well as lays the groundwork for more advanced methods.

Put yourself in a state of Mastermind submersion, and in your mind's eye pour water into a cup. Focus on the very small details without losing sight of the larger picture. Watch how the water splatters against the glass and the sound of the rising purl as the glass fills. But as you're doing so, make sure that you can see the rim of the glass too, and the reflection in the water stream.

Depending on the objects you choose, this exercise can also be used therapeutically. Your objects can be fast – wheels on a racecar, for instance – or slow. Try watching ice melt into lemonade if you want to calm down. The objects can be sharp, like a knife slicing into an onion, or relaxing, like water sprinkling onto a flower in bloom. Color your objects in stimulating reds and yellows, and see biting edges and hard angles to invigorate yourself. For calm, you'll want smooth objects in earth tones.

Get creative. When you can see these objects vividly interacting, you can add more complexity and more moving parts and diverse textures. Once you can see water sprinkling the flower, maybe add a bumblebee. Once you can see the wheel and the racecar, try adding exhaust. Or see a meadow in its entirety, and braid together the blades of glass, knot the end of it. See the whole scene as well as the details. The most important point is that whatever objects you choose to play with must be interesting enough to hold your attention. The more lifelike and multidimensional this experience becomes the more creative fulfillment and imagination you'll achieve.

Take pleasure in these challenges, and take pride in your successes.

Linger here, if you like, experimenting and combining the tools dangling from your belt. The next chapter will bring you to the terminal station of these visualization exercises, and then catapult you out into the wild blue yonder.

Item Combination - Basic Benefits

- advances your ability to focus attention
- allows for enhanced training of memory
- enhances your abilty to train your imagination
- platform for training of creativity

Item Combination - Concentrated Version

- Mask—Heavy—Warm
- Breathing
- Forehead
- Item Combination
- Exit

See Quick Reference Guide page 196 for a Therapeutic Escape lesson.

CHAPTER FIFTEEN

The Man Who Saw Many in One

In the 1970s, an inventor, scientist, and space explorer named James Lovelock began gathering together the bricks that he would eventually mortar into the Gaia theory. He studied methods of detecting life on Mars by analyzing the composition of its atmosphere, and then took a position with Shell examining the effect of fossil fuels on our own atmosphere. The way the earth recycles carbon through living creatures in trees, oceans, and reefs struck Lovelock as a single cooperative system. He compared adaptive reactions by the earth to pollution, to the reaction of the human body to poison. Lovelock's most contentious statement was that the Earth might itself be the largest life form on Earth.

It took time for Lovelock's hypothesis to be recognized, but it is now a scientifically respected model for conceptualizing the planet. Whether or not the Gaia theory seems reasonable from your perspective, at least it is a remarkable feat of imagination. What has, for the bulk of human existence, been considered incomparably diverse and countless, Lovelock saw as one. He proposed that the whole range of flora and fauna on earth could be regarded as a fragment of a single living entity, all the way from blue whales to oak trees to algae sludge – and to you. This may remind you of James Cameron's film Avatar.

You are singular. You are unique, with a body and a mind and a set of experiences distinct from everything else in the world. No one else shares your specific cumulative set of memories. They live within the wrinkles of your mind and nowhere else.

And yet you are many. You are an entire ecosystem. Your body has about ten times more bacteria – tiny individual lives – than human cells. These are the human flora. Without them, critical nutrients would flush out through your gut, undigested. Pathological microorganisms would consume you. Your immune system would cringe and flail helplessly before the invaders.

Your life, without those bacteria, would deteriorate almost immediately. In a very real sense, you are the diverse population of bacteria, and they are you.

Every unit of life is an incredible fractal that contains the whole world, if you have the awareness to see it. That, ultimately, is the real value of welcoming the world into your mind. That is why you have trained your attention to linger on things your brain has a tendency to skip past. Of course as you've already discovered, there are practical, day-to-day benefits of heightened awareness. But those advantages are underpinned by more profound life truths. When you apply Mastermind observation methods to, say, a jellyfish, that observation will inform your understanding of yourself as well as your appreciation of the jellyfish. If the bridge between your mind and the world is broad enough, these paired understandings fuel a feedback loop that enhances in leapfrogged bounds literally everything about your life and your world. All that from a spineless blob!

There are only so many ways to illustrate this and all of them pale in comparison to the actual experience. The only thing for you to do is to explore.

The two exercises in this chapter are the culmination of your Mastermind mind to world training. Until now you have probably been visualizing inanimate objects. The final challenge of specific visualization will be to see, in your mind's eye, a human face. Nothing is more difficult. Human faces are infinitely complex. They transmit such a vast load of information that visualization incorporates not only sensory detail, but mood and emotion and even memories.

The face of a stranger carries less emotional charge than a known face. For the **human faces exercise**, begin by imagining a *generic face*. You'll probably start off seeing cartoony sketches, or caricatures that lack a depth of individuality. Think of these faces as doodles. Try giving them a bit of character – a moustache, or glasses, or makeup. Watch them smile. Observe the effect of a smile that crinkles the eyes, or one that doesn't move in their eyes at all. Make them angry, or shocked, or shy, or comfortable. The face should stay whole and visual in your mind. If you find your observation slipping into abstraction, drift there for a moment, and then bring the face back.

You'll probably find that as you tweak this imagined face, it begins to resemble someone you know or have met. It may be a hair stylist, or a pet groomer, or even someone you passed by on the street today. Don't fight it. Let it become whatever it becomes. Continue studying this face from different angles. It will give you insight into his or her character. Those insights may even transform the face. If you really lose yourself in this exercise, you will find your own emotions echoing the emotions you impart onto this human face. Again, don't strain against this. Simply observe yourself and your reactions.

This exercise allows you to empathize with people in your daily life, and from there a deep and human awareness for both yourself and for the people around you. This is called *psychological mindedness*. You may notice after some practice with the human faces exercise that you pay more attention to the smallest tics and pulls on the living faces around you. Those very tics and pulls are revealing. By understanding them, you deepen your ability to empathize and communicate with others. You sense their needs and desires simply by looking at them. Their actions become glued together by an understood psyche. By knowing them, you can graduate to knowing yourself.

Once you have mastered the faces of strangers or distant acquaintances, move on to *faces of significant or meaningful people* in your life. Try your parents, or your spouse, or children, or best friends. This is more challenging. There is no part of your brain that is silent when you retrieve such an image. It requires you to be able to remember everything about this person and about the whole world all together.

At first, it is very difficult for people to be able to envision significant faces clearly. You may find it more natural to *sense the presence* of someone you love. This has no less dramatic an effect than a visual contact. Engage this sense, but work on developing new abilities. Shape faces in broad strokes at first, and allow the presence of that memory to tighten the lines until you are able to see the face in sharp relief.

Such faces, when remembered, show not just physical features, but complete lives and memories. In fact, during or shortly after practice with significant faces you may find yourself unlocking long forgotten memories. The emotional response attached to those memories or those faces can be dangerously overwhelming at first. It is very important for you to be in a perfect state of Mastermind relaxation during your early explorations of significant faces. If you find yourself shaken, remember the continuum of your mental and physical anxiety defenses. Keep working backwards through them until you are in control. Melt ice into lemonade, or observe bite marks on your pencil, or see earth tones, or focus on your diaphragmatic breathing. Or march in the other direction and begin by applying the Mask of Relaxation and move forward through the submersion exercises.

Once you have mastered the significant faces exercise, it will become a source of extraordinary comfort in even the most dire circumstances. It will also open your mind to the fullness of yourself and others. You probably know your mother (or your father, or brother, or spouse, whatever the case may be) better than anyone else in the world. Trust is in her face, and mistrust, and role confusion, and resentment, and happiness, and love, and explosive arguments, and all her flaws, and tender affection, and soft hands, and her Sunday morning waffles, and her mushy green beans, and her comb through your hair before school, and ...

Here are your deepest memories and the fount of your human understandings.

The final mind to world exercise removes that last human barrier and asks you to *understand the world itself*. This is called **empathy** and it is the beginning of a radical new approach to your exploration. On a personal level, extending consciousness allows you to become something other than yourself, and by doing so to absorb positive features from whatever you inhabit.

For instance, imagine extending your consciousness into a chair – just a normal wooden chair with four legs. It may sound strange, but marinate in the idea for a moment. If you can become a chair, you suddenly feel very stable, very sturdy. You may feel the screws and nails holding you tightly together. You may feel the purpose of serving someone, holding someone up, allowing them to rest against you. You may even be proud of your role. Imagine a chair doing its solid duty. It is honest, consistent, strong, and dependable. Those are good qualities to experience and retain.

If you can actually become a chair in your mind – to not pretend to be a chair, but to actually become it – you are empathizing with that chair. A pilot who empathizes with his airplane – someone who can feel his wings and navigation equipment, who tastes the jet fuel in his veins, who knows the feel of thrust and air resistance – ultimately becomes a better pilot than one who lacks that union with machine. The same is true of a surgeon and his scopes, or a race car driver and his vehicle. The practical benefits are numerous.

Moving beyond our day to day life, this exercise has potential to transform the way you look at even the most basic physical mechanisms. Within the same laboratory where we sterilized our fears, we can test our assumptions of the world. The discoveries that can be made within such a laboratory have a history of changing the course of human understanding.

In 1905 an anonymous loser working a dead end office job published three scientific papers with no footnotes or citations. They unveiled some of the most astonishing insights into the natural functions of the universe that have ever been achieved. His name, of course, was Einstein. He accomplished his earliest and most radical work with no scientific experimentation in university physics labs, but only with the power of what he called "thought experiments." Throughout his storied career, Einstein extended his consciousness to trains and elevators, magnets, beams of light, and photons. His mind was unchained by the dogma of the time. Now many of Einstein's discoveries have become dogma. Be careful with that. Nobody is correct about everything. The belief that Einstein told the whole truth is limiting. Your imagination is the key to these shackles. Nothing – absolutely nothing – is impossible or unimaginable for a supple mind on its own turf.

You may or may not be the next Albert Einstein. Don't despair if you're not. In the same way that not every cyclist becomes Lance Armstrong (steroids or not), extending your consciousness can effect positive change in your own life even without the intense focus and curiosity that Einstein employed. Even if we are not as brilliant as he was, at least we can imitate his brilliance. If we are only the moon to his sun, we are still shining gloriously.

*   *   *

Now come back to earth. Try being a *chair*. See the chair first, using mental observation. And then rush upon it. Inhabit it. Feel its legs as yours. Feel your skin as the rough wood grain. Once you've managed that, move on to something a little stranger. Imagine yourself as a jellyfish. Enter a state of Mastermind relaxation and see the jellyfish. Watch how he moves. Admire his grace. Now become him. Remember: Don't imagine this transformation. Don't just see it. Accomplish it.

You are soft and transparent and wobbly. You have no skeleton. You are light, rocking in the waves. Experience the current pulling you. Feel the coolness of the ocean around you. You don't have arms or legs or eyes. You are carried and carried and carried by the current, picked up by a wave and suddenly thrown on the shore.

You land on hot rocks, out of the water, dripping off your protective coating. You are splayed there, uncomfortable. Gravity flattens you and pushes you as you spread softly and shapelessly. Feel the sun drying your skin. You cannot breathe well. You're not supposed to be here. You sense the dry heat on your back and the rough wet stone beneath you.

Make the picture emotionally complete. How do you feel out of the water? Are you scared? Anxious? Helpless?

Suddenly another wave catches up with you and swirls you right back into the water. You're bathed again in a comfortable salty environment. You're carried away from the shore, into the depths of the ocean with less and less light above and deep blue darkness underneath. Feel the frustration of the near death experience and the relief of survival.

Are you happy to be alive? Or grouchy and looking for something to sting?

If you want to keep this softness in you, retain it. If you want to feel the elation of survival, hold on to this feeling. Then lead yourself out of the state of Mastermind submersion and back into human reality.

There is a whole universe of exploration. What does a liquid feel like? Or a gas? What about a piece of butterscotch candy melting in someone's mouth? Or a beam of light, or a spark of electricity? As you become more comfortable with extending your consciousness, consider larger targets. Can you become a pile of sand, or a colony of ants, or a city full of people? Can you be plural? Can you be every person in the city or every grain of sand all at once?

Can you be the whole world, with cities and fields, with oceans and deserts and mountains, with storms and skies and clouds?

This is the zenith of Mind to World methods. It's not easy. The very trial opens up your mind. Experiencing yourself simultaneously as an individual and the whole planet is something close to enlightenment. It will transform your understanding of the world and your place in it. As you experience other forms of consciousness, you will come to realize that the sense of being many and one is not a mere illusion. Remember the hundreds of trillions of bacteria living inside you. You are the world, and the world is you.

Smile.

Enjoy this.

When you move on, it is time to turn your attention inward.

Empathy Training - Basic Benefits

- allows for advanced training of intuition and insight
- promotes advanced understanding of the world outside
- Improves and advances communication skills
- Promotes training of memory, concentration and creativity
- Sharpens ability to enjoy life

Empathy Training - Concentrated Version

- Mask—Heavy—Warm
- Breathing
- Forehead
- Empathy Imaging
- Exit

PART THREE

Advanced Mastermind

Mind to Mind

CHAPTER SIXTEEN

A Man in the Storm

When his tiny boat capsized in the middle of the Atlantic, Hannes Lindemann remembered a huge wall rising up on his right side, and then sudden lack of breath. "Dead?" he thought, and then he pulled himself out of the frame and canvas boat and burst to the surface. Storm clouds roiled and thundered above him. Rain spattered down. He crawled atop the hull of his little upturned vessel – just seventeen feet long and three feet wide with a hull of rubber and canvas stretched across a plywood frame – and clung for dear and frigid life. Hannes hadn't told anyone of his plan to paddle alone across the Atlantic in a folding boat. It was an impossible project, and catastrophe had finally caught up with him.

Beneath the roof of black clouds, waves turned great shadows over him. His clothes crackled when he moved. He was literally freezing. He slipped into the water to escape the wind, but every kick and tread pulled sodden clothes away from his skin and sucked in cold water, so he forced himself to remain motionless but for the chattering and shivering. Around midnight he felt something brush against his feet – a shark, or some unknown monster of the deep coming to gnaw at a corpse. In a fright, Hannes scrambled back onto the bowed hull and into the biting wind. He thought of home and his parents. Self-pity washed over him. As the cold seeped into his bones he began to hallucinate funeral bells tolling through the night.

About a year earlier, Hannes had resolved to attempt this solo crossing to, as he said, "test the human machine." Before setting out, he researched historical and contemporary accounts of castaways, and found that those who survived had done so through strict discipline, adaptability, and calm. Those unfortunates that lacked these virtues suffered dire ends. In 1816, a French doctor recorded that during just thirteen days lost at sea; survivors of a sunken ship completely lost their minds. They committed suicide, killed one another, and ate human flesh and excrement. Of one hundred and fifty, only fifteen survived.

Hannes knew that if he even had a chance at making the Atlantic cross-ing successfully, he would have to exercise a severe power of will. In the months leading up to his departure he prayed with a great intensity. "I will succeed," he said over and over again, "I will keep going." After three months of regular repetition, the words became thought, which became in-stinct. He grew into an unruffled confidence – that is, until the days before he planned to set out. That is when doubt, creeping through the back alleys of his mind, began its assault. "Am I really doing this?" he found himself asking. And then, shockingly, from within the depths of his own mind, an answer sallied forth. "You'll make it," was the riposte. "You will succeed."

The voyage was torture from the very first day. Water leaked through Hannes' spray cover and soaked through his oilskin pants. His skin cooked under the sun so that even a gentle touch felt like a burn of hot tar. His fingertips swelled, and the constant bailing of water wrinkled his hands until they were raw and soft, and the skin rubbed apart like wet paper. Af-ter dumping forty pounds of food to lighten the boat, Hannes veered into despair. It whispered to him gently and soothingly. "Jump overboard," it told him, "who cares about you?" But like an immune response, his mind rallied against the germs of hopelessness and self-pity. "You will succeed," came the answer. "Keep going west."

After twenty days in the tiny boat he began to feel as though it were part of his body. He could feel the triggerfish gnawing barnacles off the bottom of his foldboat, and slapping at the rudder with their tails. They seemed to be attacking him. He killed one, and gnawed its flesh and scales raw, and drank up its blood. Wind blew steadily against him for days, slowing his progress. For some reason his knee swelled just below the kneecap, and he couldn't touch it without pain shocking up and down the leg. "It tried my patience," he wrote later, "made me nervous, ill-at-ease and irritable. I was ready to start an argument with myself." He teetered at the brink of losing his calm out there in the blue ocean wild, nearly giving in to the sweet whispers of self-destruction. Hannes closed his eyes and imagined civili-zation – life on his farm, and pastries topped with mountains of whipped cream. The tension drifted off, and he was peaceful again. "You will suc-ceed," his mind reminded him. "You will keep going."

Fifty days into the voyage as he clung to an overturned vessel, with salt stinging in his eyes, and cold shaking in his bones, and the bells of death tolling in his ears, his mind should have failed. It should have torn to piec-es, the forgotten mantras and prayers scattering in the wind. But it didn't. Hannes found himself muttering, "You'll get through," over and over again. "It made me a slave," he later wrote of the chant, "who was not allowed to die, a slave to an idea." As the prayer slowly beat back the funeral bells, Hannes' self-pity was replaced by a puzzled confidence. Didn't the storm know that he had no choice but to succeed? With what convulsive futility did these waves lash against him?

He clung like an animal to the hull, and survived the night.

By morning he had lost his mast and sea anchor. Every single can of food had washed away, along with his glasses, his toiletries, grappling iron, and knife. He capsized again that morning and lost his spear gun. In the last days before touching land at St. Martin in the Caribbean, he was in a state of constant hallucination, but the same words kept chanting in his head: "Keep going west. I will make it. Keep going west."

*　*　*

There are so many remedies within us, always present, if we just can recognize and grow them. You have already discovered your control over your body and your world. Those tools dangle from your belt. The dangers that Hannes faced, however, were of the mind. The whispers of suicide and despair came from within him. If he had failed to exercise control over himself then he may have paid with his life.

Hannes lived to tell his tale of mental and physical endurance. You can read about it in his book *Alone at Sea*. Through the trials of his solo crossing, he discovered that the human machine can indeed survive incredible deprivation – but only in a primed state of mind. In his darkest hours, Hannes felt the same urge to leap from his boat and swim to his death that every suffering castaway records. Without prior mental preparation on land, he may have indulged those tempting whispers of despair and self-destruction. But he had anticipated the dangers facing him, and programmed himself to survive using methods of what psychiatrists call **self-suggestion.**

The same way that chronic stress can have pathological effects on your body, extreme stress switches on extreme mental defense mechanisms, often with unpredictable results. These mechanisms need to be practiced and oiled to be of any reliable value in a crisis. Your Mastermind methods are not just spare tires to be used in an emergency. They are the regular, prophylactic tune-ups that will keep your human machine from breaking down in a cloud of dust and smoke beside the highway.

Hopefully few of us have a need to exercise mental stability alone at night in an upturned canoe in the middle of an Atlantic rainstorm. But even if we never find ourselves in as dire circumstances as Hannes, the *self-reassurance* that he employed during his seaborne trials is just as effective on a crowded public bus, or on the wrong side of an angry supervisor's desk, or when you are startled awake by a newborn's wail. The earlier you learn these methods and incorporate them into your daily Mastermind practice, the more robust preventative and therapeutic benefits you can gain from them.

Prevention is your first line of defense against doubt and despair. Avoid unhealthy behaviors. You will do this naturally as you increase your awareness of the world and yourself. Maintaining mental health through regular practice is your second line of trenches. When you are well trained, you don't *need* to ponder up a decision. You know the answer already, just like Hannes instinctively knew to stop the thoughts of "give up," and "you will die." In fact, most choices in life are based on a clear knowledge of what needs to be done. We don't waste time on finding solutions to, say, the best way to brush our teeth. We just do it. Or for even a more basic skill – imagine if you had never been potty trained and every time you needed to use a toilet you had to decide how to do it. Without knowing how to hold it in while you unbuttoned your pants, which is a learned skill, you'd never survive in the modern world.

We all live by a myriad of daily skills, ranging from keeping our balance while we walk to performing microsurgery or shaping a diamond. However different those habits might be, they are based on the same principles of repetition and development of mental and physical coordination. These skills are developed by a process called **conditioning**.

Humans are no less slaves of habit as Pavlov's dog, who learned to drool at the sound of a bell. A mischievous medical school classmate of mine in Moscow secretly trained patients to urinate each time we turned on the lights in their room. He bragged to us afterwards of his process: he'd give a water pill at a certain time, and thirty minutes later he would flip on the lights. That was about the time that the water pills started to work, so the patients would rush for the bathroom. He repeated this at least twice a day. About a week later, the poor patients were rushing to relieve themselves with the flip of a switch even without the help of a water pill. They were conditioned to do this, and had no awareness of being manipulated.

Although none of us approved of such abuse and that classmate was eventually booted from the program, it was an important lesson in the efficacy of physiological conditioning. Mental conditioning is no different. Humans by nature develop habits. If the process is unconscious, those habits can limit our ability to think in new ways or experience the world with fresh young eyes. But if we train our own habits consciously, we can program healthy mental pathways. In fact, the repetitive nature of conditioning can be applied to memory as well as emotions. A healthy amount of repetition organizes the mind, and arranges your knowledge and memories into a searchable, organized forensic grid. A well planned routine can cry halt to disaster – be it wetting your pants or an urge to just die – long before it arrives.

Thought stopping, the method Hannes practiced to eliminate fears of death or failure, guides the brain into the right direction. Ruminations and worries and hectic concern are replaced with structured activity – *a mantra*, in Hannes' case – that guides you peacefully in the direction you need. An alternative to thought stopping, which Hannes did not employ but is useful for those who frown upon eliminating rumination, is *self-talk*, wherein you dialogue with yourself. Have a conversation between the angel and the demon on your shoulder. This also brings structure and consistency to reality, and allows you to utilize a powerful combination of mind and body defenses.

An active treatment chasing down your problems should always be your last resort. The flurry of a crisis is not the best time to experiment with new methods. It is in safety and peace that mental stability is forged. It is so much easier to smother problems when they are young than when they have snowballed into crises with real bulk and momentum. For all of the stories of horror and human failure in earlier chapters, let the fact of Hannes' survival remind you of this: With awareness, anticipation, and practice, tragedy is avoidable.

So how can you improve your self-awareness?

More than two thousand and five hundred years ago, a student of Confucius wrote that every day before he went to sleep, he would think of three things that day he did poorly. In that way he became aware of his failings, and could then go on to mend his habits. It is a simple exercise that can be adapted to the present day.

Start by paying attention to your daily activities. At the end of each day, pencil down in a notebook some things you have done well, and some that you could have done better. Don't just think it. Actually *write* it. Do this every day for at least two weeks, you will notice patterns emerging. You will register strengths and weaknesses that can be acted upon.

One interesting side effect of heightened self-awareness is the sudden decrease in the number of people around you who you consider "bad." This is because the deeper you understand yourself, the deeper you understand the behavior and emotions of others. You will begin to empathize with them. When you stop judging them and stop suspecting them of constant wrongdoing, you will feel more secure. Your surroundings will seem less threatening. You may become less judgmental, more relaxed, and more self-assured. The world changes because your perspective on it is new and different. By changing yourself, you change others.

*   *   *

There are two methods of Mastermind self-reassurance – verbal and visual. Both act to change a negative perception of yourself and your circumstance into a positive one.

The verbal method of **positive self-suggestion** was first developed in the nineteenth century by a French pharmacist called Emile Coue. It had wide appeal in the early twentieth century because of its matter-of-fact simplicity. The idea was this: If you say something, it will happen. Put another way; if you oink a thousand times you become a pig.

The exercise itself is intuitive. Twice a day – just after you awake and just before you go to sleep, put yourself in a state of Mastermind submersion and chant to yourself the following recitation:

"I can.

I'm healthy.

I'm strong.

I'm smart.

I will remember."

These imperative **self-suggestions** turn you into a motivational speaker for yourself.

Some think that such a strong and pushy insistence on improvement may cause inner resistance and self-sabotage. If you don't like motivational speakers, try soothing self-suggestions in permissive self-talk, as in:

"Let me do it.

Let me be healthy.

Let me be smart.

Let me remember."

Modify the contents of this recitation according to your own needs. Hannes Lindemann prayed not for health or intelligence but to "Keep going west," and "I will succeed." You may recite for confidence, or happiness, or contentment.

This verbal self-suggestion may seem obvious – and it is obvious – but few people in the modern world actually apply it. Although we take it as our social duty to reassure our children, our friends, our peers, and our elders, we rarely reassure ourselves. It took Hannes about three months of daily practice before his prayers trickled into the deepest layers of his mind. Once they were embedded in his subconscious, the prayer became his coach, his hope, and his determination. He later described the confidence that grew out from his chants as a lighthouse. "Loud and bright, it warned me not to give in, to keep on fighting. It shouted at me, 'You will make it!'" He did not flail around or lean on others for help. Instead he programmed himself for strength and success.

The visual method is a gentler slope that eventually arrives at the same destination as the positive self-suggestion. You'll need to utilize all of your powers of visualization to create complete settings for your reassurance. There are two basic approaches to creating whole scenes. You can either begin with a complex setting and slowly zoom into it, or you can start with one simple object and piece by piece enrich it with details. For instance, you might see a forest glade from afar, and then as you draw closer see the spring leaves on the trees, and the bunnies scrambling out from their dens. Or you might begin with just a single flower and from there look around you, building grasses and a tree, then many trees, and a cool breeze. The details are as endless as your imagination. You can go under the ground and into the water. You can fly in the skies and shoot out of the atmosphere. You can write little scenarios in advance to guide you through or you can create them as you go. There is no limit. It all depends on your personal inclinations and desires.

Put yourself in Mastermind submersion and, using your tools of visualization, come to a place where you are loved and cared for – your childhood home, or an imaginary meadow of wildflowers. Explore your setting. Fill it with smells and sounds of happiness and contentment. Settle down into a leather recliner, or a bed of soft grass, and experience yourself in this contented environment of safety and comfort. You are not a detached observer, but living in this place. You are connected to it with every fiber. Know that someone who is dear to you will be coming soon to meet you. Wait for this person in anticipation. Be in control of your emotions. Feel valued and accomplished. Linger, if you like. As long as you keep exploring and fantasizing, your world will never end. Know that you have much to tell and that you will be heard. Lock onto the feeling of closeness and peace, and then slowly bring yourself out of the Mastermind submersion.

Smile when you open your eyes.

The power is not a storm outside raging upon you. The power is within you to act upon the world.

Self Suggestion - Basic Benefits

- enhances visualization
- improves effectiveness of exposure therapy
- deepens connection with the world
- helps with multitasking

Self Suggestion - Concentrated Version

- Mask—Heavy—Warm
- Breathing
- Forehead
- I can, I will, I see
- Exit

See Quick Reference Guide pages 198 through 201 for a detailed lesson on Scene Building.

CHAPTER SEVENTEEN

The Athlete Who Made it Big

Harry had been a giant back in the late sixties – nearly seven feet tall as a teenager. People back then used to call him "Mount Harry." In the photo of his high school state champ basketball team, he kneels in the front row and his head is almost level with the collars of the players behind him. He wears a stern expression. Beside him, his grinning teammates look like children.

In those days, basketball in Indiana was life. The statewide single-class high school tournament, in which small rural schools went man for man against huge urban ones, was an annual hysteria that made wicked witches and Cinderellas of Hoosier students. Harry won himself some local notoriety in his senior year when he led his team on an undefeated run to the championship. Sportswriters covering the final four of the tournament wrote of his brutish play, claiming he was a rough-and-tumble player who ought to stick to football. Although Harry was in fact a decorated downfield blocker on his school's football team, he was hurt by the suggestion that he was either a bully, or a klutz who didn't know how strong he was.

"I wasn't playing mean, was I?" he asked his dad after winning the championship. "I can't help being big."

"Son," answered his father, "you're a man among boys. It's not that you're too mean or too strong. It's that you don't know how fast you are."

Harry didn't have a mean hair on his head. He was kind, sweet, and fair-minded. Although he had grown up poor – his dad was a freelance construction worker and his mother a housewife – his parents raised him with good Christian values. Their family had migrated to Indiana in the fifties, fleeing institutionalized racism in Dixie. When Harry was a child his dad taught him to hunt squirrels and rabbits for food. Harry learned to creep through the woods quietly, to match his lungs with his movement while he was shooting, and to squeeze the trigger in the valleys between his breaths. When he hit his target, his father praised him – but if he missed, Harry would catch it good.

His dad was a perfectionist. "You've got to drain every talent in your body, son," he used to say. "You don't know when the Lord will take you up into the hereafter." And so whatever Harry set his mind to, he did it hard. He played football to the hilt, and basketball too. Harry practiced to exhaustion, and at night as he lay in bed with his eyes shut, he played out scenarios in his mind – juking and swiveling in his imagination, grabbing with his toes at the turf, or straining the seams on his shoes as he feinted back and forth on the lacquered wood. His diligence paid off. He became an All-American in both sports.

After his team won the state championship, Harry joined a squad of Indiana all-stars to take on the flower of Kentucky high school basketball in an annual two game series. The Hoosiers won the first game in Indianapolis, and then ventured across the Ohio River into Louisville for the finale. Harry's mother and father travelled down from Indianapolis to watch him play. It would be one of the best games of his life to date. Harry had a strange, one-handed shot – he balanced the ball on his huge mitt and lobbed it up – and despite the frantic swatting leaps of his defenders, he just couldn't miss. His sneakers cut and squeaked across the hardwood, his boat like feet feinting and pivoting to slip around the Kentuckians. They moved in slow motion. Harry scored just under half of the total team points. It was a massacre.

When his coach pulled him from the game in the final minutes, the crowd of nearly twenty thousand honored his brilliant play with a standing ovation. That was the first time in seven years that the Hoosiers beat the Kentucky high school all-stars. After the game, a disgruntled Kentucky sportswriter grumbled to his Indiana counterpart, "We'd have whipped you again this year if you hadn't brought along one of the Boston Celtics."

His father met him after the game, bursting with pride. "This is my boy," he shouted over the bustle of celebration, "my son!" The whole night he was glued to Harry's side. It was a glorious victory for Harry. He was Mr. Basketball, the king of his school, the hero of a state, and the apple of his father's eye. In the coming weeks, Harry knew he would have scholarship offers filling his mailbox in from colleges all across the country. That very evening, he vowed to play hard and study harder so that he could earn a living to bring his parents to a better station. After all, they had already sacrificed so much for him by uprooting the whole family from their southern home and moving all the way to Indiana.

But Harry became the man of his family sooner than he had expected. A few days after the triumph in Louisville, Harry's father slipped from scaffolding on a construction site in Indianapolis. The man who had taught Harry to work hard, to love the outdoors, and to support his family, died.

Thus at nineteen years old and with great sorrow, Harry retired his dreams of sports stardom and resolved to join the American workforce to support his mother.

But she had other ideas. She forced him to go on with school. In the haze of tragedy and emotional upheaval, Harry accepted a scholarship with a recruiter from a nearby university, and worked construction in the summertime to provide for his mom. He played college ball for just two years – one season on the freshman team, and the next on varsity – before being signed to his hometown pro team. Every single dollar he earned with his signing bonus went toward a new house for his mother.

Harry went on to have a storied career in professional basketball. He was one of the most physically dominant players of his generation. During the peaks of his run on the basketball court, he remained among the league's top five players in scoring, rebounds, assists, steals, and three point shots. Ten years later when he retired from professional basketball, he was such a beloved pillar of the community that his team retired his jersey along with him. He was a rough-and-tumble poor boy who earned for himself treasure and fame – but more importantly, who made him loved.

It should have been a storybook ending, but life doesn't follow the same rules as narrative. Today, Harry's spine is ruined. He stands at least a foot shorter now than he did as an athlete, and he walks with a crooked, teetering gait. Sitting or standing, he suffers constant scoliotic discomfort. Yet somehow, despite the steep tumble of his physical condition, Harry remains a happy and humble Midwestern man. He is not disabled by his disability; he just cannot do as much as he did before. He is loved now for his business sense, his determination to help others, and not just himself. He has gotten shorter with time, but he stands taller than he ever has.

*   *   *

All living creatures yearn to control the uncontrollable. Bugs dream that frogs will disappear, cows wish for grass to always be tall and juicy, trees hope for plentiful rain, and schoolchildren want to plug their brains into the Matrix to learn their lessons in a flash so they won't have to do homework. Maybe you wish for a stock portfolio that always pays big, or for a house that never ages. In today's world of modern marvels, such dreams may seem deceptively within grasp.

Don't be fooled. Everything changes. Sometimes it comes at the flip of a switch, and other times it is so slow that you don't see it happening except in hindsight. So happiness that depends on the stability of a healthy body, or on a fulfilling job, or on a padded bank account, is frail. Catastrophe will come to anyone who lives long enough to meet it. The control we exercise over our lives does have limits. What is within your power is to moderate the risk of disaster, while at the same time preparing for the tiger's pounce as you stroll through life's tall grasses.

Although your Mastermind practice has shown you tools for self-management that you may not have known you had at your disposal, even now you are not in perfect control of your life. No one is. Jesus Christ himself, in the garden of Gethsemane, prayed in vain that he might sidestep the suffering he was bound to face. But like the true Mastermind he was, he eventually realized in the end that all that he had to do was to bear his burdens with aplomb. During the torture of the crucifixion, his pain did not overwhelm him. He died without moans or complaints, training his attention on the positive end rather than the discomfort at hand.

Your Mastermind training so far may have given you some confidence in your powers of self-control. Maybe it has shown you a depth of unexplored realms within you. What it should not have done is convince you of anything like invincibility. There is a word for someone who trusts to his own omnipotence: narcissist. And a great fall awaits every narcissist on the day he becomes self-aware.

Harry's sense of self-worth didn't collapse after his spine degraded. He hadn't pinned his happiness to performance on the basketball court. He only wanted to provide a comfortable life for his family, and in that he had already succeeded. Some professional athletes do lash their whole identity to their physical prowess. When their health declines, as it inevitably does, they find themselves floundering.

So how was Harry able to stay happy?

Well, as you may have guessed, Harry is a Mastermind.

*   *   *

On those late high school nights that Harry spent awake in bed after practice, imagining his moves on the football field or the basketball court, he was practicing a Mastermind method called **ideomotor training**. Ideomotor training has several incarnations that can be tailored to your specific purpose. In its simplest form it is a practical skill. But like most things, if you spend time and imagination on it, it can become transcendent.

You can use a basic form of ideomotor training when you are trying to track down your missing keys. If your grandmother was anything like mine, she taught you that when something is lost you must not frantically dart around the house, but instead calm down and retrace your steps. The job is made even easier if you apply your new skills of observation and visualization. The next time you misplace your keys, sit down and close your eyes. Start by recreating the scene of the last point you remember having them.

So they were in your right hand when you walked in the front door. Hear the creak of the floorboards, and feel yourself slap the door shut behind you, locking the latch. See the keys in your hand. Then what? You see the cat slinking across the floor and leaping up on the sofa. Examine your sensory memories. What exactly do you feel, standing there in the doorway? Can you hear your keys jangling? Is there dinner on the stove top – or do you smell the litter box? That's it. Instead of hanging your keys where they belonged, you went to the restroom to clean the litter box. That is where the keys are, on the counter beside the sink! Open your eyes and go get your keys.

Vivid visualization is critical. That is the first step. Visualization becomes ideomotor training when you enter the scene and begin exercising within it. You can train any kind of physical ability here in the laboratory of your mind. You are safe and free in your holodeck. You can be a surgeon making a precise incision, or a welder joining rails together, or a folk guitarist finger picking his strings, or a hunter knocking squirrels off tree limbs. In Harry's case, he would lie in bed, close his eyes to better see and smell and feel the basketball court – and then work three pointers until he fell asleep.

Obviously you can't substitute ideomotor training for a real work out. Use it instead to complement your physical tasks. You'll find that mental practice improves your coordination and helps you use your strength more efficiently. In the athletic arena, it is an invaluable tool to shave milliseconds off your personal records. You can also use ideomotor training to improve your mental stamina. You might imagine yourself sweaty and exhausted, with your attention crashing from a caffeine high two hours before, and you haven't slept for a day and half – and in spite of your weariness, still sinking those three point shots. Do it over and over and over and over again. Feel the hard-won success, again and again and again. Taste it, bite after bite after bite. Make it your best friend.

You may actually break a sweat or feel an increased heart rate during your practice of the ideomotor exercise. That's because of the bridge between body and mind. What you convince the mind of becomes the true reality of your body. If the mind experiences exercise with enough vivid sensation, the body actually feels as though physical exercise is occurring. Remember hysterical pregnancy, in which the mind causes the body to undergo dramatic physical change.

As always, don't be afraid to trim your ideomotor training to your own needs. There are infinite applications. You may have heard of miracle cancer survivors visualizing their immune defenses careening into their tumors like torpedoes destroying it, and the cancerous cells dissolving and leaving the body. Well, if you're a cancer sufferer, imagine scooping that bleeding tumor out from your body. Suck it out through a catheter, or cut it away with an invisible knife.

There are many practical incarnations of the ideomotor method that will help you in your daily life. But as you've discovered, when you accept a role or assume a persona separate from your own, you gain a sublime kind of understanding that is only possible in the laboratory of your mind. You can use the physicality of ideomotor training to further enhance the experience of your visualizations and to experience different forms of existence.

Put yourself into a state of Mastermind submersion, where you are who you want to be. Your body is absent. Your mind is in charge. Allow yourself to encounter a complex experience. Become a creature moving through space – maybe a bumblebee. Remember – you are not imagining. You are being a bee. Feel your six legs, your stinger, the little whisks of hair all over your body, and your crispy wings. See the world through the 1,000 facets in your eyes.

Fly around. Feel your strength. Feel the muscles in your back beating the wings, and the rush of air fanning your body. Rise up and sink down. Find a pleasant flower and land on it. Rub against the soft pollen. You are not allergic to it. Sniff the sweet nectar. There is nothing wrong with your bumblebee body. Drink the nectar down. Taste it. Fly away again toward some other bumblebees. Touch them with your antennae to sense what they feel like. Come home and meet hundreds and hundreds and hundreds of your brothers and sisters. They nuzzle up to you as you enter the hive. You are comfortable surrounded by them.

Be creative. Feel whatever else you want. Be as true a bumblebee as possible. And don't be passive! Get involved in your adventure. When it gives you enough satisfaction, become a human again and sense yourself floating over the surface. Recognize the increase in your physical strength – you absorbed it from a bumblebee. Retain the syrupy nectar in your mouth.

Now, imagine yourself lifting weights, or using an exercise machine, or just running, or whatever task you choose. Experience in full the pleasure of physical movement within your mind. This practice actually improves blood flow to the muscles and develops stamina. Feel your body strong and fit, moving with increasing speed and strength. Be an Olympic champion and beat everybody in your sport. See it. Experience it. Enjoy the victory. Do it with pleasure and confidence.

When you are done with being a super hero, let the excessive warmth and heaviness leave your body. Remain strong and confident, fast and capable.

Count to three.

Inhale deep and fast in your chest, and then forcefully exhale.

Stretch and open your eyes.

Smile.

Ideomotor Training - Basic Benefits

- improves physical performance
- counteracts future uncertainties
- builds stamina
- improves visualization skills

Ideomotor Training - Concentrated Version

- Mask—Heavy—Warm
- Breathing
- Forehead
- Be whatever you want
- Exit

Ideomotor Training Method

- assume a state of Mastermind submersion
- without moving the body, perform an exercise in the minds eyes
- this could be any task to be done in the future – riding a bike, shooting a basketball, or firing a weapon
- always do the task *perfectly* in inner vision

Tips

- try inhabiting other creatures: a bumblebee, or a hummingbird, or an elephant
- feel the motions of their bodies as they move throughout the world

CHAPTER EIGHTEEN

The Man with Sex and Money

"Remind me of your name, Private," snapped the lieutenant.

"Anton, sir."

"Well. The inspection has succeeded," said the lieutenant. "Your sprayer worked."

"Yes sir," said Anton.

The fall inspection by the regional political delegation had come and gone. Just before the politicians had arrived, the lieutenant noticed that the changing leaves on the bushes around the barracks looked drab and untidy. Anton, in almost no time at all, had managed to cobble together a kind of rudimentary pressure sprayer to paint the leaves crispy and green. It had been the final touch that really made the base sparkle.

"So what else can you do?" said the lieutenant.

"What can I do?" repeated Anton slowly.

"That's what I said, damn it. Are you deaf? What else can you do?"

Many years later, the memory of this question would make Anton laugh until he cried. As a young man he was small, weak, and ugly. He had no girlfriends, no skills and no money. Of course, no one had any money in the U.S.S.R. back then. No one had anything. The most that common people could do was offer favors to powerful Party members – but Anton didn't know anyone in the Party.

He wasn't a good soldier. He couldn't keep the scuffs off his boots, and his marches were always a little out of step. He didn't like the physical training, or the weapons drills, or the endless digging that formed blisters and then calluses on his hands. But as a lowly private he had no say in the matter. When the officers said, "Dig," he dug, and that was his whole life. So when the lieutenant asked him what else he could do, Anton didn't know how to answer. He could dig, that was for sure. He'd never been asked to do anything more.

Scrawny Anton shrugged, and sniffled, and kicked his shoes a little against the floor, and finally said, "I can do anything, sir."

Anton accepted a position in the lieutenant's administrative staff, where he made small tweaks to their operations that had a big impact on efficiency. He perfected a filing system, and streamlined reporting. He improved the lighting, and decorated the offices with handsome images of Soviet leaders. The leaves outside the barracks were always green.

Before next year's inspection, Anton sculpted Communist figures in relief – Brezhnev, Lenin and Politburo members – to hang on the walls of the battalion headquarters. They were a real hit with the commissars. Other bases commissioned reliefs of their own from Anton, and then a general wanted one for his home. Anton even heard that one of his reliefs made it to the Kremlin, which made him chuckle.

His newfound skills earned him better rations and easier hours. He wasn't sweating alongside the other soldiers any more. He ate well and slept long. The calluses on his palms peeled away. He saw firsthand an officer's leisurely life – their vodka fueled romps with fast women. Once he saw the lieutenant dismiss a blushing young woman with rumpled hair from his office. The lieutenant wore a superior grin. "The doctors say to bump a woman twice a week," he told Anton. "Keeps your prostate healthy."

It was Anton's first exposure to what counted as success. Although it was this same lieutenant that had improved his station, he disliked him. He was arrogant and brusque. "I'll have hundreds of girlfriends someday," Anton said to himself, "a hundred for each one that these officers plow."

When his service ended, he was honorably discharged. By then he had a reputation as a political artist, and his work was in high demand. His patrons paid him very, very well, and Anton learned quickly that good money meant lots of women. He would have three, four, or even five women in a single day. "But five girls in one day," he admitted to me later, "is too many. Three is enough. More than that and you don't have time for anything else."

Anton liked sex and not love, but the young and beautiful girls he bedded didn't always appreciate the distinction. So he used them as bridges to seduce their mothers. They were often less lovely, but more amenable to a strictly physical relationship. After all, Anton wasn't trying to start a family. He was just exercising a healthy concern for the state of his prostate.

Of course, shameless philandering in Soviet Russia was a dangerous lifestyle. After a post-coital disagreement with the wife of a Party commissar – a triumph which under the sheets had seemed like a sign of how high his station in life had risen since his days of digging trenches, but afterwards threatened to turn Pyrrhic – he realized that he couldn't safely achieve the measures of success he so urgently wanted. And so, smuggling what cash he could with him, Anton fled for New York City, without a second thought for the mess of broken families, jilted lovers, and swollen bellies he left behind.

Manhattan was a return to an enlisted man's life. Anton spoke no English, knew nothing about American society, and furthermore competed for work with hundreds of thousands of Russian émigrés like him. He shaped a few reliefs of J.F.K. but found Americans less enamored with their political leaders than he expected. Soon he didn't have enough money to attract any women to his bed, not even homely ones. Visions of a swollen prostate haunted his dreams. He had to marry.

These were dire times for Anton. After window shopping up and down 5th Avenue hunting for the flash of inspiration that would bring him the wealth he needed, he spotted a birdcage in an upscale shop. It was woven of bent wicker and sprayed with golden flecks, but Anton saw splinters near the knots. He knew he could make a better birdcage than that.

He bought some scraps of mahogany, carving and gluing them into an ornate birdcage with miniature columns and flowered gabled ends, and he brought this back to the shop. In his stammering English he turned the cage around in his hands, explaining the different features. The owner didn't understand at first. "It's a lovely cage," he said, "but we don't sell that model here."

"No, no," said Anton. "I sell you."

"Who is the artist?" asked the owner.

"I make it."

"*You* made this? How much are you asking for it?"

Anton, who was canny even with his broken English, asked in return, "How much do you buy for?"

The owner named a price ten times higher than Anton had ever imagined. They had a deal. "So what else can you do?" asked the owner.

Anton shrugged and answered, "I can do anything."

So Anton made larger and more elaborate cages, with secret doors and latches, and rounded perches, and nooks where the birds could stash their seeds. He made a cage that looked like the Parthenon and another like a Japanese pavilion, and a neck-high freestanding behemoth that looked like the Taj Mahal. The last one made it into the front window of the shop, and was bought in a few days by an Arab prince. As time passed, Anton built a client list of wealthy bird lovers. He made cages to order and on spec. And the more he got paid, the more women he seduced. His marriage notwithstanding, the trail of pregnancies he left behind him grew longer.

After several years he moved out to California. He didn't like the weather in the northeast, and furthermore the rent of his apartment and the apartments of all his girlfriends was too high. On the west coast he bought an apartment complex and rented the rooms to other Soviet émigrés. He reserved the penthouse suite, though, to fulfill an adolescent fantasy – a dream over so many years had somehow never matured. He wanted a harem. For that he had to divorce. His wife had too many headaches and he became fearful of his prostate's possible unhealthy swelling.

Anton was tired of taking his girlfriends out one by one on different days of the week. He wanted a one stop sex shop all for himself and his prostate. At first the harem wasn't a popular idea among the prospective concubines. His girlfriends took some cajoling, but because they were all dependent on the monthly stipend he gave them, they eventually broke down and agreed to move in together to satisfy him and bear his children.

But even this extraordinary lifestyle still wasn't enough for Anton. He needed more. "I can do anything," he told himself. "I am not rich enough or successful enough if I can't maintain a healthy prostate. I will just have to think of a way to have more sex." Thus began the strangest chapter in his strange life. Anton began a fertility business. Dry, old, desperate women, from New York and Russia and all over the world, paid to reserve timeslots in Anton's schedule. They would fly into California on their own expense to sleep with him in the hope that he might seed a child in them. And if you believe him, he was successful. Anton, the enlisted soldier who didn't like digging, *impregnated barren women.*

By then he was in his fifties. The constant sex was a chore. He slept with scores of women with the same enthusiasm that he paid the bills. What pleasure and novelty his conquests once had, wore off years ago. It was a duty, now. A soldier digs. A successful man maintains a healthy prostate by sleeping with many women. And Anton knew he was successful – a hundred times more successful than the Soviet officers who had looked down on him. Most importantly, his prostate was healthy.

"If only those bastards could look at me now," he says to me, laughing. "I can do anything, Dmitry. Don't you see?"

*   *   *

Anton, in his life so far, has achieved his dreams. He has more money than he can spend, more women than he can ever satisfy, and more sex than any man needs in ten lifetimes. His prostate is healthy. Like Hannes Lindemann, Anton's answer to every challenge is, "Yes, I can." This confidence and ambition, at least, we can admire – in the same way that we admire the self-control of an anorexic. Anton's self-assurance is a slave to shallow motives. He has ignored the truth that sex and money alone do not bring lasting happiness. Instead he is propelled by his *likes, wants, and needs.* His prostate is healthy, though.

Once upon a time, western medicine believed that these three psychological functions existed separate from the body, but research over the last 30 years has traced them down to specific neurochemical bases. What we experience as likes, wants, and needs are *physical functions*. They are the product of a complex reward mechanism in the central nervous system. In the same way that you learned to control your circulation, a study of the anatomy and neurochemistry of this reward mechanism gives you the power to influence your likes, wants, and needs through concentrated power of thought. In other words, where Anton is the slave, you can be the master.

One of the most important neurochemicals involved in this reward mechanism is **dopamine**. Picture a neuron, a cell like a fried egg with long strands branching off in every direction. In order for neurons to operate cooperatively and manufacture a concerted reaction to a foreign stimulus, they must communicate with one another. As we know now, the cells surrounding neurons, or glia, which in the past were thought to provide only supporting matrix like Styrofoam packaging, are indeed as active in the brain as the actual nerve cells and use neurochemicals as routinely as the neurons. But between the neuron appendages – axons and dendrites which connect the cells – lies a gap called a synaptic cleft which must be crossed somehow in order for neurons and glia to send messages back and forth. Here is dopamine's turf. Dopamine shoots through the synaptic cleft, bearing communications from one cell to another.

Besides dopamine, the brain has several dozens of such messengers, which neuroscientists call neurotransmitters, released into synaptic clefts as well as into surrounding area. Whereas dopamine relays messages specifically to excite cognition and relax muscles, other neurotransmitters relay other messages, depending on the stimulus. Imagine a planet wide civilization of cells – three hundred billion of them, all jabbering to one another with neurotransmitter messengers. The scene is so complex and the variables so many that parsing apart the exact effects of various neurotransmitters on a specific individual is, like most things in life, a game of probabilities. The relationship between neurotransmitters and our individual *likes* is based on a complicated network of biological predisposition and factors associated with our upbringing. But for everything we don't know, the basics are understood.

The brain has to be stimulated to make dopamine levels rise. Any activity can produce a strong stimulation. Musical tension and resolution – that flight of goose bumps you get when you hear a stirring love song, for instance – has been indirectly linked to dopamine. So has gambling, bungee jumping, and other risky behaviors. Addictive substances like alcohol, drugs, and even food can raise dopamine directly. The lack of dopamine in the *nucleus accumbens* area of the brain moves people to do everything they can to increase it.

The nucleus accumbens is in charge of the marvel we describe as **liking**. If you like a certain stimulus, neurochemically speaking, it is because the stimulus kicks off an increased production of dopamine. If some activity prompts dopamine, that means you *like* it. That is why some people *like* gambling, or binge eating, or excessive sexual activity. A severe deficiency in dopamine motivates people to take drastic measures to maintain their dopamine levels. Consider Anton's increasingly outlandish sexual conquests of daughters, wives, and mothers.

The more deficient dopamine is in the nucleus accumbens, the more someone is prone to addictions. Addictive medications are addictive specifically because they induce *liking*. Unlike a simple blood pressure medication or an antibiotic, people who take opiates such as morphine, fentanyl, or oxycodone; benzodiazepines like Xanax, Klonopin, and Valium; or amphetamines like Ritalin, Adderall, and Concerta, will wait for the next dose. They are frequently aware of the time remaining until that dose is due. As the addiction settles in, these people do not experience a "high." They just *like* taking the medicine. Cocaine, heroin, LSD, and other street drugs do the same thing, in principle. All of this is based on direct stimulation of the brain by chemical substances. When *liking* stops, *want* grows, and over time hatches *need*. Addiction becomes dependence.

It is not just dopamine volume that defines our reactive experience to various stimuli. The difference in reactivity is crucial. The faster dopamine builds up in your nucleus accumbens, the more you'll like something. Psychopathic and antisocial people are especially prone to a rapid increase in dopamine when they do something which is useful to them. Theft or assault can be gratifying to such people. One pharmaceutical treatment is a class of antipsychotic mood-stabilizing medicine that blocks dopamine in the brain. While on these medicines, theft will cause less spurt of dopamine to the nucleus accumbens, and the patient will not *like* stealing as it could happen otherwise. But pharmaceutical agents block dopamine everywhere in the brain, and can compromise or alter other behaviors beyond the predatorial ones specifically targeted.

The function of **wanting** is managed in a different part of the brain called the *amygdala*, in which the neurotransmitter **GABA** is particularly active. When you *want* something, the nerve cells in your amygdala are firing rapidly, shouting, "Gimme, gimme, gimme GABA!" Social restraints that might otherwise hold you back from abnormal behavior become less important. You become impulsive. Inhibition falls away. You are single minded in the chase for whatever it is that you *want*. Imagine a hungry man bursting into a cafe, shoving to the front of the line and ordering a dozen turkey clubs – "on the double, damn it, faster, faster, faster!" His voice may be quavering or his hands shaking, both outward signs of low GABA in the amygdala.

You have already learned the method of regulating GABA in the brain: Stop shaking, relax your muscles, and control breathing. When you feel heaviness, GABA is increasingly released into the brain. The firing of neurons is normalized, which in turn stabilizes mental function and physical regulation.

The third important drive circuit in our brain manages **need**. Need is more than just a desire. It is a demand to have what you *want* because you *like* it. The integration of these three functions was crucial to our development as a species. We know that water sustains life, but what mental process convinces our tongues of the need for water? Working backwards, you *need* to drink water so you must *want* to drink it, and to *want* to drink water you must *like* doing it. Doing anything out of obligation is a chore, while doing something you like to do is pleasurable.

Need is based deep in the brain, in the so-called *brain pons* around a chamber filled with cerebro-spinal fluid on top of the brain stem and beside the cerebellum. It is connected to chambers above through what neuroscientists called an *aqueduct*. The grey matter layered around this aqueduct is where *endorphins* work.

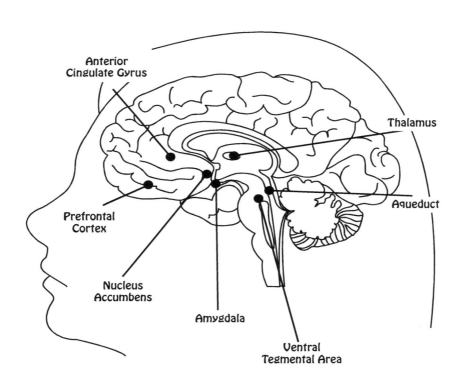

Endorphins are a third kind of reward neurochemicals. If we don't have enough of them, we can't feel good about ourselves or the world. They, among other things, regulate mood, pain, mental integrity, and pleasure. Endorphins are potent in immune cells and the blood stream and other tissues in the body – so happy people are healthier overall and recover quicker from illness than pessimists. For the same reason, hepatitis, lung, and pancreatic cancer are associated with depression. Psychological defense mechanisms can, in extremity, release endorphins to protect your mental wellbeing. The need to have a high level of these natural opioids is so pressing that, in dysfunctional cases, some people may cut or otherwise harm themselves so that they feel physical pain, thereby releasing the endorphins in their brain, which makes them pathologically feel better.

Many other neurochemicals, including **serotonin** and **norepinephrine**, also relay important messages across our brain. They help with the modulation of the nucleus accumbens, the amygdala, and the brain pons. *Serotonin*, when produced in a sufficient amount, makes us feel optimistic. It is also involved in digestion. You have already begun to manipulate your serotonin levels by the abdominal warmth exercises. *Norepinephrine* works as a thermostat, setting energy and initiative just right. A third chemical, **histamine**, seems to be the motivation fuel of the brain. *Histamine* is connected with the *initiation* of higher cognitive function. When you feel yourself saying, "Let's go, let's do it," that is histamine squirting about the prefrontal cortex.

Mastermind exercises can change brain chemistry the same way as psychostimulants and amphetamines and other psychiatric mood-altering medications. Diaphragmatic breathing, for example, influences the level of many of your neurochemicals and produces improvements in global functioning. Prescription medication that targets just one brain function – what psychiatrists call single action medication – sometimes improves that function at the expense of all others. Serotonin reuptake inhibitors, SSRIs, such as Prozac, Paxil, and Zoloft are especially guilty of this, and must be combined with other medications to tinker with additional neurochemicals. They disturb the balance of brain chemistry – if something goes up here, something else over there has to go down. This is why *when serotonin goes up* and eases depression, *norepinephrine and dopamine go down*, decreasing motivation and vibrancy of life, often muting creativity and zest. This is why many people say they do not want to continue antidepressants because they feel indifferent to life. Mastermind methods, on the other hand, affect the complete brain function simultaneously, without creating hazardous changes in individual neurotransmitters at the expense of the others. It is a natural and healthy way of regulating your mind.

Our wants – for example, the desire for a kiss when your spouse returns home from work – can seem awfully dry, looking through the lens of neurochemistry. But a foundational knowledge of the origin of our likes, wants, and needs shouldn't subtract from the authenticity of the *experience* of those functions. After all, we can still enjoy the majesty of a sunset even though we know the sun is a thermonuclear inferno.

You may or may not have noticed that by smiling after your Mastermind practice, you have been training yourself to draw satisfaction from self-regulation. The constructive pleasure of learning can be *induced on purpose*. Consciously or unconsciously, Anton trained himself to need sex and money. Maybe you like a cigarette after dinner, or sleeping on a full stomach. Replacing your dysfunctional wants with healthy ones is the first step to eliminating bad habits (which we will examine in further detail in the following chapter.)

Simply put, the more you understand the processes and functions of the brain, the more you will be able to handcraft your likes, wants and needs. For example, bringing regular warmth to the nucleus accumbens after a behavior you'd like to encourage will, over time, increase the production of dopamine in reaction to that stimuli. Cooling it will have the reverse effect. Don't forget that dopamine, GABA, and the rest of the neurotransmitters are not agents but heralds. They are the starting points of a complex chain of events in the brain cells. The actual changes are made by proteins within the neurons, and it may take up to several weeks to alter their production and build new proteins for you to feel the effects. This is no different than healing a kitten's scratch: for a cut to heal new proteins have to be produced, which takes some time.

* * *

Think of all the people who want to lose weight. Most Americans turn to surgery, or trendy diets, or snake oil. Really, the only healthy way to lose weight and keep it off is to control your appetite and make a habit of exercise. If you know how to motive yourself, physical exercise can become a pleasure and not a chore. A decrease in appetite is no different. Hunger – even starvation – can be pleasant. Consider religious fasts. Are they torturous or pleasant? Or both? The conscious manipulation of your wants, likes, and needs is called **pleasure manipulation**.

Try it. Put yourself in a state of Mastermind submersion. Build yourself a comfortable environment, and then inhabit it. Create some elixir of hunger. It should be something that makes you feel good. Maybe it looks like a pitcher of fresh squeezed lemonade, cold and refreshing and pulpy. Or it is a swimming pool of sparkling, clear water, or maybe it is just the rays of the sun beating down on your shoulders in a tropical paradise. Use your creativity to tailor the elixir to your own mental associations. Then pick up the pitcher and gulp that hunger down, or dive into the pool of hunger, or spread your arms and close your eyes and feel the hunger soaking into you. Make it pleasurable and perfect. It is precious. Cherish it. Absorb it. Smile when you come out of your submersion. Keep the pleasure of hunger with you as you awake.

Hunger is just an example. You can bring any abstract categories into the physical world within your mind. Give physical substance to anything you want to like: love, creativity, intuition, intelligence, persistence, independence, anything. Any virtue, if you give it a palpable objective form, is easily handled and regulated. You could even simplify the above exercise by giving hunger a shape – maybe a shiny fluorescent cloud – and when you want to remind yourself of the virtues of hunger, close your eyes and immerse yourself in this cloud of hunger.

Be realistic with your implementation of this exercise. Know the difference between a *desire* and a *want*. Desires are dreams. Wants are practical actions. You may *want* to lose weight, but you *desire* immortality. It is good, generally, to have unreasonable desires if you recognize them for what they are. It is bad to have unreasonable wants. If you want something that is impossible, you will obviously fail. Your wants must be in the range of your grasp. If you clearly label your *wants* and *desires*, you spare yourself potential disappointment. Actually use a pen and paper. Write it down. Make it visible. Create your own notebook of little wants and big wants, little desires and huge desires and impossible desires.

Effective pleasure manipulation cannot be achieved in one session. The key is repetition. You consistently need to keep in mind what you are trying to accomplish. Even if your end goal is weight loss, the purpose of this exercise must remain pleasure manipulation. Associate the pleasure of eating less with the feeling of power over your urges. It's fun. Look at it like a game – a mental game that changes your reality the longer you play. Remember: You cannot *not* do something; you can only *do something else instead*. The goal is not to *not eat*. The goal is to *enjoy hunger*.

Pleasure Manipulation - Basic Benefits

- improves physical performance
- counteracts future uncertainties
- builds stamina
- improves visualization skills

Pleasure Manipulation - Concentrated Version

- Mask—Heavy—Warm
- Breathing
- Forehead
- Pleasure manipulation
- Exit

Physical Form to Abstract Categories Method

- give any desired virtue a palpable form: a shiny cloud representing courage, for instance
- in a state of Mastermind submersion, bring the cloud around the body
- see it secreted or being absorbed into the body
- feel it pleasant and life giving
- by physically controlling a virtue, it becomes something palpable that can be summoned on command

- if a diffuse substance is too difficult to imagine, try keeping a concentrated pool of a virtue in the heart or in the mind or the solar plexus, the main hubs of human energy
- may be easier to imagine or control, depending on visualization skills

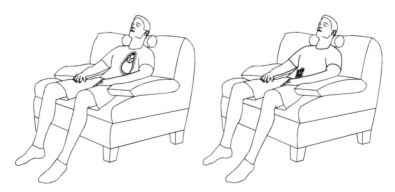

Tips

- give physical form to anything desired: love, creativity, intelligence, persistence, anything
- any category, if it acquires a palpable objective form, is easier to handle and regulate

CHAPTER NINETEEN

A Boy Who Found Treasure

I must have been eleven or twelve years old when I remembered my hidden treasures. The memory burst into my dreams in the middle of the night and shot me upright. At first I could only remember in dim smudges – a thrill of excitement, hunching over a bit of lined notebook paper tracing the outline of a mysterious coast, a time in my childhood when the whole world was fresh and new – but the longer I dwelled on it, the more I recalled of the whole childhood adventure. It had been the project of an idle summer years earlier – inventing obscure hieroglyphs, scrawling treasure maps, sealing them into homemade chests, and scurrying all around the neighborhood secreting my treasures in any dark, dank holes I could find.

The whole thing had all begun with bit of wisdom from my grandmother, who told me that she was the luckiest person in the world, because she did so many nice things for others – who then gave back more in return. She almost felt selfish helping people, because she knew that the goodness would return to her tenfold. I pondered the strange idea for an hour or two. At the time I badly wanted to find hidden treasures. I was always getting in trouble with the neighbors for digging holes under the bushes in search of pirate booty. The worry that all of the treasure in the world had already been discovered kept me awake at night. But with my grandmother's advice, the solution seemed clear: I would bury treasures for others to find, and then wait for someone to bury a treasure for me.

The first week I experimented with cryptology – a simple code like applying a number to each letter of the alphabet and then writing a secret message in numbers. I rolled my message up, tied it with a scrap of yarn, and dropped the little scroll into a glass bottle. When my mother came home, she gave me a cork and helped me to seal it with wax. I wrote out a codebreaker too, and packaged it separately in its own bottle. Under the cover of a moonless night, I crept outside to hide the two treasures. I dropped one in the hole of a tree, and the next I hid under a bush.

All next week I made more treasures. I hid old toys in wooden boxes lined with plastic wrap, and nailed the lids shut. I wrote little clues in more elaborate codes: seek more treasures under such and such bush, or in the walls of such and such apartment building. I wrapped an old plywood box in faded cloth and sutured it shut with a thick thread, and then painted some red nail polish on the outside to look like blood was spilled. (Treasure can be a bloody business, as I knew from my books.)

I put one of my baby teeth in a pill bottle, wrapped it in gauze, stuffed it in an old sock, gauzed the sock, hid the whole lumpy thing in a bigger box which I smudged all over in nail polish, and secured the whole thing with a dozen nails. I imagined hundreds of years later, some future archaeologist would discover the treasure, unwrapping layer by layer with increasing anticipation. He would see the tooth and understand immediately the depth of this revealing part of me. Maybe he would be able to grow me out of the tooth, and we could have a little chat.

I hid these treasures in construction sites, in cable trenches, in the gardens of unsuspecting neighbors, in parks, and in the crooks of tree roots. And then I waited. Years passed – an eternity, really – and I never heard of anyone finding any of my treasures. I would remember them every once in a while, and happily imagine them aging, dust accumulating on the bottles, the dirt working into the old sacks. I gave some hints to friends and adults about good places for treasure hunting, but no one took the bait. Eventually I forgot the messages, the codes, and the contents of my treasure chests. When I suddenly remembered the treasure project, I had even forgotten my carefully selected hiding spots – all but one.

For a single special treasure, I had cryptified an important bit of advice, sealed it into a bottle, and taken it into the basement of my apartment building. This was a treasure for me to find. I couldn't sleep all night. The next day after school, I went down into the basement. It smelled like cat urine, and after just three or four steps I was picking cobwebs out of my eyebrows. I found my treasure bottle standing upright in a mildewed corner behind a boiler. It was preserved, untouched, and mysterious. It could have been there for hundreds of years, maybe left by an ancient warrior who died on this very plot of land.

This was the first real treasure I had ever found. My heart ached. My hands shook. I carried the bottle up to our apartment, holding it with two fingers on the neck so the ancient dust wouldn't wipe away the illusion that I had uncovered some ancient artifact. The wax had cracked off long ago, and the cork was crumbling and scored by rats' teeth. Piece by piece, I plucked it out with tweezers and a penknife. Squeezing an eye shut, I peeked down the mouth of the bottle. The thread binding the message had rotted and was lying in pieces on the bottom of the bottle. My scroll had unrolled inside, and was too wide to get through the neck.

All of a sudden, like a weathered treasure hunter, I knew exactly what to do. I went outside and smashed the bottle – and then immediately realized my error. School notebook paper was not designed for carrying messages through the times, especially not in a humid basement. My scroll was yellowed with age, which I liked, but when the bottle shattered the message inside broke into pieces.

I crouched to gather up the fragments, but each piece of paper I touched crunched into even smaller bits, and on top of that I cut my finger on broken glass. Then a gust of wind blew. In a panic I tried to spread out my jacket to shield the message, but most of it was picked up in the breeze and confettied away into oblivion. My secret message would never be reassembled.

I could see faded blue marks on the few remaining scraps of scroll. It was broken gibberish. I remembered then that I had hidden a code breaker somewhere to translate the message, but I couldn't think of where it might have been. My treasure, then, was a few chicken scratches on brittle corners of paper. The mystery was no longer manufactured. This was a genuine puzzle. I stamped my foot and cursed the wind. "If it weren't for you," I shouted, "I could have broken the code!"

Looking back, I think the wind saved me from failure. I may not have been able to decipher my message, even if I had managed to completely reassemble it. But more importantly, by blowing away half of my scroll it made my treasure *real*. I hid that treasure those years ago in the hope that someday someone would leave a treasure for me to find – only to realize that I didn't need to depend on others, but could create my treasures all on my own.

*　*　*

To the ears of an adult, digging for treasure in the gardens of a Soviet apartment complex sounds like a waste of time or even a punishment. But as a child, I dug randomly with the full expectation that all I had to do was scrape away a bit of earth beneath any old bush to find something wonderful. Children have a naturally hopeful curiosity.

As we grow older we convince ourselves that we know everything and have seen it all – but that's a trick of the mind. We still know practically nothing about the world around us. We just adapt to our surroundings and stop paying attention. It is an efficient use of brainpower to identify patterns and then devote attention elsewhere. Sometimes, though, seeing the world with a child's wide-open eyes can help you take pleasure in your daily life.

Much of our day is taken up by unconsciously rigid habits. You wake up, boil some water, brush your teeth, have breakfast tea, wash the dishes, and then hit the gym. You'll shower after that, and drive to work. Or maybe every morning for the last fifteen years you have sat on the porch and smoked a cigarette. Whatever the case, the longer we stay in these holding patterns, the more deeply grooved our habits become. Scrabbling out of those grooves to experience a fresh new world becomes increasingly difficult. To embrace a child's creativity and freedom of thought, we need mechanisms that allow us to temporarily wipe that rigidity away, and have a fresh look around.

You may have heard of **déjà vu** (literally "already seen") – the feeling that you already experienced something that has never happened before. The lesser known **jamais vu** (literally "never seen") is exactly the opposite: the feeling that a familiar happening or object seems completely new. This is a real phenomenon. You may be able to experience it yourself. Take out a piece of paper and write the word "door" as many times as you can in sixty seconds. You could try typing it into your iPad too. At some point, maybe around forty five seconds in, you may start thinking that "door" is a pretty strange word. Its pronunciation may change in your mind to "dure" or "doer" or "dür." How could that be? Only one minute earlier, you knew exactly how to read "door."

That's jamais vu.

Uncontrolled, it can be quite a frightening disorder. But you can apply jamais vu purposefully to douse boring daily tasks in a fresh curiosity. You can experience old things anew, over and over again, day after day. When I was growing up, it took me several years before the message I'd hidden for myself became a real discovery. What if you could make that transformation in just a day? Or an hour? Ordinary things or even ugly things – like a dusty bottle in a dank basement, or a sink full of dirty plates – can become honest-to-goodness treasures.

So doing the dishes doesn't have to be a chore. It *shouldn't* be a chore. We make the most of our lives by having fun and being joyful. You can experience pleasure from anything and everything. If you can find little joys in little things, then great joys and great things will happen more readily. That is why all the Mastermind methods and all the imagery exercises should lead to pleasure, to the fun of seeing something in your mind, and the novelty of doing something you could not do before, and the excitement of strengthening yourself, and the perfect bliss of life.

Controlled jamais vu is one way to help you accomplish that. The method is rather simple. It is based on not letting any moment pass by unexamined, but rather to consciously focus when you feel your attention slipping. The moment you have a fleeting sensation that what is happening now has already happened, you need to open your eyes and your mind to delve into the event. So if you're standing before a sink of dirty dishes, for example, observe the scene carefully. You may think that doing the dishes is a brainless obligation – and it is if you don't pay attention. But in fact *each time you wash them is different.* Watch how the bristles on your sink brush bend as you press them against the plates, and how the soap bubbles foam, and the path of the water as it drains. Imagine you have never seen a brush stroking against a dirty dish prior to this very moment. What a marvelous adventure! This awareness will help you discover small, fresh treasures after each meal. In this way you can break out from the canyons of your habitual thoughts, and see the world with the fresh curiosity of a child.

Often building a new habit is the best way to eliminate bad ones. Here is a silly challenge to illustrate my point. Grab an egg timer, set it for three minutes, and find a comfortable place where you can sit quietly. All you have to do is close your eyes and *NOT* think about elephants wearing tutus. Ready, set, go.

It's not easy, is it? Even if you were able to distract yourself somehow, I'll bet that no matter how hard you tried to distract yourself, a troupe of elephants in tutus were pirouetting at the edges of your mind, trumpeting for your attention. If you want to be successful in not thinking about elephants wearing tutus, you need to think about something else instead – bunny rabbits in tuxedos, maybe, or a kangaroo in a knit sweater. Similarly, all reformed smokers know that the best way to quit smoking is not to go through daily life agonizing over not smoking. ("Don't smoke, don't smoke, don't smoke, please don't smoke.") Instead, you take an active role and replace the smoking habit with a chew of nicotine gum, or jumping jacks, or any new habit to supplant the old.

Your biggest challenge when building new habits is inconsistency. Until a new habit feels natural, it is not a habit but a staged event. For instance, you probably have the habit of brushing your teeth twice a day, no matter what external circumstances conspire against you. If, for whatever reason, you don't brush your teeth in the morning, you will feel uncomfortable all day. You must persist in your habit building exercises until *not* doing whatever habit you're creating makes you feel strange and unnatural. Don't let up your training until you've reached that point.

If you don't think you have any bad habits that need replacing, try building a new habit just for fun – something pleasant and interesting. Play the harmonica for twenty minutes each evening, or go for a fifteen minute run every morning, or tell your spouse you'll do the dishes for the next two months. Test out your pleasure manipulation and jamais vu methods. That way, when you have a real habit that needs elimination or adjustment, you'll have trained with the tools that will help you accomplish your goal.

If, on the other hand, you do have some bad habits you'd like to eliminate, why not start today? Even if it seems daunting, you'll certainly never take two steps before you take just one. When you successfully trade a bad old habit for a good new habit, the sense of fulfillment and possibility is over-whelming. You realize that you have deep control over yourself, and are not a slave to whims or distractions. You appear more healthy and happy. You are the master of your mind. You don't need to dig for buried treasures on deserted coasts – you need only to dig within yourself.

Controlled Jamais Vu - Basic Benefits

- increases the brain's flexibilty
- promotes the training of curiosity

Controlled Jamais Vu - Concentrated Version

- Submerge
- See yourself doing something you want
- Exit

CHAPTER TWENTY

The Doctor Who Never Swore

I have never heard my friend Grigory utter a four letter word, not in English nor Russian. He'll groan if he stubs his toe, and when he gets cut off in Chicago traffic his mouth gets tight and he'll beep his horn – but he never swears. I asked him about it once.

"When I was seven," he said, "I cursed all up and down the street. Hanging out with the neighborhood gang, you know. We roamed around climbing on things, breaking sticks against trees, what have you. And gosh, did we have foul tongues. Blank this, blank that, blank you, look at that blanking cat."

"Really?" I asked. "You did that?" Grigory is a respected neurosurgeon and one of the smartest men I know. For the life of me, I couldn't imagine him hanging out with ne'er-do-wells.

"I had been different," he said, "so different from the other kids for so long. I guess I wanted to adapt, that's all."

Grigory, you see, was a wunderkind. Before his first birthday he had learned the names of all the pieces on the chessboard. When he was three, he had an audience with the Ministry of Health to prove the rumors about his native genius. They gave him a newspaper and listened to him read. To this day he remembers feeling embarrassed because although he knew his letters and numbers, he had never learned Roman numerals and so he read them as letters.

On his fourth birthday when his family was quizzing him on his earliest memories, the conversation somehow came to the question of how he was born. Grigory's brow furrowed. His uncle, trying to smooth the situation over decently, said, "Surely you were carried to your mother by a white kitten weren't you? Isn't that it?"

"A kitten?" said Grigory. "No." He went on to give an anatomy lesson on the uterus, ovaries, placenta, and birth canal. When he finished, the listeners were stunned. The uncle who had brought up the kitten asked in a small voice how the baby ended up in the abdomen in the first place. Grigory answered with regret, "I'm sorry, uncle. It's a good question, but the book didn't say."

The next year, he finished first, second, third, and fourth grade. He could have skipped more, but his parents drew the line. "This is it," his mother decided. "He is just a boy. He has to be in school." Of course she knew he was special. In fact, she believed that any child could learn anything, given the opportunity and the right tools. But she didn't want her son to grow up too fast either. Most children who are savants at age three do not continue to experience endless progress. She knew that humans have jumps in development, sometimes phenomenal leaps forward. These accelerations could happen at any age. The older a person underwent a jump, the more likely he or she was to remain ahead of the crowd. Einstein and Darwin, for instance, were regular kids, not hidden treasures. Grigory's mother feared that a jump too early might end up disabling his mind rather than enhancing it. So Grigory had to have a normal life. Now, he supposes that he could have graduated high school by ten if his mother hadn't insisted that he have a childhood.

Instead he stayed in school, and ran around with neighborhood kids, and when he was seven years old he was swearing like a sailor. One of his neighbors overheard him, and told his mother. She wasn't happy.

"Where did you learn those words?" she asked.

"From the older boys."

"You're only seven years old," she said. "Why do you need to talk that way?"

"Everyone does."

"So?"

"It is language," explained Grigory. "I never learned those words before, but that is how the other boys talk. I have to talk like they do if I will be in their group."

When he told me this story, Grigory took pains to emphasize that he wasn't angry or talking back. He didn't wrestle against his parents for freedom of thought. He was too smart for that. He *knew* too much to get swallowed into a battle of wills. The only time he really got in trouble was when he was thirteen years old and graduating from high school. He went to the beach against his mother's orders, and came home sunburned. Because he had disobeyed her, she scolded him badly. (She later apologized.) But typically, Grigory was just a good kid. He was emotionally stable. He listened to his parents. He studied hard, and he didn't have a swollen ego. "If you are lucky and smart," his mother told him, "enjoy it. But don't rub your classmates' noses in it."

After high school, which he finished way too early, medical schools didn't want to accept Grigory because he was so young. But he wouldn't be dissuaded. He wrote a complaint to the Ministry of Education, which issued a memo reiterating that anyone who graduated from high school and otherwise fulfilled the necessary criteria could not be denied admission to medical school. In response, the school objected to Grigory's enrollment because he was *too short*. Undaunted, Grigory contacted the Ministry of Education, which reminded the medical school that there were many short doctors practicing fine medicine. They also suggested that Grigory probably had growth spurts ahead of him, because he was only thirteen years old. The school gave in.

By the time he was twenty, Grigory was indeed much taller. He was already in his second year of a neurosurgical residency and only a few courses away from a Ph.D. He served on the editorial boards of several international journals, and had presented important neurosurgical works at international symposiums. When he decided he wanted to immigrate to the U.S., several Nobel laureates testified on his behalf to the U.S. government, submitting affidavits claiming that Grigory was of irreplaceable value to the United States. He was granted a green card, he immigrated, he passed the necessary licensing exams, and was accepted to his second neurosurgery residency.

In America he spent seven more years fulfilling required neurosurgical post-graduate training, and at the age of 27 he became a neurosurgeon for the second time in his life. Now he lives and works in Chicago. He has an adorable wife and two teenaged children who are as American as apple pie: a rebellious son and an introspective daughter. Both are smart kids like their father and mother.

If you didn't know who Grigory was, you wouldn't guess his success. You would have never heard of him, first of all, if you hadn't read this book. He is not an athlete or an entertainer. He doesn't buy into the same cult of leisure as broader society. But it seems to me that a man of his intellect ought to be lauded. Everyone should know Grigory. He prospers in one of the few professions where skill and intelligence mean the same thing. He is a brilliant child who grew up to become a brilliant doctor, a brilliant husband, and a brilliant father. He is a man who fulfilled his potential, and an example of everything that any of us can become.

And why?

Because of what his mother told him about bad language.

"Do you know how many obscene words I know?" she asked. "Have you ever heard me saying them? Surely you know that many adults use foul words, but I don't do what others do. I do what is right. Have you ever heard me curse?"

"No, mama," answered little Grigory.

"Then I want you to do the same," she said. "Use your judgment. Don't blindly follow the standards of those around you."

That small lesson would define his whole life.

He saw no boundaries in the world to pin him in place, and that has made him the man he is today.

*　*　*

Picture yourself strolling through the woods and finding an old hardwood log lying on the forest floor. You might climb on top and walk back and forth to test your balance. You might even bear walk across the length of it, or stand up and run, or hop on one foot up and down from root to treetop. The worst that will happen is that you may fall and skin your knees. But imagine that same log is spanning a canyon. You probably would not play on top of it. You would cross with tingling feet, hands a-quiver, hearing with your heart in your throat the distant rush of rapids far down through the yawning space beneath you. Why the difference? Nothing has changed except your perspective. You have turned a plaything into torture.

This log is your life. You might dance across it, or you might make every step sweating, timid and fearful. Some among us may even commit horrific atrocities so that we and those we love might not face the terror of the log. Remember Ivan the submariner? His life became a nightmare of his own making, all because he wasn't able to change his perspective on the challenges ahead of him.

My friend Grigory, on the other hand, has lived a fairy tale. That is not to say he has never struggled or faced uncertainty – of course he has – but rather that he always knows which boundaries are real, and which can be breached. With the outward and inward awareness that grows alongside your Mastermind training, you are gaining a similar faculty.

The keystone of successful application of the Mastermind method is the ability to achieve a balance between the desirable and the possible. For example, Grigory would have been a hopeless fool if he had striven to sprout wings and fly to the moon. On the other hand, medical school at thirteen was a reasonable goal for him. Maybe with training you can match Grigory's accomplishments, or maybe you can't.

Don't worry if his feats seem out of reach for you. The greater part of strength is knowing your own limitations. No one is superman, not even Grigory. (His tennis game could use a lot of work, for example, and he is a lousy carpenter.) Your control over yourself does have limits. Your job is to find those limits.

The fact is you are capable of more than you think. The exercises you have learned thus far have given you a peek through the cracks of possibility. If you can consciously control your heart rate, your attention, and your desires, what else might be attainable? In the words of Grigory's mother, don't blindly follow the standards of those around you. Experiment with the Mastermind methods and determine for yourself what is reasonable and what is not.

You will find that almost any kind of adjustment of your own mind or body is possible. You could convince yourself that apples are blue, if you liked. You could program yourself to love vegetables and hate steak, or vice versa. In the next two exercises, you will learn to occupy your mind for your own benefit, and to empty it for the same. You will slip a bridle over the heads of your wildest, unharnessed thoughts.

More than any other, the brain of an insomniac never stops for rest. It keeps running and running, like a generator that won't shut off. Insomniacs depend on pharmaceuticals – sleeping pills, specifically – to stop the thoughts running endlessly through their minds. The **Spinning Wheel** exercise is a way to control those convulsive thoughts always bubbling at the back of your mind.

As we learned with the example of the elephant in a tutu, it is useless to try to stop your thoughts with negative commands like, "Stop thinking about that!" Instead you need to do something about the process generating those thoughts. You must redirect it somehow. But the language of the mind, as you know, is sensation. So don't just think your thoughts. Watch them. Visualize them. Imagine them as something tangible, like typed lines, or skeins of yarn twisting together, or rainbowed waves of light. You could even use simple colors. Pick a visualization that seems natural to you.

Start weaving your thoughts onto a spinning wheel, moving them in a circle in a steady motion. Any time you begin thinking a thought rather than watching it, it will fray off from the wheel. You need to send it into the vortex to be sucked back and turning along with the rest of your thoughts. Slowly, see them flushing away into nothing. If there is a particular thread or thought you would like to focus on, leave it off the wheel. Or if you just want everything to be silent, spin it all together and watch it twirl away to black. A brain devoid of thoughts cannot stay awake. You will fall sleep. The spinning wheel has become your sleeping pill.

If you have the opposite problem – if you don't have enough waking hours to mull over whatever problem you happen to be facing – you can program your dreams to plumb your unconscious for answers. In 1869, a Russian chemist named Dmitri Mendeleev spent four sleepless days shuffling notecards containing the chemical properties of all the known elements, trying desperately to organize them logically. It was like a jigsaw puzzle. He was sure that there was some overarching principle, but there were too many factors jostling around in his conscious mind.

"It's all formed in my head," he told a friend, "but I can't express it." Shortly thereafter, Mendeleev fell asleep at his desk. His unconscious somehow managed to sort through the mess in a way that the wakeful chemist could not. "I saw in a dream," said Mendeleev later, "a table where all the elements fell into place as required. Awakening immediately I wrote it down." The result was the Periodic Table of Elements.

Mendeleev's dream seems to have been an accident, but it is not the only dreamy eureka in the history of scientific revelation. August Kekule, the 19th century German chemist, famously gave birth to the modern theory of chemical structure in his sleep, when he dreamed of a snake biting its tail. Kekule awoke knowing the molecular structure of benzene. (Its carbon skeleton is built in a ring, and not a chain of atoms as commonly believed at the time.)

It is possible to intentionally exercise control over your dreams, this last and woolliest realm of the unconscious. You can use a dream to become something or even just to watch something. It is another laboratory to inhabit. You can stage threatening scenarios to see how you will respond. You might even move your ideomotor training into a dream.

The actual **Dream Programming Exercise** is simple. Give yourself the detailed plan of a dream. When you are in bed with the lights off, close your eyes and visualize whatever it is you would like to experience – a problem you've been unable to sort through at work, shooting a basketball, or challenging a coworker. Your script can be as detailed or vague as you like. Build a scene in your conscious mind, and play it out. Put it on a repeating loop, so it runs over and over again until you fall asleep. You will find yourself immersed in at least some form of that dream. At first, it may not be exactly what you imagined. You'll likely encounter bizarre or shocking twists – more so than anything you could consciously create.

Play with this method. If you have less luck with pre-sleep visualization, try chanting to yourself: "Give me a dream that makes me feel confident," or "Let me travel in time," or, "What am I going to do about so and so?" As you experiment you will become familiar with your own triggers. With regular practice you will be able to use your unconscious as another tool to help you navigate the shoals of life.

Spinning Wheel - Basic Benefits

- helps with falling to sleep
- clears the mind
- improves focus and self-control

Spinning Wheel - Concentrated Version

- Submerge
- Plan for anything you want and see it happening
- Engage a spinning wheel and suck everything you see & think into it
- Do not exit, just fall asleep after removing excess warmth and heaviness

Spinning Wheel Method

- give thoughts a shape: colored yarn, or typed lines, or rainbowed waves of light
- weave the thoughts onto a spinning wheel
- move the wheel in a steady circular motion
- give any new thoughts a shape, and feed them into the wheel
- flush away the thoughts at a vortex in the center of the wheel
- try to suck everything away – the wheel, and everything
- continue feeding newly arising thoughts into the wheel
- a brain devoid of thoughts will fall asleep naturally very soon
- move not just thoughts within the wheel, but the wheel itself as well

CHAPTER TWENTY-ONE

The Magic of Cooking

There is an old Indian story about a sage who asks his disciple to cover the whole world in leather – the mountains, and the prairies, and the fields. The disciple measures the average size of a cow skin, and travels to other wise men to investigate the total surface area of the world as compared to the number of cows in it. Eventually he concludes that the task before him is beyond his powers. He returns to the sage begging that such an ambitious project requires the expertise of the sage himself.

The sage scoffs. "Where would I possibly find enough leather with which to cover the surface of the earth?" he asks. "But wearing just leather on the soles of my shoes is equivalent to covering the earth with it."

That sage was a Mastermind. He knew what you know now: You are the only unique thing on earth. Everything else is a repeat of something that came before it. You alone are unlike anything before you or after you. By changing yourself, you change the whole world.

So if you know unhappiness, change yourself.

If you know dissatisfaction, or anxiety, or tragedy, change yourself.

If you want to be happy, be happy.

If you want to be healthy, be healthy.

If you want to be rich, then be rich.

If you want to find treasure, find it.

Some years ago in a small village far from the bustle of cities and industry, I sat with my new friend Masha in her restaurant. Here, deep in the rural heartland of Russia, an assembly of luxurious cars were parked on a gravel lot – shining Bentleys, a Lamborghini, and others gleaming under the bright summer sun. Men in suits and women with big sunglasses and impeccable hairstyles lounged about. The muffled melody of French conversation drifted from outside.

"You mean there was nothing here?" I asked. "Just this old cottage in the hills?"

"Yes and some farmland just beyond the grove. None of the other vacation homes had been built yet."

"But Masha," I asked, "what on earth made you think you could start a fine dining restaurant in a place like that?"

"To tell you that," she said, "I would have to start from the beginning. It's not so exciting."

"But I really want to know how all this was possible," I said.

Masha made an innocent face, formed a little ribbon out of her lips, and looked at me kindly. "Well, okay," she said. "Just give me a minute."

She stepped aside and asked her husband Jean-Pierre to look after the kitchen, and then returned to begin her tale. "I was young when I went to Paris," she said. "It was a good place for artists. I had dreams of singing, but then I met Jean-Pierre, and … well, things change. We married and began a family. For 18 years everything was well. We bought a chateau not far from Paris, and had a lovely little life. But one day I was cleaning my husband's desk and I stumbled upon a letter from the bank saying that if a mortgage payment wasn't made within the next two weeks, our house would be repossessed.

"Two weeks! Have you ever heard people say their legs felt like they were made of cotton? That is what I felt, reading the letter. I had to sit down and look stupidly at it for a few minutes before it truly sank in. We would lose everything – the herb garden I had planted, the walls Jean-Pierre had painted, all of it. I took the letter to Jean-Pierre. He was shy and defensive. 'It's true,' he said. 'I didn't want to tell you. Yes, I've lost my job, and I've lost our savings. I don't know, my love – I just didn't want to disappoint you. I am so sorry, my darling.'

"I thought, Sorry? Disappoint me? And just like that, goodbye to all the comforts we had grown accustomed to! I was stunned. The ground was going out from under my feet. The world crumbled. That night in bed I closed my eyes, but I didn't sleep for even ten seconds. My throat spasmed. My ears rang. It was like my brain had vanished. My head was just an old, empty cigar box. I didn't want to open my eyes. Jean-Pierre had completely given up. He had surrendered. Only I could steer us away from disaster – but how? A housewife of fifteen years with no income? What could I do? Go to Paris and sing in the metro? Would that feed two children?"

"I didn't know what to do the next morning, so I got up bleary-eyed and did what a housewife does – I went to the stove and began to cook. Doing something familiar, that is what saved me. All of a sudden I began to feel better, even as questions rattled about in my cigar box of a brain. How could I earn money? How to make this payment? How could I survive this ordeal?

"But why was I feeling so content doing something so common? What was I doing right? Then it hit me. What was happening was that I was *cooking*. That was the answer. After all, my pierogies were famous among our friends. So there was my plan. Wonderful! I would earn money with my food. It was only after the pierogies were finished did I realize the absurdity of my simple idea. The French palate couldn't appreciate a hearty Russian pierogie, especially not within the next two weeks between my family and total financial collapse. I closed my eyes again and called for a solution – and would you believe, it came to me! A smell of something baked, something sweet, something tasty.

"Ah, I never enjoyed baking as much as I did that day. I mixed and kneaded and then set the dough to rise. I cut the fruit, and put it all together as an ornate tart. It was delicious. 'I can do this,' I thought. An image came to me, of an airy, whimsical dessert – I could see the layers, puffing up with curls of orange peel and candied ribbons, the fruits gleaming in infused syrups, a cloud like stage of sweets.

"I cooked all day and through the night. This night, though, was not filled with despair but hope. In the morning when I looked at my finished desserts, the tarts were so unlike anything I'd seen before that doubts left me for a moment. I packed the tarts as delicately as I could and drove to Paris with the idea of selling them at the open market. On the way, the silliness of my faith crept into mind. I had never sold anything before. How could I possibly hope to sell my own cooking at the open market? Surely I should have offered my desserts to a baker, right? But then again, could a baker pay the mortgage?

"I was concerned enough that along the way I stopped at a bakery and opened one of the boxes. The baker's eyes widened and he offered me 50 euros on the spot. I was flattered, but for that price I'd never make enough money to make ends meet. So I turned him down, and drove on to Paris, biting my nails and cursing myself for letting a bird fly out of my hands.

"The market was busy. I unfolded a card table and laid two tarts on top of it. There was no room for more. After fifteen minutes my heart began to sink, as realization of the whole futile endeavor became more and more obvious. I closed my eyes, as I was doing way too frequently lately, but still saw light shining behind my eyelids. It reassured me in some small way that everything would be alright.

"A few minutes later, a beautiful and richly dressed woman stopped at my little table. She asked a few questions, and hearing my accent, explained that she was a Russian countess, descendant of a noble family which relocated to France after the Bolshevik revolution. She was preparing a dinner party for some notables, and felt that God sent my tarts to her as an exclusive and unusual gift she could surprise her friends with. She bought all three of my tarts and paid 400 euros for each, and promised she was interested in more in the future.

"The price was ridiculous. 400 euros for a fruit tart, three times over? But do you know what? Somehow, I expected the whole thing to play out as it did. The countess called me the next day and said that her guests were so astonished with the sight and taste of my desserts that they wanted tarts for themselves. My business took off.

"Well, we made the mortgage payment and I opened a small bakery which became famous and fashionable enough that money was not an issue any longer. A few years later, I was still happy with my life but acutely aware that my French cooking was not as good as my Russian cooking. My heart told me that I had to cook Russian dishes, and what better place for that than back home? By then, my children were on their own, my husband retired, and I decided to return. Jean-Pierre wrote his books and didn't care in which country he would live as long as he had a chance of writing without thinking of money.

"We packed and moved to Moscow. But the city life was too expensive and hectic for our tastes. I thought that if I really loved what I was doing, I could be anywhere enjoying culinary art. We bought a house, this countryside cottage in the sticks, and transformed it into a little restaurant. Nothing was here then, but for some reason, shortly after we opened people began building here. This became a sort of rustic getaway for wealthy businessmen and politicians."

Masha gestured at the walls covered in framed newspaper articles and clippings from glossy journals with pictures of her, Jean-Pierre, and her cooking. In one framed photo, I recognized the Russian President sitting at the same table we were chatted over, smiling over a delicious plate.

I finished my meal and we went outside. From the top of a hill where I stood we overlooked a plush valley and grassy meadows surrounding newly built rich and beautiful cottages.

"Oh Masha," I said. "*You* brought all this life here. You and your kitchen."

She tutted and shrugged my words away, but when I returned inside to gather my things, she stayed on the patio for a while with her arms folded, breathing in the fresh air and looking out upon the world that she had wrought around her.

*   *   *

Happiness and tragedy, unhappiness and treasures – we seed all these within ourselves. The knowledge of how to pull up the weeds and nurture whatever fruits you choose empowers you. No longer will you wander aimlessly through the woods hunting for roots and grubs. You can live with purpose.

The deeper you explore the potentials of self-mastery, the more you will realize that the question is more than, "What can I do?" but "When should I do what?"

Just as there is no dogma or ideology that fits all of life's circumstances, you must read no hard and brittle strictures into the Mastermind methods you have been practicing. In some situations you must consciously plot out a route to guide your body and mind away from dysfunction. In other situations you must be loose and supple, living by the whims of spontaneous circumstance. It is not necessary to use your full powers in every interaction in the same way that you do not always drive as fast as your car can go. It is good to idle at times. It's okay to let edges blur. Your behavior and your thoughts and your feelings should reflect you and your surroundings, not contradict them. Random pleasures are crucial to the human experience. Part of healthy control is being able to loosen your grip on yourself when you can afford to. Only your sense of balance and healthy judgment can be your guide to when and where that is. From here and forward, there are no simple answers.

And yet – it *is* simple. Be in control when you need, and lose control when you can.

You, and by extension your Mastermind methods, are in equal parts simple and complex. Is it more interesting to watch a raindrop or the ocean? Try inhabiting them both. You will find that both have their own simplicities and complexities. If something seems too simple, then you are not examining it closely enough. Look at the city and see the buildings, look in the buildings and see the people, look in the people and see yourself, look in yourself and see the tissues, look in the tissues and see the cities of cells, and so forth.

The ability to see everything in anything will guide you over the last horizon. Your final task is to stretch out further than you know you can. You'll need to be psychologically primed to climb this mountain of your mind. There is no helicopter that can spin you straight up to the mountaintop. You must climb step by step, building sufficient strength to claw up the slope toward **Answers of the Unconscious**.

- Start with the usual. Submerse yourself.
- Face.
- Heaviness.
- Warmth.
- Breathing.
- Heart.
- Forehead.
- In control. Calm.
- Happy.
- You know this place well. This is home.
- Now, with the power of mind, create an emotion in your home.

- Feel yourself – *be* yourself standing on the rocks at the edge of a roaring ocean spray.
- A storm blasts around you. The swirling salty mist catches in your hair.
- Cheeks are hot with the gusty wind.
- Lungs are full with the freshness and power of nature. This is a hallucination. But it is not a disease. It is a sign of your power of creation.
- It's vivid. It's real. You've made this. You are the trigger.
- Open your mouth and taste the drizzling seawater.
- Let your heart beat in excitement, your chest rise and fall.
- Feel your body tense up, resisting the elements.
- Lean against the pressure of the wind.
- Be there. Be in the midst of this mighty storm in the world.
- Now, be the world.
- The storm is a part of you, only a distant whisper.
- You are strong.
- You are in a safe world of your power, hanging in the awesome silence of the cosmos.
- In this soft space, ask yourself:
- Who am I?
- What is death?
- What is God?
- What is eternity?
- What is time?
- What is endlessness?
- What is life?

Here, at last, it is time to stop guiding yourself. Whatever happens, let it happen. Let the tools and habits you have built guide you. Experience yourself. Experience life. Experience God and eternity, if you believe in it. Let them be in you. Let the answers come to you. They are there, deep in your brain, mulled in your thoughts and your emotions and your work and your life. They are yours. Allow your mind to reach up and show you the answers through feelings or fantasies or memories. No one's telling can match the depth or significance of your own discovery. It will be time for you to share them with others when you *understand*.

For now, be the master of your mind.

Everything is within you.

Answers of the Unconscious - Concentrated Version

- Submerge
- Ask the questions
- Exit

Creating Emotions Method

- assume a state of Mastermind submersion
- create a scene of extraordinary force: a crashing ocean, a craggy peak above the clouds with the earth around you, or any other magnificent scene
- continue adding visceral sensory details until it is true to life
- when a scene is staged with enough vivid detail, the mind will believe it is true and form emotions to match the scene
- place yourself in a position of power and excitement and your mind will rise to the occasion

AFTERWORD

Say you want to hang a mirror on the wall. You have all the right tools: a nail, a hammer, and a stud finder. But if you bash at the wall with the hammer to find the studs, you'll bust the wall down. Instead of hanging a mirror, you'll earn for yourself an extra trip to the hardware store. So it's not enough to have the right tools, and it's not enough to use them. You need to employ these tools purposefully.

The same is true of the Mastermind methods you have learned. Think of when and for what purpose you might use warmth, or coolness. What condition or process do you want to alter? Why do you want to do it? Will it help you or hurt you? You must understand the problem you are dealing with. Know your relationship with it. This is called *insight*, and without insight your tools are useless.

You have been indirectly training your insight with every Mastermind story and method in this book. Insight allows you to turn things upside down and look at them from different angles. It shows you, among other things, that symptoms like depression and paranoia and hallucination and pain can actually be a part of health and not a disease. What you have accomplished in the final method is to use a hallucination, commonly considered a symptom of a mental disorder, to trigger an emotion through a conscious, self-regulated process. With creativity, you can use many such symptoms as protective reflexes. A fever, after all, warms you as part of the natural human process of self-healing. Diarrhea flushes your intestines clean. Let that be a lesson as you move forward: No condition is a disease unless it impairs your normal function.

Your understanding of the function and fluctuation of your own body is maintained by the practice of Mastermind submersion. If you only spend one minute flying through the submersion method once a day, or once a week, or even once a month – as long as you are setting time aside for formal practice, it is beneficial. In fact, if you've arrived at the end of this book and learned nothing but abdominal breathing, your health will be transformed. Teach abdominal breathing to your friends and your children and your parents. Proper breathing powerfully affects one's life.

If, on the other hand, you have arrived here as the master all of the methods, remember that whenever you feel on top of the world you may indeed be only at a summit. Use your visualizations as a staircase climbing up and away from your normal conception of the world around you. Try mixing senses. What does a sound look like? How does a color taste? Experiment.

Another way to continue improving your own insight is to go on exploring yourself. Choose any of the higher level Mastermind exercises and perform them, only this time without any agenda. For instance, don't try to achieve a specific scene – just wipe your mind clean, and see what fills the space. Experiment how readily your mind can bring images and emotions to you. Or come up with an abstract category you want to envision – maybe some hope or determination or disappointment from your life right now – and let yourself associate freely about this subject while in a state of Mastermind submersion. This is called **free association**, and is related to certain meditative methods. Remember: Don't force yourself to see something. Rather, allow images to surface from the trackless seas of your unconscious mind. You'll never fill in all the blank spots on the map. You shouldn't want to. Self-discovery is an endless joy.

Close your eyes, drift up from your body, and observe what arises from the depths.

- A scaly kraken?
- Or long lost treasure?
- Go find out.
- Know yourself.
- Smile.

* * *

There was a river once, with glittering clear water. At night fish turned and flopped as they fed, and in the day they hung still and silver in the eddies of the rocks. On bright summer days farmers' children would slide down the banks to dabble in the shallows. The water they splashed up would glint in the sunlight like a handful of scattered sterling coins.

I worked at a hospital in the village beside the river. Daily decisions of life and death were routine. I remember many of my patients from that unit – one was Anna, the asthmatic child who didn't draw noses (until she did, and then she drew nothing else.) I was schooled to save these children's lives. I had studied my lessons exhaustively through sleepless nights and endless exams to earn that responsibility. But sometimes the most pivotal events of a life have nothing to do with your field of training.

On a day off I took a walk along the river. It was a perfect afternoon during the short Russian summer. The clouds were plush and cottony. Grasshoppers thrummed in the bulrushes, and dragonflies darted amongst the nodding reedy spires. The footpath snaked along the water at times, and then turned into the weeds and bushes. Where the path drew near the river, I liked to slow my pace and watch the fish.

As I passed the pebbled bank at one of these lookouts, I saw *under* the surface of the water a boy floating on his back with dazed eyes watching me. He wore swimming trunks, navy blue with stripes. His mouth was open and full of water. No bubbles broke the water's surface.

The current had brought him to me at the exact moment when I was within arm's reach. There was no time for emotion. Before the river carried him away, I stepped closer to the water, grabbed his hair, and lifted out his head. Then, squeezing his cold arm, I hauled him onto the river bank. He lay there slender, gasping. He blinked. He clambered to his feet and stood stiffly for a second, then whipped about and dashed off in his bare feet, disappearing down the path. He hadn't said a word. Neither had I.

For a long time I didn't share the story. The telling could paint the incident in the colors of a banality: I saw a drowning boy, and then pulled him to safety. The whole encounter only took about ten seconds from start to finish. But that young life would have ended if I'd loitered any longer or shorter at another of the lookouts, or if I had delayed my walk by savoring each bite of my lunch earlier that day, or if I had decided to nap instead of stroll. The turns of the world come in such delicate intervals, and the difference of life and death can hang in the balance. They are intimate acquaintances, those two, joined in a simple, mindless tangle of complexity.

I turned the incident over in my head, year after year. I felt sure that it meant something, but I wasn't sure what. The child's blue eyes live in my memory – the stunned look in them while he died underwater, and then how they blinked to life on the shore – and after that I remember how the sunlight marbled through the water onto the sand and stones of the river floor, how the wisp like minnows flitted from rock to rock, how in the belly of the river the water went so deep that you couldn't see what was hidden beneath, but only the color of a flat and silty green. I remember drying the wetness from my hands onto the thighs of my pants as I contemplated the damp spot on the bank where the boy had breathed again. Meanwhile his footsteps, skipping down the path, faded.

How easy it is to die – and also how extraordinarily simple to walk into your own life.

Quick Reference Guide

GUIDELINES FOR SELF-SUGGESTION

Understand. No work should be done without thought of the end point. The "end point" is the goal: Do you want your face to warm up, or cool down?

Feel. No thought should occur without a sensation. Consider sensation a language. "Be relaxed" is a good thought, but to actually enact it you must use a sensation and to materialize the thinking.

See. No sensation should be detached from an image. An image creates the sensation. For instance, an image of a cool towel on the head creates the sensation of a cool forehead.

Attach emotion. No image should be detached from emotion. Without an emotional association, the sensation is aimless. A wet towel on the head can be either a five-star luxury sauna, or waterboarding. It is crucial to know what emotion you want to associate with each sensation.

How to Practice

For the best effect:

- practice two or three times per day, for five to fifteen minutes
- keep a detailed journal
- combine the exercises creatively and monitor the results

BASIC MASTERMIND
Body to Mind

Mask of Relaxation

- calms nerves
- gives you a sense of control over yourself

On the floor

- body perfectly flat
- supportive roll under the neck and knees
- do not cross arms, legs, fingers, or anything else
- arms beside the body, slightly bent, palms down

Seated

- hands in lap
- don't hang arms off armrests
- do not cross arms, legs, fingers, or anything else

Method

- eyes close and roll up to focus on bridge of the nose
- jaw relaxes and unclenches
- tongue rests on inner side of upper teeth
- slow, deep breaths

Heaviness

- counteracts physical stress response
- eases muscle tension

Basic Heaviness Method - Hands

- squeeze a fist in the dominant hand for sixty seconds
- relax the muscles
- allow dominant hand to fall to the lap
- feel heaviness
- repeat with other hand
- repeat with both hands simultaneously

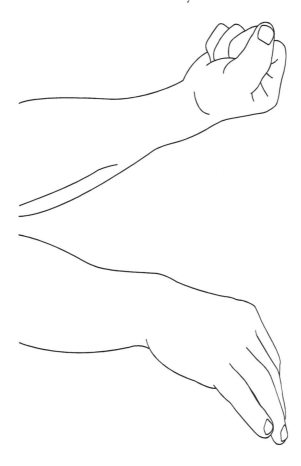

Basic Heaviness Method - Arms

- flex both arms for one minute
- relax the muscles
- allow arms to fall to your lap
- feel heaviness in the muscles of the arms

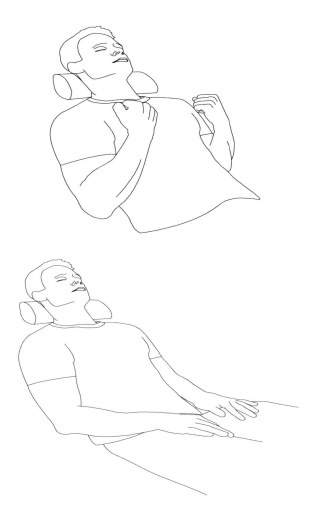

Basic Heaviness Method - Feet

- extend legs
- move the toes up toward the face as much as possible
- feel tension in the feet and ankles for one minute
- drop legs down
- feel heaviness in the feet

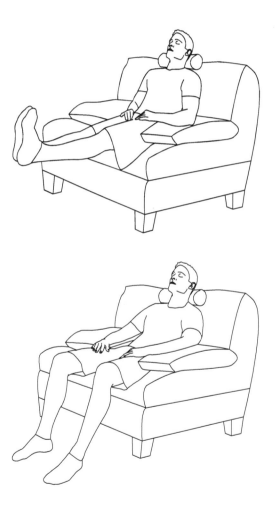

Basic Heaviness Method - Legs

- lift legs as with feet, as high as possible
- squeeze muscles for one minute
- drop legs to the floor
- feel heaviness in the legs

Basic Heaviness Method - Neck and Shoulders

- shrug and tense the neck and shoulders for one minute
- release the tension
- feel heaviness in the neck and shoulders

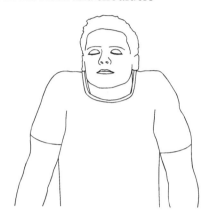

Basic Heaviness Method - Back

- squeeze shoulder blades together and arch the back for one minute
- release the tension
- feel heaviness in the back

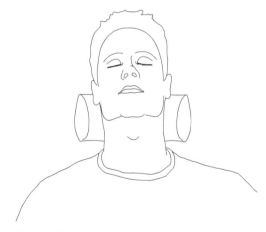

Basic Heaviness Method - Buttocks

- squeeze buttocks for one minute
- release the tension
- feel heaviness in the buttocks

Basic Heaviness Method - Face

- tense the face in a spasmed grimace for one minute
- release the tension
- feel heaviness in the face

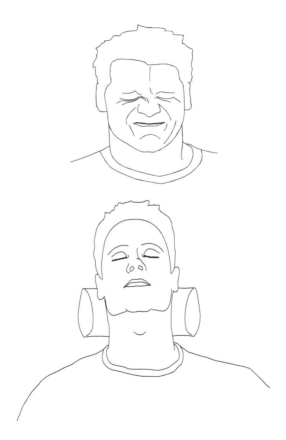

Basic Heaviness Method - Full body

- feel heaviness everywhere
- heaviness is not soreness but relaxation
- heaviness can come easier for some practitioners who imagine themselves squished by a heavy force
- feel your belt unhooked

- feel flanks spreading outside the body
- feel the belly flattening out like a frog belly

- feel flattened, liquefied

Advanced Heaviness Method

Full body heaviness

- progress through the muscle groups without tensing, only feeling heaviness
- always use the same order:
  - dominant hand
  - both hands
  - arms
  - feet
  - legs
  - neck
  - shoulders
  - back
  - buttocks
  - face
  - everywhere

Warmth

- increases metabolism
- manages circulation
- countless applications for health

Warmth Method - Warm hands preliminary exercise

- imagine hot blood pouring into hands
- imagine hands warming from the inside, like hot water filling a bal-loon
- use a hand held thermometer to measure the warming of hands

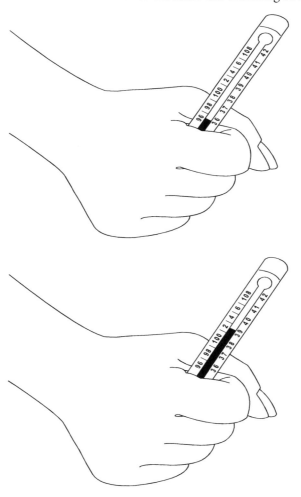

Warmth Method

- hands and feet are warm
- arms and legs are warm
- neck and shoulders are warm
- back and buttocks are warm
- face is warm
- whole body is warm
- imagine yourself lying on a sunny beach covered to the chin in hot, dry sand
- feel warm inside and out
- feel relaxed, pleasant, and peaceful
- once you have mastered body warmth, integrate a sensation of heaviness alongside warmth with each muscle group

Removing warmth

- removing sensations is as important as creating them
- count to three, removing excess warmth and heaviness
- imagine warmth and heaviness spilling out, evaporating, leaving behind a strong, springy, healthy body

Abdominal Breathing

- can change the course of events when feeling out of control, anxious, or fearful
- cannot hyperventilate
- actively prevents anxiety
- communicates peace to the brain

Abdominal Breathing - Basic Method

- bulge the abdomen out and suck it back in toward the spine, just to feel the movement

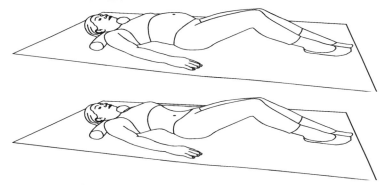

- repeat ten times
- inhale when abdomen bulges

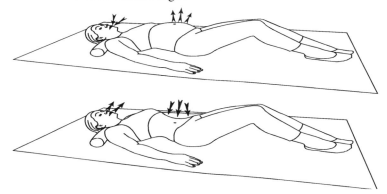

- exhale when abdomen sucks toward spine
- repeat as frequently as possible, any time and in any position
- eventually the body will switch to permanent abdominal breathing
- as that change takes place the diaphragm breathes and not the abdominal wall, so there is no unwanted belly bulge

Abdominal Breathing - Integrated Method

- assume Mask of Relaxation
- hands and feet are heavy and warm
- arms and legs are heavy and warm
- neck and shoulders are heavy and warm
- back and buttocks are heavy and warm
- face is heavy and warm
- whole body is heavy and warm
- "I am relaxed. I am at ease. It is pleasant, and peaceful. I am in control."
- breathe with the abdomen, slowly and evenly
- remove warmth and heaviness once practice is finished
- continue breathing with the abdomen

Warmth in Upper Abdomen

- increases blood flow to the gut
- improves nervous system function at the hub of the solar plexus
- improves digestion
- further manages physical stress response
- increases awareness of your body

Warmth in Upper Abdomen - Basic Method

- collect saliva on tongue
- feel its warmth
- swallow
- follow the warmth with your hand as it moves through the upper abdomen, or "epigastric area"
- feel the warmth travel down your esophagus and spread into the stomach

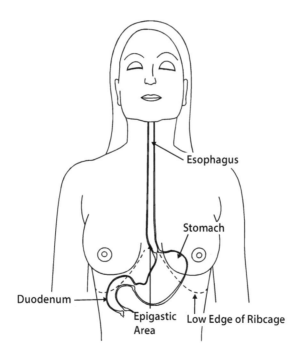

Warmth in Upper Abdomen - Basic Method (continued)

- linger here for a moment, at the solar plexus
- trace the warmth with your hand through the duodenum and through the loops of the small intestine until it reaches the large intestine at the right bottom side of the abdomen
- feel the warmth building as the intestine ascends and turns to the left, crawls along, and spills into the descending colon

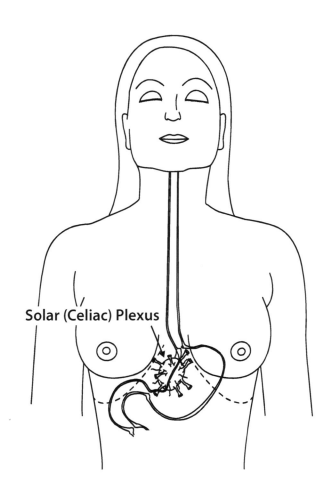

Solar (Celiac) Plexus

Warmth in Upper Abdomen - Basic Method (continued)

- feel the warmth floating down to the rectum and the anal sphincter
- the whole continuum should feel warm
- hold the warmth a moment
- release the warmth

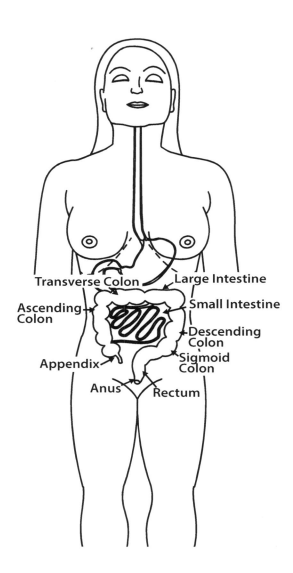

Warmth in Upper Abdomen - Integrated Method

- don't use your hand or your saliva to feel warmth
- instead use inner vision and visualization
- feel arms and legs heavy and warm
- feel neck and shoulders heavy and warm
- feel back and buttocks heavy and warm
- feel face heavy and warm
- feel warmth in the mouth, esophagus, and stomach
- imagine a heating pad on your solar plexus, or a warm water bottle

- feel warmth moving through the intestines to the rectum
- imagine a warm coiled garden hose in your gut, filled with hot floating gel

- imagine floating in a hot tub full of steaming water
- feel the heaviness and warmth all around you, inside and out

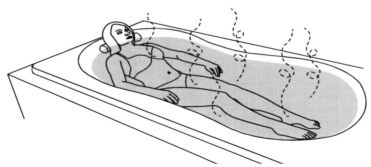

- when you decide to surface, imagine excess warmth and heaviness oozing out of you
- muscles are strong and healthy
- body temperature returns to normal
- breathing remains abdominal and stomach remains warm

Warmth in the Heart

- regulates heart rate
- improves circulation efficiency
- further counteracts physical stress response
- communicates peace to the mind

Tips

- sensation of warmth in the heart slows heart rate
- slow abdominal breathing slows heart rate
- heart quickens during an inhale, so by prolonging an exhale, heart rate slows further
- coordinate warmth in heart with the complete integrated method
- if your pulse quickens during the exercise, that means you are fighting with yourself; try soothing yourself instead

Warmth in the Heart - Integrated Method

- eyes focused on the bridge of the nose, tongue on the upper teeth, jaws unlocked,
- hands and feet are heavy and warm,
- arms and legs are heavy and warm,
- neck and shoulders are heavy and warm,
- back and buttocks are heavy and warm,
- face is heavy and warm,
- abdominal breathing is easily and effortless
- tongue is warm
- upper abdomen is warm
- gut is warm
- use the warmth in the esophagus as a heating element
- shift the warmth into your heart
- prolong your exhale and continue warming the heart
- imagine floating in a hot tub or any other visualization which feels safe
- "I am comfortable. I am in control. I am peaceful and rested."
- when coming out of the submersion, state your goals
- maintain that conviction as warmth and heaviness oozes away

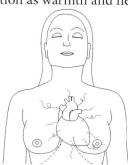

Coolness of the Forehead

- regulates blood flow to the brain
- manages brain metabolism and function
- influences physiological activation of the brain
- only use after mastering earlier methods

Tips

- in the beginning stages of this exercise, ask a friend to wave a fan over the forehead to feel the draft of cold air
- or put a wet cloth or drops of water on the forehead
- as the sensation of coolness internalizes, physical crutches are no longer necessary

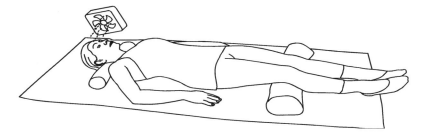

Mastermind Submersion Method

- hands and feet are heavy and warm
- arms and legs are heavy and warm
- neck and shoulders are heavy and warm
- back and buttocks are heavy and warm
- abdomen is heavy and warm
- face is heavy and warm
- abdominal breathing
- warm upper abdomen
- warm esophagus and stomach
- warm intestines
- warmth from esophagus spreads to the heart
- whole left side of the chest is warm
- forehead is chilled
- imagine the whole body heavy and warm, floating in a hot tub with a cold towel on the forehead
- thoughts are slow, pleasant, and comfortable
- don't fall asleep
- feel confident and safe and powerful
- remove excess heaviness and warmth upon completion
- increase alertness and sensation of lightness in muscles
- clear the mind

Stages of Mental Submersion
- sensations to expect during Mastermind Submersion:

- Body asleep while consciousness is fully awake.
  - body is completely relaxed, but mind remains awake
  - mental state is close to meditation
  - what began as heaviness and warmth becomes replaced by a sensation of lightness or weightlessness
  - frequently brings the feeling of hovering above the surface or attached by a few points like the shoulder blades and tailbone

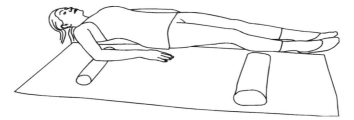

Changes in body structure

- arms and legs may feel elongated, or head drifts back and away from the body
- hands or feet may feel huge
- different sort of Alice-in-Wonderland metamorphosis may take place
- spatial relationship to the world may be disturbed

Total disappearance of the body

- the mind seems to continue on its own
- physical form seems unnecessary, transitory, or nonexistent
- can be a dissociative and unhealthy experience when it emerges spontaneously, but is gratifying when achieved intentionally and then reversed in a timely manner
- can be achieved with only a few weeks of training

Inner Flashlight

- bridges gap between body and mind
- the culmination of mental control over physical processes
- can be used for countless therapeutic self-treatments

Inner Flashlight Method

- assume a state of Mastermind submersion, using a boil down of the suggestion routine
  - face
  - calm
  - whole body is heavy and warm
  - warmth in upper abdomen
  - warmth in left chest
  - cool in forehead
- imagine a spot of light positioned on the palm of the hand
- feel the warm circle of light
- move the light along the arm leaving a warm trace behind or just keeping warmth at the illuminated spot
- brings localized warmth, or increased blood flow and healing power, to any place in the body

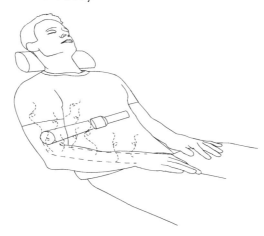

Tips

- with a working knowledge of anatomy, the inner flashlight gives control over internal organs
- with a working knowledge of brain function and physiology, can stimulate or inhibit different areas of the brain to influence vision, smell, pain, emotions, memory, and so on if to focus ray of light on particular parts of the brain
- try replacing the warmth with a spot of icy cool light to constrict blood vessels in targeted areas

TRANSITIONAL MASTERMIND
Mind to World

Continuous Observation

- improves awareness
- enhances memory
- extends attention span
- stretches the mind

Continuous Observation Method

- choose an object
- observe it for 5-15 minutes
- focus on the details
- what makes this object different from others like it?
- what makes this object similar to others like it?

Tips

- if the mind wanders, gentle nudge it back to the object of your attention
- do not let the mind think about work or chores; instead direct it toward tangential wonderings about the object itself

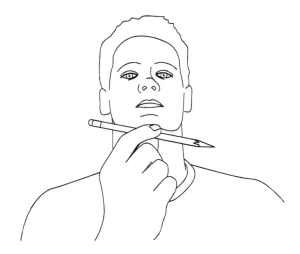

Intermittent Observation

- improves memory
- strengthens architecture of the mind
- calms the mind
- extends attention span

Intermittent observation method

- assume a state of Mastermind submersion
- inspect an object with eyes open
- commit details of that object to memory
- close eyes and recreate object in inner vision
- repeat this process several times

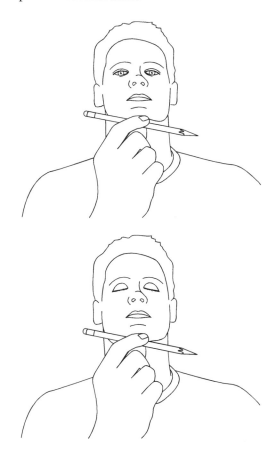

Mental Observation

- improves intuition
- hones visualization capabilities
- enhances awareness
- can be used to vaccinate against fears

Mental observation method

- assume a state of Mastermind submersion
- think of an object and recreate it in your inner vision
- conjure it with as many tactile details as possible
- add smells, or sounds if applicable

Tips

- different objects can be used to calm or excite the mind
- red and yellow colored objects are stimulating
- greenish, yellowish, and brownish colors are relaxing
- sharp edged objects stimulate, smoothed objects relax
- fast moving objects stimulate (like the cheetah below)
- peaceful objects relax (like the flower example)
- target imagery for therapeutic goals depending on the circumstance

Mental Exposure

- eliminates fears without trauma
- smothers anxiety
- promotes a calm interaction with the world

Mental exposure method

- imagine the object of fear using the mental observation method
- when this becomes endurable graduate to intermittent observation of the object of fear, retreating back into the inner vision if feeling anxiety
- when this becomes endurable, graduate to continuous observation of the object of fear

Tips

- remember that the mind is a safe and comfortable place
- if intermittent observation is too traumatic, begin with pictures or representations of the object of fear rather than the object itself

Therapeutic Escape

- changes perception of a stressful event from the past
- can alter the very memory of that situation in a therapeutic way

Therapeutic escape method

- using visualization methods, replay the events of the traumatic event in inner vision
- feel the fright, or anger, or outrage
- at the point of trauma, change the outcome

- whatever the desired ending, see it in inner vision
- repeat again and again
- the new and imaginary reality has the effect of neutralizing the wounds of the original offense, healing trauma and improving confidence

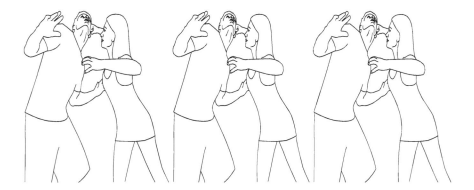

ADVANCED MASTERMIND
Mind to Mind

Ideomotor Training

- improves physical performance
- counteracts future uncertainties
- builds stamina
- improves visualization skills

Ideomotor Training Method

- assume a state of Mastermind submersion
- without moving the body, perform an exercise in the minds eyes
- this could be any task to be done in the future – riding a bike, shooting a basketball, or firing a weapon
- always do the task perfectly in inner vision

Tips

- try inhabiting other creatures: a bumblebee, or a hummingbird, or an elephant
- feel the motions of their bodies as they move throughout the world

Scene Building

- enhances visualization
- improves effectiveness of exposure therapy
- deepens connection with the world
- helps with multitasking

Details from the Big Picture Method

- in a state of Mastermind submersion, choose a scene to create in inner vision, say a town by a river and a hill far off
- see the scene generally at first

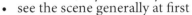

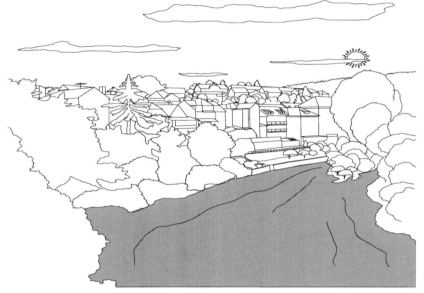

- continue adding details to the original scene: separate flowers and grasses, insects and birds, and fish, and frogs, and worms, and clouds

- make the scene as vibrant and involved as possible

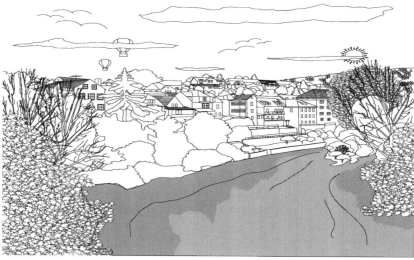

- continue adding details until there are separate feathers on each bird, a shimmer in their eyes, and crunchy dry leaves with sharp veins

Big Picture from Details Method

- in a state of Mastermind submersion, build a scene from the details
- begin with a wet rock, then see the bush beside it, and the white walls of a house by the river

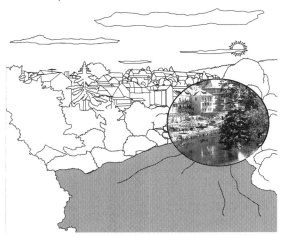

- build another house, or another spot along the river
- realize each scene as viscerally as possible
- keep several focus of attention simultaneously
- eventually join the disparate scenes together into one world

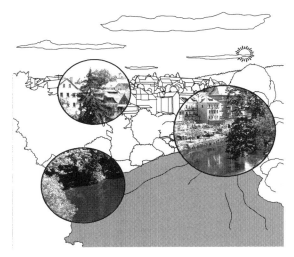

Tips

- the details of the scene you build are as endless as an imagination
- go underground, or underwater, or anywhere imaginable or un-imaginable
- try to expand the scope of your scenes
- see more than one action and item at a time, and manipulate them together
- keep the mind sharply on the whole and divided among many all at once
- imagine that the whole consists of many parts, with the parts not be-ing separate from the whole

Physical Form to Abstract Categories

- a part of pleasure manipulation
- absorbs desired values
- helps program the mind and the self
- a practical approach to acquiring intangible goals

Physical Form to Abstract Categories Method

- give any desired virtue a palpable form: a shiny cloud representing courage, for instance
- in a state of Mastermind submersion, bring the cloud around the body
- see it secreted or being absorbed into the body
- feel it pleasant and life giving
- by physically controlling a virtue, it becomes something palpable that can be summoned on command

Physical Form to Abstract Categories Method (continued)

- if a diffuse substance is too difficult to imagine, try keeping a concentrated pool of a virtue in the heart or in the mind or the solar plexus, the main hubs of human energy
- this may be easier to imagine or control, depending on visualization skills

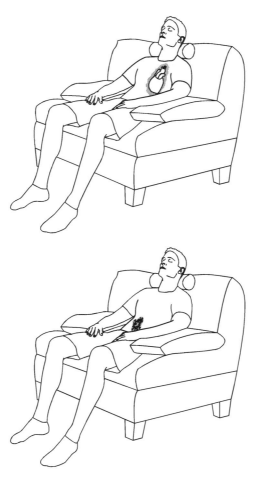

Tips

- give physical form to anything desired: love, creativity, intelligence, persistence, anything
- any category, if it acquires a palpable objective form, is easier to handle and regulate

Spinning Wheel

- helps with falling to sleep
- clears the mind
- improves focus and self-control

Spinning wheel method

- give thoughts a shape: colored yarn, or typed lines, or rainbowed waves of light
- weave the thoughts onto a spinning wheel

- move the wheel in a steady circular motion
- give any new thoughts a shape, and feed them into the wheel
- flush away the thoughts at a vortex in the center of the wheel
- try to suck everything away – the wheel, and everything
- continue feeding newly arising thoughts into the wheel

- a brain devoid of thoughts will fall asleep naturally very soon
- move not just thoughts within the wheel, but the wheel itself as well

Creating Emotions Through Self-Suggestion

- trigger emotions
- a demonstration of the power of self-suggestion
- a powerful confidence builder

Creating emotions method

- assume a state of Mastermind submersion
- create a scene of extraordinary force: a crashing ocean, a craggy peak above the clouds with the earth around you, or any other magnificent scene
- continue adding visceral sensory details until it is true to life
- when a scene is staged with enough vivid detail, the mind will believe it is true and form emotions to match the scene
- place yourself in a position of power and excitement and your mind will rise to the occasion

HEALTH APPLICATIONS
OF MASTERMIND

Health Applications of Mastermind as Reported in World Medical Literature

Neurology

- Bowel incontinence
- Chronic daily headache
- Chronic pain
- Dizziness
- Epilepsy
- Extrapyramidal movement disorders
- Fatigue
- Functional dysphonias
- Meniere Disease
- Menstrual headache
- Migraines
- Motor control in cerebral palsy
- Multiple Sclerosis
- Neuromotor rehabilitation after anoxic head injury
- Nighttime urinary incontinence
- Phantom limb pain
- Quality of life in MS
- Reflex neurovascular dystrophy
- Reflex sympathetic dystrophy
- Spinal myoclonus
- Stiff man syndrome
- Stuttering
- Tension headaches
- Ticks in Tourette's syndrome
- Tics in children
- Tinnitus
- Traumatic head injury
- Vascular headaches
- Volitional sympathetic control
- Writer's cramp

Health Applications of Mastermind as Reported in World Medical Literature

Psychiatry

- ADHD
- Adjustment disorder
- Alcoholism
- Anorexia
- Anxiety
- Anxiety in pregnancy
- Bedwetting
- Borderline personality
- Character disorders
- Chronic pain
- Cocaine craving
- Concentration problems
- Depression
- Drug abuse
- Dying and critically ill children and their relatives
- Fear of snakes
- Functional dysphonia and aphonia
- Group psychotherapy
- Increase in will power
- Insomnia
- Intractable depression
- Learning
- Modification of consciousness
- Night terrors
- Obsessions
- OCD
- Panic disorder
- Perception of well being
- Phobias
- Premature ejaculation
- Psychosomatic disorders
- PTSD
- Schizophrenia
- Sexual disorders in women
- Sleep disorders
- Sleep problems in adolescents with diabetes
- Stage fright
- Stress
- Substance abuse in adolescents
- Suicidal thoughts
- Test anxiety
- Tobacco smoking

Health Applications of Mastermind as Reported in World Medical Literature

Medicine

- Abdominal pain
- Aerospace medicine
- Anesthesia in labor
- Asthma
- Atopic dermatitis
- Atrial fibrillation
- Bleeding disorders in children
- Breast cancer
- Bronchitis
- Cancer chemotherapy
- Cancer therapy
- Cardiac arrhythmias
- Chest pain
- Chronic diarrhea
- Chronic obstructive bronchitis
- Chronic pain
- Cold hands or feet
- Collagen vascular disease
- Constipation
- Decrease in inflammation
- Decrease in sexual desire
- Dermatosis, skin dryness and itching
- Diabetes
- Diabetic intermittent claudication
- Diet in obesity
- Disabled war veterans
- Dysmenorrhea
- Ear, nose, throat disorders
- Eczema
- Fibromyalgia
- Gastric motility disorders
- Gastritis and stomach spasms
- Glaucoma
- Glucose regulation in diabetes
- Hair loss
- Heart attack recovery
- Hypertension
- Hyperventilation
- Infertility
- Irritable bowel
- Labor pain
- Leg claudication in diabetes
- Maternal and fetal distress during labor
- Myocardial infarction
- Myofacial pain
- Obesity
- Pain in rheumatoid arthritis
- Postsurgical pain
- Problems with esophageal motility
- Prophylaxis of gastric ulcers disease
- Racing heart and irregular heartbeat
- Renal failure
- Rheumatoid arthritis
- Scleroderma
- Teeth grinding
- Thyroid problems
- TMJ
- Ulcerative colitis
- Ulcers
- Voice pathology
- Vomiting due to chemotherapy

Health Applications of Mastermind as Reported in World Medical Literature

Athletics

- Alpine competition skiing
- Athletic performance
- Competitive performance
- Exercise recovery
- Improvement in performance in biathlon
- Improvement of dexterity in athletes
- Motion sickness
- Performance improvement in competing athletes
- Reduction of injury in ballet dancers
- Relaxation in soccer players

Miscellaneous

- Brain mapping on EEG
- Captivity surviving
- Caregivers' health in elderly
- College performance
- Communication with Gods
- Finding one's self
- Increasing work capacity in air force personnel
- Job stress
- Maintaining pilots' work capacity during long flights
- Orthostatic intolerance in aerospace crews
- Pilot performance
- Preparation for skydiving
- Promote Breastfeeding
- Sailors' health on prolonged cruises
- Sustaining humans in space
- Test anxiety
- Wintering in Antarctica

Endless other life and health problems in children, adolescents, adults, and the elderly individually and in groups

FOUNDING PRINCIPLES OF MASTERMIND

Origins of Mastermind

- Autogenic Training
- Hypnosis
- Medieval Martyrs
- Meditation
- Self-Suggestion
- Yoga

Components of Mastermind

- Acceptance
- Assertiveness Training
- Behavioral Modification
- Breathing Retraining
- Conditioning
- Controlled "Jamais Vu"
- Creative Imagery
- Creativity Training
- Distraction from harm
- Exposure Therapy
- Forgiveness
- Functional restoration
- Hope installation
- Identification of Functional Cognitions
- Imaginary play
- Insight Training
- Intuition Training
- Memory Training
- Mindfulness
- Modification of Unrealistic Assumptions
- Night Dreams Programming
- Not blaming
- Optimism
- Physical combat systems
- Play Therapy
- Positive Thinking
- Prayer
- Progressive Muscle Relaxation
- Psycho education
- Psychological Mindedness
- Role Reversal
- Alternatives Creation
- Repetition
- No Failure Environment
- Reframing
- Registration of strengths and weaknesses
- Reprocessing of Traumatic Memories
- Self-Talk
- Therapeutic escape
- Thought Stopping

ACKNOWLEDGEMENTS

There is no accident that this book was written by a doctor, whose heritage is Russian, Jewish, French and German and edited by a journalist with Dutch and Indian ancestry, an American upbringing, and a Chinese wife. The fusion of cultures, ideas, wisdoms and approaches that define the content of the Mastermind Method was shaped and solidified by my friends and colleagues to whom I am deeply thankful.

My gratitude to Matt Jager is endless. He baked my raw book and managed to make it into what I wanted it to be. Even before him, Paul Adams saw that the book was possible and, while giggling, supervised its maturation from a toddler into a teenage delinquent. And before Paul, Nancy Noel encouraged me to pursue my old dream of writing this book and shamed me into actually writing it. She gave this book its face, painting the cover image, and bringing to me the name of this book from my beloved grandmother who passed away thirty years ago. Thank you all, thank you from the depth of my heart.

This book would be impossible without Bobby Laikin, who managed to read the first ten pages before advising me to work with a professional editor; Christina Bodurow, who suggested the illustrations; Robert Wagner, Esq, who read the whole book when it was not readable and gave me a hope that it could be made into something of value; and Jeremy Cranfill and Christy who worked on illustrations in spite of all the catastrophes in their life at the moment. Thank you!

My wife Elaina deserves special appreciation. She helped me to select stories for the book, knowing first-hand what was important to me. Thank you, Mom, for praying for me. Thank you, Dad, for still seeing me as an adolescent.

Thank you books and teachers who gifted me with all I know. Thank you.

REFERENCES

Akimenko MA; Gromov SA "Adaptive biocontrol in the system of treating epilepsy patients" Zh Nevropatol Psikhiatr Im S S Korsakova 1995; 95(3): 45-48, Russian

Ball, Phillip. The elements: a very short introduction. New York: Oxford University Press, 2002.

Benson H "Hypnosis and the relaxation response" Gastroenterology 1989 June; 96(6): 1609-1611

Bluminstein B; Breslav I; Bar-Eli M et al. "Regulation of mental states and biofeedback techniques: effects on breathing pattern" Ribstein Center for Research and Sport Medicine Sciences, Wingate Institute, Israel Biofeedback Self Regul 1995 Jun, 20:2, 169-183

Coincidence Studies, Psychiatric Annals, Dec.2011;41:12

Cott A; Parkinson W; Fabich M et al. "Long term efficacy of combined relaxation: biofeedback treatment for chronic headache" Department of Medicine, McMaster University, Ontario, Canada Pain, 1992 Oct, 51:1, 49-56

Covington EC; Kotz MM (2009) "Psychological issues in management of pain" in Ries RK; Miller DA et al "Principles of addiction medicine" 4th ed. 1297-1316 Philadelphia, Lippincot, Williams and Wilkins

Cowings PS; Toscano WB; Miller NE et al. "Autogenic-feedback training: a potential treatment for orthostatic intolerance in aerospace crews" J Clin Psychopharmacol, 1994 June, 34:6, 599-608

Cox, M; Theilgard, A, "Mutative metaphors in psychotherapy" London: Jessica Kingsley Publishers Ltd, 1997.

De Punzio C; Neri E; Metelli P at al. "The relationship between maternal relaxation and plasma beta-endorphin levels during parturition" Department of Gynaecology and Obstetrics, University of Pisa, Italy J Psychosom Obstet Gynaecol 1994 Dec; 15 (4): 205-210

Diehl BJ; Meyer HK; Ulrich P et al. "Mean hemispheric brain perfusion during autogenic training and hypnosis" Psychiatry Res 1989 Sept; 29(3): 317-318

Dierks T; Maurer K; Zacher A "Brain mapping of EEG in autogenic training (AT)" Psychiatry Res 1989 Sept; 29(3): 433-434

Draaisma, Douwe "Why life speeds up as you get older". Cambridge University Press, 2004

Duckett S; Kramer T 'Managing myoclonus secondary to anoxic encephalopathy through EMG feedback" Physical Therapy Department, Bryn Mawr Rehabilitation Hospital Brain Jnj 1994 Feb-Mar; 8(2): 185-188

Ehlers A; Stanier U; Gieler U "Treatment of atopic dermatitis: a comparison of psychological and dermatological approaches to relapse prevention" Department of Psychiatry, University of Oxford, Great Britain J Consult Clin Psychol 1995 Aug, 63:4, 624-635

Engel JM; Rapoff MA; Pressman AR "Long term follow up on relaxation training for pediatric headache disorders" Headache, 1992 Mar, 32:3, 152-156

Expert consensus "Treatment of PTSD" J Clin Psychiatry, 1999;60 (suppl 16)

Farne M; Corallo A "Autogenic training and signs of distress: an experimental study" Boll Soc Ial Biol Sper 1992 Jun; 68(6):413-417

Friebel V "Relaxation training for children, a review of the literature" Prax Kinderpsychol Kinderpsychiatr 1994 Jan; 43 (1); 16-21, German

Haustein UF; Weber B; Seikowski K "Substance P and vasoactive intestinal peptide in patients with progressive scleroderma. Determination of plasma level before and after autogenic training" Klinik and Poliklinik fur Hautkrankheiten, University of Leipzig, Hautarzt 1995 Feb; 46 (2) : 102-106, German

Henry M; de Rivera JL; Gonzalez-Martin IJ, at al "Improvement of respiratory function in chronic asthmatic patients with autogenic therapy" University Hospital of the Canary Islands, Faculty of Medicine, University of La Laguna, Santa Cruz de Tenerife, Spain J Psychosom Res 1993 Apr; 37(3):265-270

Jacobs GD; Lubar JF "Spectral analysis of the central nervous system effects of the relaxation response elicited by autogenic training" Behav Med 1989 Fall; 15(3): 125-132

Kaufman KL; Tarnowski KJ; Olson R "Self regulation treatment to reduce the aversiveness of cancer chemotherapy" J Adolesc Health Care 1989 Jul; 10(4): 323-327

Kaufmann C; Barolin GS "Psychorehabilitation aspects in older age groups" Ludwig Boltzmann Institute for Neurorehabilitation and Prophylaxis, Rankweil, Austria

Kaufmann C; reiter N; Barolin GS "Comparative analysis of mental health treatment of various groups of competitive athletes" Ludwig-Boltzmann-Institut fur Neuro-Rehabilitation und Prophylaxe'" Feldkirch, Wien Med Wochenschr 1995; 145(10): 227-235, German

Kawano M; Matusuoka M; Kurosawa T et al. "Autogenic training as an effective treatment for reflex neurovascular dystrophy: a case report" Acta Pediatr Jrn 1989 Aug; 31(4): 500-503

Kiroi VN; Tambiev AE; Melnikov EV "Reorganization of the spatio-temporal structure of the electric field of the human brain as a result of psychotraining" Fisiol Cheloveka 1994 Sept-Oct; 20 (5): 133-136, Russian

Kleinsorge H "Hypnosys and other active relaxation procedures" Z Arztl Fortbild (Jena) 1993 Jun 12; 87(6):501-507, German

Labb EE "Treatment of childhood migraine with autogenic training and skin temperature feedback; a component analysis" Headache, 1995 Jan, 35:1, 10-13

Lehrer PM; Carr R; Sargunaraj D at al "Stress management techniques: are they all equivalent, or do they have specific effects?" Department of Psychiatry, Robert Wood Johnson Medical School, Biofeedback Self Regul 1994 Dec; 19(4): 353-401

Lindeman, Hannes "Alone at sea" Random House, 1958

Linden W "Autogenic Training: a narrative and quantitative review of clinical outcome" Department of Psychology, University of British Columbia, Vancouver, Canada Biofeedback Self Regul 1994 Sept ;19(3):227-264

Lobzin BS; Reshetnikov MM "Autogenic Training" Medicine, Moscow, 1986, Russian

Long N "Labeling relaxation procedures: impact on adolescence self report of effectiveness" J Adolesc Health, 1992 Dec, 13:8, 686-692

Lovelock, James "Gaia: a new look at life", Oxford, 1979

Margolin A; Avantis SK; Kosten TR "Cue-elicited cocaine craving and autogenic relaxation. Association with threatment outcome" Department of Psychiatry, Substabce Abuse Treatment Unit, Yale University School of Medicine, J Subst Abuse Treat 1994 Nov-Dec; 11(6): 549-552

McDanal C., "Comment on Hypnosis and Self hypnosis in the management of nocturnal enuresis" Am J Clin Hypn 1995 Apr; 37(4):343 Comment on Am J Clin Hypn 1993 Oct; 36(2): 113-119

Maurer, Michael "19 stars of Indiana: Exceptional Hoosier Men" Indiana Historical Society, 2010

Moskowitz L. "Psychological management of postsurgical pain and patient adherence" Hand Clin, 1966 Feb, 12:1, 129-137

Paulman, Paul M., Abdul Sadat "Pseudocyesis" Journal of Family Practice May, 1990

Pert, Candace "Molecules of Emotion", Scribner, 2003

Rama, Swami, Rudolph Ballentine, Alan Hymes "Science of Breath: A Practical Guide", 1998

Rivera, JLGde:.Autogenic psychotherapy and psychoanalysis. In: «The body in Psychotherapy», pp. 176-181. Editor: J. Guimón. Karger, Basilea, 1997.

Sadigh MR; Mierzwa JA "The treatment of persistent night terrors with autogenic training: a case study" Biofeedback Self Regul, 1995 Sept, 20:3, 205-209

Sakai M "A clinical study of autogenic training-based behavioral treatment for panic disorder" Department of Psychiatry, Saga Medical School, Japan Fukuoka Igaku Zasshi, 1996 Mar; 87:3; 77-84

Sakakibara M; Takeuchi S; Hayano J "Effect of relaxation training on cardiac parasympathetic tone. Department of Psychology, Aichi Gakuin University, Japan Psychophysiology 1994 May;31(3): 223-228

Saunders JT: Cox DJ; Teates CD et al "Thermal biofeedback in the treatment of intermittent claudication in diabetes: a case study" Biofeedback Self Regul, 1994 Dec, 19:4, 337-345

Seager, Allan "The old man of the mountain and seventeen other stories" , Simon and Schuster, New York, 1950

Seikowski K; Weber B; Haustein UF " Effect of hypnosis and Autogenic Training on acral circulation and coping with the illness in patients with progressive scleroderma" Klinik and Poliklinik fur Hautkrankheiten, University of Leipzig, Hautarzt 1995 Feb; 46 (2) : 94-101

Spinhoven P; Linssen AC Van Dyck R et al "Autogenic training and self hypnosis in the control of tension headaches" Gen Hosp Psychiatry 1992 Nov; 14(6): 408-415

Stetter F; Walter G; Zimmermann A et al "Ambulatory short-term therapy of anxiety patients with autogenic training and hypnosis" Psychiatrische Universitatsklinik Tubingen Psychother Psychosom Med Psychol 1994 Jul; 44(7);226-234

Ter Kuile MM; Spinhoven P; Linssen AC at al "Autogenic training and cognitive self hypnosys for the treatment of recurrent headaches in three different subject groups" Department of Psychiatry, University of Leiden, The Netherlands Pain 1994, Sept;58(3):331-340

Teshima H; Sogawa H; Mizobe K et al. "Application of psychoimmuno-therapy in patients with alopecia universalis" Psychoter Psychosom 1991; 56 (4): 235-41

The Analects of Confucius, translated by Burton Watson. 2007, Columbia University Press. New York.

Tonnesen S "Diffuse suffering. Rehabilitation of patients with fibromyalgia" Sykepl Fag 1993 Dec 7;81(6):11-15

Van Dyck R; Zitman FG; Linssen AC et al. "Autogenic training and future oriented hypnotic imagery in the treatment of tension headache: outcome and process" Int J Clin Exp Hypn 1991 Jan; 39(1): 6-23

Winterfeld HJ; Siewert H; Bohm J et al "Autogenic training in hypertensive dysregulation after aortocoronary venous bypass operation of coronary heart disease" Poliklinic fur Physiotherapie, Medizinischen Fakultat, Humboldt-Universitat zu Berlin Z Gesamte Inn Med 1993 Apr; 48(4):201-204

PUBMED PUBLICATIONS

(listed in chronological order)

The effects of progressive muscle relaxation and autogenic relaxation on young soccer players' mood States.
Hashim HA, Hanafi Ahmad Yusof H.
Asian J Sports Med. 2011 Jun;2(2):99-105

Behavioural modification of the cholinergic anti-inflammatory response to C-reactive protein in patients with hypertension.
Nolan RP, Floras JS, Ahmed L, Harvey PJ, Hiscock N, Hendrickx H, Talbot D.
J Intern Med. 2012 Jan 31

Psychosomatic approach for chronic migraine.
Hashizume M.
Rinsho Shinkeigaku. 2011 Nov;51(11):1153-5.

The application of autogenic training in counseling center for mother and child in order to promote breastfeeding.
Vidas M, Folnegović-Smalc V, Catipović M, Kisić M.
Coll Antropol. 2011 Sep;35(3):723-31

Treatment of psychological factors in a child with difficult asthma: a case report.
Anbar RD, Sachdeva S.
Am J Clin Hypn. 2011 Jul;54(1):47-55

Chronic daily headache: helping adolescents help themselves with self-hypnosis.
Kohen DP.
Am J Clin Hypn. 2011 Jul;54(1):32-46

Relaxation techniques for chronic pain.
Diezemann A.
Schmerz. 2011 Aug;25(4):445-53

Mind-body interventions during pregnancy for preventing or treating women's anxiety.
Marc I, Toureche N, Ernst E, Hodnett ED, Blanchet C, Dodin S, Njoya MM.
Cochrane Database Syst Rev. 2011 Jul 6;(7

Application of autogenic training in patients with Ménière disease.
Goto F, Nakai K, Ogawa K.
Eur Arch Otorhinolaryngol. 2011 Oct;268(10):1431-5

Cognitive-behavioral therapy and hypnotic relaxation to treat sleep problems in an adolescent with diabetes.
Perfect MM, Elkins GR.
J Clin Psychol. 2010 Nov;66(11):1205-15.

Nonpharmacological treatment of tics in Tourette syndrome adding videotape training to self-hypnosis.
Lazarus JE, Klein SK.
J Dev Behav Pediatr. 2010 Jul-Aug;31(6):498-504

Psychophysical and physical methods in treatment of dermatoses, accompanied by skin dryness and itching.
Tsiskarishvili NV, Eradze MSh, Tsiskarishvili TsI.
Georgian Med News. 2010 Apr;(181):28-32. Russian

Behavioral neurocardiac training in hypertension: a randomized, controlled trial.
Nolan RP, Floras JS, Harvey PJ, Kamath MV, Picton PE, Chessex C, Hiscock N, Powell J, Catt M, Hendrickx H, Talbot D, Chen MH.
Hypertension. 2010 Apr;55(4):1033-9

Intractable depression successfully treated with a combination of autogenic training and high-dose antidepressant in department of otorhinolaryngology: a case report.
Goto F, Nakai K, Murakami M, Ogawa K.
Cases J. 2009 Aug 14;2:6908.

Effects of supportive-expressive group therapy on pain in women with metastatic breast cancer.
Butler LD, Koopman C, Neri E, Giese-Davis J, Palesh O, Thorne-Yocam KA, Dimiceli S, Chen XH, Fobair P, Kraemer HC, Spiegel D.
Health Psychol. 2009 Sep;28(5):579-87

A new mind-body approach for a total healing of fibromyalgia: a case report.
Cuadros J, Vargas M.
Am J Clin Hypn. 2009 Jul;52(1):3-12

Perceived changes associated with autogenic training for anxiety: a grounded theory study.
Yurdakul L, Holttum S, Bowden A.
Psychol Psychother. 2009 Dec;82(Pt 4):403-19

Intensified voice therapy: a new model for the rehabilitation of patients suffering from functional dysphonias.
Fischer MJ, Gutenbrunner C, Ptok M.
Int J Rehabil Res. 2009 Dec;32(4):348-55

Predictors of the efficacy of methods for psychocorrection in patients with irritable bowel syndrome and constipation.
Aĭvazian TA, Zaĭtsev VP, Pakhomova IV, Gusakova EV.
Vopr Kurortol Fizioter Lech Fiz Kult. 2008 Sep-Oct;(5):6-8. Russian

Self-care for job stress in the workplace.
Ishikawa K, Saito M.
Sangyo Eiseigaku Zasshi. 2008 Jan;50(1):4-10

Response of spinal myoclonus to a combination therapy of autogenic training and biofeedback.
Sugimoto K, Theoharides TC, Kempuraj D, Conti P.
Biopsychosoc Med. 2007 Oct 12;1:18

Psychological intervention programs for reduction of injury in ballet dancers.
Noh YE, Morris T, Andersen MB.
Res Sports Med. 2007 Jan-Mar;15(1):13-32

Stress management in the treatment of essential arterial hypertension.
Schwickert M, Langhorst J, Paul A, Michalsen A, Dobos GJ.
MMW Fortschr Med. 2006 Nov 23;148(47):40-2; quiz 43. Review. German

Autogenic training for tension type headaches: a systematic review of controlled trials.
Kanji N, White AR, Ernst E.
Complement Ther Med. 2006 Jun;14(2):144-50. Epub 2006 May 18. Review

Autogenic training as a therapy for adjustment disorder in adults.
Jojić BR, Leposavić LM.
Srp Arh Celok Lek. 2005 Nov-Dec;133(11-12):505-9. Serbian

Effect of autogenic training on cardiac autonomic nervous activity in high-risk fire service workers for posttraumatic stress disorder.
Mitani S, Fujita M, Sakamoto S, Shirakawa T.
J Psychosom Res. 2006 May;60(5):439-4

Autogenic training to reduce anxiety in nursing students: randomized controlled trial.
Kanji N, White A, Ernst E.
J Adv Nurs. 2006 Mar;53(6):729-35

Therapy of unspecific tinnitus without organic cause.
Frank W, Konta B, Seiler G.
GMS Health Technol Assess. 2006 Aug 30;2:Doc17

A randomized controlled trial of Japanese patients with obsessive-compulsive disorder--effectiveness of behavior therapy and fluvoxamine.
Nakatani E, Nakagawa A, Nakao T, Yoshizato C, Nabeyama M, Kudo A, Isomura K, Kato N, Yoshioka K, Kawamoto M.
Psychother Psychosom. 2005;74(5):269-76

Relaxation and health-related quality of life in multiple sclerosis: the example of autogenic training.
Sutherland G, Andersen MB, Morris T.
J Behav Med. 2005 Jun;28(3):249-56

The effect of the definition of menstrually-related headache on the response to biofeedback treatment.
Blanchard EB, Kim M.
Appl Psychophysiol Biofeedback. 2005 Mar;30(1):53-63. Review

Sleep management training for cancer patients with insomnia.
Simeit R, Deck R, Conta-Marx B.
Support Care Cancer. 2004 Mar;12(3):176-83

Complementary and alternative medicine for bronchial asthma: is there new evidence?
Györik SA, Brutsche MH.
Curr Opin Pulm Med. 2004 Jan;10(1):37-43. Review

Effects of autogenic and imagery training on the shooting performance in biathlon.
Groslambert A, Candau R, Grappe F, Dugué B, Rouillon JD.
Res Q Exerc Sport. 2003 Sep;74(3):337-41

Effectiveness of a stress management program for family caregivers of the elderly at home.
Mizuno E, Hosak T, Ogihara R, Higano H, Mano Y.
J Med Dent Sci. 1999 Dec;46(4):145-53

Autogenic Feedback Training Exercise and pilot performance: enhanced functioning under search-and-rescue flying conditions.
Cowings PS, Kellar MA, Folen RA, Toscano WB, Burge JD.
Int J Aviat Psychol. 2001;11(3):303-15

Hypnorelaxation as treatment for myofascial pain disorder: a comparative study.
Winocur E, Gavish A, Emodi-Perlman A, Halachmi M, Eli I.
Oral Surg Oral Med Oral Pathol Oral Radiol Endod. 2002 Apr;93(4):429-34

Predictors of response to a behavioral treatment in patients with chronic gastric motility disorders.
Rashed H, Cutts T, Abell T, Cowings P, Toscano W, El-Gammal A, Adl D.
Dig Dis Sci. 2002 May;47(5):1020-6

Effect of autogenic training on glucose regulation and lipid status in non-insulin dependent diabetics.
Kostić N, Secen S.
Med Pregl. 2000 May-Jun;53(5-6):285-8. Croatian

Autogenic-feedback training exercise is superior to promethazine for control of motion sickness symptoms.
Cowings PS, Toscano WB.
J Clin Pharmacol. 2000 Oct;40(10):1154-65

Stress reactivity to and recovery from a standardised exercise bout: a study of 31 runners practising relaxation techniques.
Solberg EE, Ingjer F, Holen A, Sundgot-Borgen J, Nilsson S, Holme I.
Br J Sports Med. 2000 Aug;34(4):268-72

Self-hypnosis training and captivity survival.
Wood DP, Sexton JL.
Am J Clin Hypn. 1997 Jan;39(3):201-11

Two cases of panic disorder treated with autogenic training and in vivo exposure without medication.
Sakai M, Takeichi M.
Psychiatry Clin Neurosci. 1996 Dec;50(6):335-6

The effect of autogenic training and biofeedback on motion sickness tolerance.
Jozsvai EE, Pigeau RA.
Aviat Space Environ Med. 1996 Oct;67(10):963-8

The treatment of persistent night terrors with autogenic training: a case study.
Sadigh MR, Mierzwa JA.
Biofeedback Self Regul. 1995 Sep;20(3):205-9

The augmenting role of biofeedback: effects of autogenic, imagery and music training on physiological indices and athletic performance.
Blumenstein B, Bar-Eli M, Tenenbaum G.
J Sports Sci. 1995 Aug;13(4):343-54

Comment on "Hypnosis and self-hypnosis in the management of nocturnal enuresis".
McDanal C.
Am J Clin Hypn. 1995 Apr;37(4):343

Effect of hypnosis and autogenic training on acral circulation and coping with the illness in patients with progressive scleroderma.
Seikowski K, Weber B, Haustein UF.
Hautarzt. 1995 Feb;46(2):94-101

Effects of self-relaxation methods and visual imagery on IOP in patients with open-angle glaucoma.
Kaluza G, Strempel I.
Ophthalmologica. 1995;209(3):122-8

Adaptive biocontrol in the system of treating epilepsy patients.
Akimenko MA, Gromov SA.
Zh Nevrol Psikhiatr Im S S Korsakova. 1995;95(3):45-8. Russian

Thermal biofeedback in the treatment of intermittent claudication in diabetes: a case study.
Saunders JT, Cox DJ, Teates CD, Pohl SL.
Biofeedback Self Regul. 1994 Dec;19(4):337-45

Autogenic-feedback training: a potential treatment for orthostatic intolerance in aerospace crews.
Cowings PS, Toscano WB, Miller NE, Pickering TG, Shapiro D, Stevenson J, Maloney S, Knapp J.
J Clin Pharmacol. 1994 Jun;34(6):599-608

Therapy of Raynaud's syndrome.
Creutzig A.
Dtsch Med Wochenschr. 1993 Oct 15;118(41):1487-90. Review. German

Self-hypnosis and computer monitoring in the management of obesity.
Alman BM.
Am J Clin Hypn. 1992 Jul;35(1):77

Effect of autogenic respiratory training on labor pain. Use of the Vaona algometer.
Cattani P, Sina P, Piccolboni G, Dell'Angelo M, Zanarotti R.
Minerva Ginecol. 1991 Nov;43(11):525-8. Italian

Emotional-volitional training in the combined treatment of patients with rheumatoid arthritis.
Siniachenko VV, Leshchenko GIa, Melekhin VD.
Ter Arkh. 1990;62(1):58-62. Russian

Autogenic training as an effective treatment for reflex neurovascular dystrophy: a case report.
Kawano M, Matsuoka M, Kurokawa T, Tomita S, Mizuno Y, Ueda K.
Acta Paediatr Jpn. 1989 Aug;31(4):500-3

Two studies of the potential mechanisms of action in the thermal biofeedback treatment of vascular headache.
Morrill B, Blanchard EB.
Headache. 1989 Mar;29(3):169-76

Pillars of therapy of chronic obstructive bronchitis.
Karrer W.
Schweiz Rundsch Med Prax. 1989 Feb 7;78(6):121-5. Review. German

A psychological approach to bruxism--application of muscle relaxation training and autogenic training.
Ujihara T, Tsuga K, Akagawa Y, Tsuru H, Tatara M.
Hiroshima Daigaku Shigaku Zasshi. 1987 Dec;19(2):480-5. Japanese

Application of psychoimmunotherapy in patients with alopecia universalis.
Teshima H, Sogawa H, Mizobe K, Kuroki N, Nakagawa T.
Psychother Psychosom. 1991;56(4):235-41

Psychotherapy in the treatment of a patient with chronic renal failure.
Seregina OV.
Zh Nevropatol Psikhiatr Im S S Korsakova. 1991;91(12):91-3. Russian

The state of professional psychological guidance for patients with multiple sclerosis.
Kiessling WR, Weiss A, Raudies G.
Rehabilitation (Stuttg). 1990 Aug;29(3):201-3. German

Psychotherapy in multimodal treatment of diabetes mellitus.
Shcherbak AV.
Sov Med. 1990;(11):38-41. Review. Russian

Autogenic training with chronically ill children. Application in kidney diseases and in asthma.
Fuhrmann M.
Dtsch Krankenpflegez. 1989 Nov;42(11):766-70. German

Sustaining humans in space.
Hubbard GS, Hargens AR.
Mech Eng. 1989 Sep;111(9):40-4.

Brain mapping of EEG in autogenic training (AT).
Dierks T, Maurer K, Zacher A.
Psychiatry Res. 1989 Sep;29(3):433-4

Dietotherapy of obesity combined with group autogenic training exercises at a sanatorium.
Panchenko MF, Doronina EL, Panfilov VI.
Voen Med Zh. 1989 Feb;(2):45. Russian

Physiological mechanisms of autogenic training and its use with sailors on a prolonged cruise.
Pogorelov IA, Shimanovich EG.
Voen Med Zh. 1988 Jul;(7):57-8. Russian

How and when are we successful in weaning from cigarette smoking?.
Wieser O.
Prax Klin Pneumol. 1988 Jun;42 Suppl 1:242-4. German

Encopresis in children.
Zernov NG, Sashenkova TP, Torchinskiĭ MIu.
Pediatriia. 1988;(12):62-6. Russian

A psychological approach to bruxism--application of muscle relaxation training and autogenic training.
Ujihara T, Tsuga K, Akagawa Y, Tsuru H, Tatara M.
Hiroshima Daigaku Shigaku Zasshi. 1987 Dec;19(2):480-5. Japanese

Problems in implementing a pain management program for rheumatoid patients and studies of its effectiveness.
Cziske R, Jäckel W, Jacobi E.
Z Rheumatol. 1987 Nov-Dec;46(6):328-32. German

Effect of psychoprophylactic training in classes on labor on selected aspects of breast feeding. II.
Sendecka A.
Ginekol Pol. 1987 Aug;58(8):540-3. Polish

Autogenic training in gerontology.
Hirsch RD.
Z Gerontol. 1987 Jul-Aug;20(4):242-7. German

Stress and fertility: some modalities of investigation and treatment in couples with unexplained infertility in Dublin.
Harrison RF, O'Moore RR, O'Moore AM.
Int J Fertil. 1986 May-Jun;31(2):153-9

Experience in using autogenic training to treat World War II disabled.
Nagornyï LA, Shmulevich VL.
Vrach Delo. 1986 Jan;(1):99-100. Russian

Limits, conditions and possibilities in the use of high level autogenic training in aerospace medicine.
Korn F.
Psychiatr Neurol Med Psychol (Leipz). 1985 Dec;37(12):727-33. German

Insomnia: nonpharmacologic management by private practice physicians.
Nicassio PM, Pate JK, Mendlowitz DR, Woodward N.
South Med J. 1985 May;78(5):556-60

Individual and typological characteristics of autonomic reactions in the autogenic training of polar researchers during wintering in the Antarctic.
Sidorov IuA.
Fiziol Cheloveka. 1985 Jan-Feb;11(1):121-8. Russian

Current status of conservative therapy of extrapyramidal movement disorders in childhood and adolescence.
Widhalm S.
Wien Med Wochenschr Suppl. 1985;88:1-23. German

Relaxation in voice pathology.
Marvaud J.
Rev Laryngol Otol Rhinol (Bord). 1985;106(4):299-300. French

Autogenic training in the combined treatment of the temporomandibular pain dysfunction syndrome.
Egorov PM, Karapetian IS, Egorova IP.
Stomatologiia (Mosk). 1984 Sep-Oct;63(5):49-51. Russian

Evaluation of the measures for the psychological rehabilitation of myocardial infarct patients.
Bluzhas IuN, Goshtautas AA, Kuzmitskene AA.
Kardiologiia. 1984 Sep;24(9):76-81. Russian

Improving competitive performance with hypnotic suggestions and modified autogenic training: case reports.
Krenz EW.
Am J Clin Hypn. 1984 Jul;27(1):58-63

Methods of preventing overfatigue (a review of the literature).
Protasov VN.
Voen Med Zh. 1984 Feb;(2):36-9. Review. Russian

Methods and means of increasing the work capacity of air force personnel.
Bodrov VA.
Voen Med Zh. 1983 Nov;(11):40-4. Russian

The will and relaxation.
Lebzeltern G.
Psychother Psychosom Med Psychol. 1983 Mar;33(2):48-55. German

Autogenic training in a drug abuse program.
Roszell DK, Chaney EF.
Int J Addict. 1982 Dec;17(8):1337-49

Biofeedback treatment of dysmenorrhea.
Balick L, Elfner L, May J, Moore JD.
Biofeedback Self Regul. 1982 Dec;7(4):499-520

Autogenic training in the treatment of schizophrenic patients.
Kraft H, Schötzau P.
Fortschr Neurol Psychiatr. 1982 Sep;50(9):297-304. German

Indication of autogenic training in childhood concentration disorders.
Kröner B, Langenbruch B.
Psychother Psychosom Med Psychol. 1982 Sep;32(5):157-61. German

Psychosomatic autoregulation, an effective method of maintaining pilot work capacity during long flights.
Mel'nik SG, Shakula AV.
Voen Med Zh. 1982 Apr;(4):47-50. Russian

Use of various programs of autogenic training in test anxiety.
Kröner B, Frieg H, Niewendiek U.
Z Klin Psychol Psychother. 1982;30(3):254-66. German

Autogenic training in the combined treatment of sleep disorders.
Beznosiuk EV.
Med Sestra. 1982 Jan;41(1):28-33. Russian

Collagen vascular disease: can behavior therapy help?
Keefe FJ, Surwit RS, Pilon RN.
J Behav Ther Exp Psychiatry. 1981 Jun;12(2):171-5

Psychotherapeutic care of dying and critically ill children and their relatives (author's transl).
Henningsen F, Ullner R.
MMW Munch Med Wochenschr. 1981 Feb 13;123(7):247-50. Review. German

Psychotherapy in complex treatment of functional dysphonia and aphonia.
Goncharuk LE.
Vestn Otorinolaringol. 1981 Jan-Feb;(1):23-6. Russian

A behavioural approach to the treatment of obsessional rituals: an adolescent case study.
Green D.
J Adolesc. 1980 Dec;3(4):297-306

Volitional sympathetic control.
Blacker HM.
Anesth Analg. 1980 Oct;59(10):785-8

A new treatment method for sensation of dizziness (author's transl).
Norré ME, De Weerdt W.
Laryngol Rhinol Otol (Stuttg). 1980 Aug;59(8):472-6. German

Longitudinal study of the effect of autogenic training on various forms of subjective perception of relaxation and the sense of well-being.
Kröner B, Beitel E.
Z Klin Psychol Psychother. 1980;28(2):127-33. German

Anesthesia in labor.
Chernukha EA, Rasstrigin NN.
Feldsher Akush. 1980;45(6):21-7. Russian

Therapy of vomiting due to cytostatic treatment.
Bruntsch U.
MMW Munch Med Wochenschr. 1979 Nov 2;121(44):1450-1. German

Impotence and frigidity. The power of autogenic training.
Breulet M.
Rev Med Liege. 1979 Sep 1;34(17):743-7. French

Psychotherapy of psychosomatic disorders such as non-organic painful temporo-mandibular joint dysfunction in adolescents. Part 2.
Morin L.
J Can Dent Assoc. 1979 Jun;45(6):290-5. Review. French

Autogenic training in psychophysiological preparation for parachute jumps.
Reshetnikov MM.
Kosm Biol Aviakosm Med. 1978 May-Jun;12(3):67-9. Russian

Psychotherapy of various functional otorhinolaryngologio disorders.
Shkundin MP.
Vestn Otorinolaringol. 1977 Sep-Oct;(5):44-7. Russian

Psychotherapy for suicidal inclinations.
Kulawik H, Ott J, Geyer M.
Psychiatr Neurol Med Psychol (Leipz). 1977 Aug;29(8):490-7. German

Psychological aspects of cardiac arrhythmia.
Lynch JJ, Paskewitz DA, Gimbel KS, Thomas SA.
Am Heart J. 1977 May;93(5):645-57

Autogenic training in courses at a local college as psychotherapeutic prophylaxis (author's transl).
Kluge PA.
Psychother Med Psychol (Stuttg). 1977 Mar;27(2):64-6. German

Augmented feedback training of motor control in cerebral palsy.
Harrison A.
Dev Med Child Neurol. 1977 Feb;19(1):75-8

Some aspects of psychosocial rehabilitation under conditions of relaxation therapy-autogenic training- in borderline psychiatric diseases.
Meiu G, Pătraşcu F, Arion J, Zahariade S.
Rev Med Interna Neurol Psihiatr Neurochir Dermatovenerol Neurol Psihiatr Neurochir. 1976 Oct-Dec;21(4):291-4. Romanian

Functional speech system disorder in stuttering.
Beliakova LK.
Zh Nevropatol Psikhiatr Im S S Korsakova. 1976;76(10):1555-8. Russian

Ulcerative rectocolotis: autogenous training. On several serious cases (author's transl).
Degossely M, Koninckx N, Lenfant H.
Acta Gastroenterol Belg. 1975 Nov-Dec;38(11-12):454-62. French

Relaxation effect of autogenic training on esophageal motility.
Berner P, Fink G, Naske R, Stacher G.
Z Psychosom Med Psychoanal. 1974 Oct-Dec;20(4):384-90. German

Reduction of test anxiety via autogenic therapy.
Reed R, Meyer RG.
Psychol Rep. 1974 Aug;35(1 Pt 2):649-50

The importance of autogenic training in "finding one's self" (author's transl).
Iversen G.
Z Psychother Med Psychol. 1973 Sep;23(5):206-9. German

Analytical psychotherapy and training methods in sexual disorders of the woman.
von Schumann HJ.
Med Monatsschr. 1973 Jul;27(7):308-9. German

Learned control of ventricular rate in patients with atrial fibrillation.
Bleecker ET, Engel BT.
Psychosom Med. 1973 Mar-Apr;35(2):161-75

Creativity and modification of consciousness.
Leuner H.
Confin Psychiatr. 1973;16(3):141-58. German

Psychological assistance for the Alpine competition skier.
Abrezol R.
Minerva Med. 1972 Jul 14;63(54):2956-62. Italian

Possibilities of use of hypnosis in the training of athletes in sports requiring dexterity.
Calderaro G.
Minerva Med. 1972 Mar 3;63(16):986-7. Italian

Symptoms and treatment of the hyperventilation syndrome.
Beumer HM, Hardenk HJ.
Minerva Med. 1971 Nov 3;62(83):4111-3. Italian

The treatment of a patient with phobias with hypnotherapy by reciprocal inhibition.
Viëtor WP.
Ned Tijdschr Geneeskd. 1970 Dec 19;114(51):2144. Dutch

Systematic desensitization of snake-avoidance following three types of suggestion.
McGlynn FD, Mapp RH.
Behav Res Ther. 1970 May;8(2):197-201

Regular use of suggestibility by pediatric bleedings.
LaBaw WL.
Haematologia (Budap). 1970;4(3):419-25

Clinical and therapeutic studies in premature ejaculation.
Cooper AJ.
Compr Psychiatry. 1969 Jul;10(4):285-95

Psychogenic aspects in the stiff-man syndrome. Presentation of a clinical case.
Casati C, Rossi R.
Encephale. 1969 Jul-Aug;58(4):349-59. French

Group psychotherapy aspects in conducting autogenic training with patients suffering from seizures, especially patients with brain injuries and epileptics.
Binder H.
Z Allgemeinmed. 1969 Mar 31;45(9):407-8. German

Phantom limb pain.
Scherzer E.
Hefte Unfallheilkd. 1969;100:127-33. German

Autogenic training in the treatment of character disorders.
Crosa G.
Minerva Med. 1968 Oct 27;59(86):4611-3. Italian

Autogenic training in the treatment of psychosomatic disorders.
Crosa G.
Minerva Med. 1968 Oct 27;59(86):4606-10. Italian

Communion with the gods among the ancient and autogenic training.
von Schumann HJ.
Med Monatsschr. 1968 Mar;22(3):122-9. German

The treatment of tics in children by autogenous training.
Sichel JP, Durand de Bousingen R.
Rev Neuropsychiatr Infant. 1967 Dec;15(12):931-7. French

Reduction of examination anxiety and 'stage-fright' by group desensitization and relaxation.
Kondas O.
Behav Res Ther. 1967 Nov;5(4):275-81

Apropos of various treatments by autogenic training and brief psychotherapy of competing athletes.
Cachard C.
Rev Med Psychosom Psychol Med. 1967 Oct-Dec;9(4):277-81. French

Development of a case of anorexia nervosa in a 16-year old adolescent treated by relaxation. Recovery in 2 years.
Berges J.
Rev Neuropsychiatr Infant. 1964 Jul-Aug;12:451-5. French

Autogenic training in the treatment of graphospasm.
Cividini E.
Neuropsihijatrija. 1963;11(3):375-80. Serbian

WEBPAGE LINKS

1. www.mhni.com/cd.aspx

2. www.coedu.usf.edu/zalaquett/relax/About_Relaxation.htm

3. www.catalog.arizona.edu/faculty/courses/984/PExx.html

4. www.wcsu.edu/ihhs/index.html

5. www.lib.bioinfo.pl/meid:69609

6. www.eprints.soton.ac.uk/42896/

7. www.buchta.lib.bioinfo.pl/meid:8895

8. www.matusevicius.lib.bioinfo.pl/meid:8895

9. www.swedish.org/111953.cfm#ref56

10. www.chisuk.org.uk/bodymind/whatis/autogenic.php

11. www.iaath.com/autogenic.htm

12. www.innerhealthstudio.com/relaxation-response.html

13. mhni migraine headache and head pain treatment - mhni relaxation and pain management strategies cd

14. http://sportsillustrated.cnn.com/vault/cover/featured/8457/index.htm

15. www.psychologicalscience.org/onlyhuman/2008/10/and-i-feel-like-ive-been-here-before.cfm

16. www.deja-experience-research.org/

INDEX

A

abdominal breathing 33, 34, 35, 37, 43, 56, 63, 165, 181, 187, 189
addiction 40, 41, 42, 139
ADHD 77
Albert Einstein 116, 117, 152
Alexander the Great 25
Alice in Wonderland 70
Allan Seagers 100
altruistic 62, 84, 100
amygdala 139, 141
anger 62, 84, 102, 109, 110, 196
Answers of the Unconscious 162, 164
anticipation 10, 40, 82, 84, 124, 126, 146
anxiety 10, 11, 32, 33, 34, 35, 43, 54, 63, 84, 88, 115, 158, 181, 195
appetite 39, 41, 42, 43, 50, 142
Army 92
arthritis 71
assertion 33
assumptions 69, 86, 116
attention enhancing 95
August Kekule 156
Avatar 113
aware 16, 34, 69, 88, 93, 102, 103, 124, 130, 139, 161

B

behavior therapy 111
bipolar disorder 38, 77
blood flow 25, 42, 43, 44, 63, 64, 72, 132, 183, 188, 191
body structure 70, 190

C

D

E

I

J

K

L

M

memory retrieval 95
Dmitri Mendeleev 156
mental exposure 100
Mental Observation 101, 104, 194
mental power 54, 78
mind period 94
mistakes 42, 68, 69, 71
mobilize for action 34, 35
movie 5, 85, 86

N

narcissist 130
neurotransmitters 138, 139, 141, 142
norepinephrine 141
nucleus accumbens 138, 139, 141, 142

O

obsessive compulsive disorder (OCD) 53, 100, 109

P

paradise 35, 142
Pavlov's dog 123
phobias 100, 101
pleasure manipulation 142, 143, 149
plural 117
pneumonia 71
positive self-suggestion 124, 125
post-traumatic stress disorder (PTSD) 23, 77, 100
preparing for the future 85
progressive muscle relaxation 19
psychiatry 8, 38, 66, 76, 77
psychological mindedness 115

R

religious fasts 142
role-play 78
Teddy Roosevelt 78
running horse 93

ABOUT THE AUTHOR

D r. Dmitry M. Arbuck was born in Tbilisi, Republic of Georgia. He received his Medical Degree in Yaroslavl, Russia, where he also completed a Pediatrics Internship and residency in Psychiatry

After moving to the United States in 1990, he completed a residency in Psychiatry at Indiana University School of Medicine. Upon completion of his continued studies, Dr. Arbuck started a pain management facility, which grew to become one of the most comprehensive pain management facilities in the U.S. He is certified by the American Board of Psychiatry and Neurology and the American Academy of Pain Management.

He is a founding member and former president of the Russian American Medical Association. He holds Clinical Assistant Professor positions with Psychiatry and Medicine at Indiana University.

29529196R00141

Made in the USA
Charleston, SC
15 May 2014